DEVELOPING CHRIST *in* OUR THREEFOLD EGO

Rudolf Joseph Lorenz Steiner
February 27, 1861 – March 30, 1925

FROM THE WORKS OF DR. RUDOLF STEINER

DEVELOPING CHRIST *in* OUR THREEFOLD EGO

Dr. Douglas J. Gabriel

Our Spirit, LLC
2024

OUR SPIRIT, LLC

P. O. Box 355
Northville, MI 48167

www.ourspirit.com
www.neoanthroposophy.com
www.gospelofsophia.com
www.eternalcurriculum.com

ISBN: 978-1-963709-06-3

Book Cover art by Charles Andrade at www.lazure.com

CONTENTS

From Group-Soul to Life-Spirit

Do humans have a Group-Soul? To answer the question of whether humans have a Group-Soul requires an answer based upon a broad evolutionary perspective that would necessitate a sort of biography of the human "I Am," which derives its nature from the "I Am" of the Cosmic Being of Christ, the second person of the Holy Trinity. Thus, a biography of the Cosmic Christ is also necessary to understand from whence came the human "I Am," made in the 'image and likeness of God.' As a quick overview, one could say that the human "I Am" biography might begin with Christ's creation of every human "I Am" through the combined efforts of the seven major Spirits of Form (Elohim) when the True "I Am" (self) of each individual human "I Am" was created and held back in the Heavenly realms on the Sun. Then, individual human souls began to descend to Earth through the four archetypal Group-Soul expressions (Angel, Eagle, Lion, Bull). The vision of Ezekiel's fiery wheels of beasts is an image of the archetypal human Group-Soul configuration as seen in the astral light. So, the answer is: Yes, humans derived from a Group-Soul and will evolve into a Christened-Group-Soul as Archangels in the realm of Life-Spirit, as Rudolf Steiner called that realm, in the far distant future.

Over millennia, individuals developed their personal "I Am" (ego/self) to the point that they could leave behind the vestiges of race, tribe, nation, and even family to develop the personal Ego through freedom. Individuals began to have free thoughts, independent of the transcendental, divine world which they could experience directly through a dull, natural clairvoyance. Christ then incarnated on Earth

1

in a physical body, once and only once, to bring to birth the personal Ego of every free human being from that time forward. With further spiritual development of the personal Ego, each liberated Human-Ego can rise into the astral light (Spirit-Self), Lower Devachan (Life-Spirit), and Higher Devachan (Spirit-Human) to reclaim the three Higher-Egos that reside in the three supersensible realms where our older siblings, the Angels, Archangels, and Archai live and help sustain the astral, etheric, and physical bodies of all humans. Ultimately, the free human individual, acting out of the impulses of Christ's love, returns to the place from whence they have come; but now with the gifts of personality and individualized distinctiveness that make each person a unique facet of the divine jewel of Heaven.

Rudolf Steiner's Spiritual Science informs us that in ancient times, during the Old Moon Planetary Incarnation of the Earth, the Ego of the human being was part of a Group-Soul configuration of Ego-consciousness based upon a division of the starry realms into four regions of space. We often see these four archetypal images, known collectively as the 'tetramorph,' represented in cathedrals; which as a group combined to create the Group-Soul of man. These are the four 'Fixed Signs' of the Zodiac:— Scorpio (Eagle), Leo (Lion), Taurus (Bull), Aquarius (Angel/Man). Rudolf Steiner makes it clear that the 'Man' of Ezekiel is the human "I Am" before the fall into matter (from the astral realm). This 'Man' is more like an Angel-Man according to Spiritual Science. Thus, the Eagle of Scorpio represents 'thinking in the head,' the Lion of Leo represents 'feeling in the heart,' the Bull of Taurus represents 'willing in the metabolic/limb system.'; while the 'Man' of Aquarius represents the "I Am" as the archetypal synthesis manifesting as a human being. It took all four, the archetypal human and the three soul forces of thinking, feeling, and willing, to create a free and independent human being.

The biography of the human being is interwoven with the pre-earthly, earthly, and etheric deeds of Christ that have given humans the gift of standing upright, speaking, thinking, and memory. The Human-

Ego is the carefully created, planted, and tended seed of Christ who gardens the soul-seeds into spirit-blossoms (Tree of Life) that reunite the "I Am" of the human being with the World-Ego—the Christened-Group-Soul of Humanity which is the future Life-Spirit (according to Rudolf Steiner). Life-Spirit is also the realm of the Archangels; whereby the etheric body of each human individual is maintained by the prototype that is the etheric body of Christ, manifesting through the agency of the Archangels, and their helpers. This re-enlivened and 'resurrected' etheric body is turned into the Life-Spirit (Christened-Group-Ego) of the individual which takes its life directly from Christ—the Solar Logos—Who tends the etheric body of the Earth, and each individual's etheric body, with the loving care of a gardener. For we are the offspring of Christ; and when we rise into the realm of the Archangels—we will become 'Christened Beings' who are part of the Group-Soul of Christ—the Macrocosmic-World-Ego.

In the selections from Rudolf Steiner below, there is a progression of this biography of the human "I Am" in full detail. Dr. Steiner tells us that to advance on the path of personal initiation, the aspirant must understand the full nature of the human Group-Soul and its evolution into a free, individualized thinker. In light of this, even some of the most experienced students of Rudolf Steiner are confused about the nature of the three Egos. For Rudolf Steiner refers to this topic in only a few lectures, and to further complicate the issue it undergoes a gradual metamorphosis over time.

The prolific anthroposophical author Sergei O. Prokofieff has written a book that highlights these indications in a most useful and illuminating fashion. Suffice it to say, the three Egos are basically the human:—

Spirit-Self (Higher-Ego/Reincarnating-Ego, united with Holy Spirit).

Life-Spirit (World-Ego/Christened-Group-Ego, united with Christ).

Spirit-Human (True-Ego/Cosmic-Ego/Zodiacal-Ego, united with Father God).

According to Rudolf Steiner the Earthly-Ego ultimately arises during the Intellectual-Soul Period (747 B.C.-1,414 A.D.); coinciding in stages with the Mystery of Golgotha, and over time, from within the Intellectual-Soul, there arises the Higher-Feeling-Soul. These preliminary stages of development lead us to a critical transition between the Grail events of the 9th century and the beginning of the Consciousness-Soul Period in 1,414 A.D. This, in turn, subsequently leads to the development of the Consciousness-Soul, which ultimately becomes transformed into the Spiritual-Soul to serve as a 'Grail' to receive the Spirit-Self in the Sixth-Post-Atlantean Period (beginning in 3,574 A.D.) that will stream in from the Angelic realm above mankind as an expression of the Universal Law and Eternal Wisdom. For, as said above, this activation of the Consciousness-Soul transformed it into what Rudolf Steiner called the Spiritual-Soul. The transformed Spiritual-Soul as a result becomes capable of retaining the spiritual elements the soul has forged on Earth—*that can as supersensible wisdom cross over the threshold between the physical and Spiritual Worlds.* This spiritual activity within the Spiritual-Soul is the humble beginning that serves as a form of sheath to receive the inpouring of the Spirit-Self (Higher-Ego) which, in-turn, further transforms the human astral body into higher, living thinking called Moral Imagination.

The Earthly-Ego begins to disenchant matter through finding spiritual content reflected in the physical world; which rises-up to receive the Microcosmic-Angelic impulses from the astral realm (astral light) in preparation for the full incorporation of the Macrocosmic-Spirit-Self in the distant future of the Jupiter Planetary Condition (the Christian Heaven). This is essentially the beginning development our reincarnating Ego, which travels from life to life.

The second Ego is found when the Spirit-Self (Manas), called the Virgin Sophia by Spiritual Science, prepares for the wedding described in the picture language of the *Book of Revelation* by St. John. Wherein the purified and prepared 'bride of the soul' marries the Lamb of God (hero of the *Apocalypse*)—Christ—who gains victory over evil and harvests the fruits of ascension. The Higher-Ego sings the 'New Song' of the 'Eternal Gospel' of the Lamb of God and is wedded in New Jerusalem as a bride to the groom in a celestial marriage. This spiritual communion is similar to the return of the 'prodigal son' to the Father. It is the 'mysterious conjunction' of the soul wedding the spirit—*a true Christian spiritual alchemy.*

There is a third stage of Ego development that Rudolf Steiner refers to as the 'third current' which can see the physical and the supersensible at one time. This third current is the third stage of Ego development called Spirit-Human (Atman). This level of consciousness is almost indescribable and far beyond what a human mind can cognize. Rudolf Steiner refers to this stage of Ego development as 'becoming a Zodiac.' The True-Ego, at this stage, takes responsibility for a sphere of activity called a 'Zodiac' as the individual becomes a Christ Being working consciously with an entire Zodiac. This stage of cosmic transcendence makes the individual into a co-creator with the Father God principle.

The Spirit-Self (Manas), Life-Spirit (Budhi), and Spirit-Human (Atman) directly relate to the Holy Spirit (Spirit-Self), Christ (Life-Spirit), and the Father God (Spirit-Human). Each individual, over multiple incarnations on the Earth entailing vast amounts of time, has the possibility of rising through these three realms to ascend back to the Throne of the Creator (Father God) to fully redeem the 'fall into matter' and claim Christ's further gifts that accompany ascension.

The image of the twelve-fold Zodiac, at this third and highest level of the development of the three Egos, brings to mind the four fixed astrological constellations represented in the four Group-Souls that humanity evolved from:— Taurus (Bull), Leo (Lion), Scorpio (Eagle), and Aquarius (Man/Angel). From the impulses of these initial four signs of the Zodiac, through the beginning of human development, to the twelve signs found within the Zodiacal stages of Ego development, we see a type of 'prodigal son' returning home. We began as donations from the spiritual hierarchies who were working from the realm of the stars, and, in the end, we return by ascending to our home in the stars—the whole Circle of the Zodiac. This type of conscious awareness is far beyond what the human soul can strive to understand about our Earth, our planets, the stellar world, and our loving Sun-Being. For Christ is the 'Sun' that dwells on the Solar System's throne, as well as the throne of the heart for anyone who has given their Ego over to selflessness and the love of others—the Christ deed of 'loving your neighbor.'

Christ's sustaining love works partially from the realm of the Spirits of Form, the Beings who help maintain the planets in our solar system and donated the 'Egos' for each human being. Christ also works from the realm of the Holy Trinity and the entire second rank of the hierarchy (Kyriotetes, Dynamis, Exusiai/Elohim). The kingdom of Christ's Father is 'not of this world'; for it is the world of the stars (Zodiac) from whence came the life of the human body that is the vessel of the Human-I (Human-Ego)—the heart of love, the gift of the "I Am" of Christ made personal and individualized from of the donations of the entire Cosmos.

The Human I as Ego Development

In pre-historic times, ancient tribes, peoples, nations, and cultures were led by spiritual leaders and priest/kings who were in direct communication with the Spiritual World. Humans did not have a Personal-Ego, per se. They followed the wise leadership of those who could directly communicate with the divine and bring down to Earth the Wisdom of the gods. Rudolf Steiner tells us that humanity was strongly organized into Group-Souls up until the time of the fourth subrace of Atlantis (Turanian). For the initial phases of the individuation of the Human-Ego only began in the fifth subrace of Atlantis onward (Ur-Semites).

The human physical body became a blended merger of the etheric formative forces underlying the three archetypal Group-Souls of Bull (during Lemurian Period), Lion (late Lemurian and throughout Atlantean Period), and Eagle (a third influence during Atlantean Period). The three influences flowed together and were balanced in the fourth Group-Soul of Man, or what Steiner calls 'Man before the Fall.' The Bull influence worked most strongly on the physical body of the human being, the Lion on the etheric, and the Eagle on the astral body.

In each human being a unique mixture of the four Group-Souls was developed. An over-emphasis of one or the other force created the different races and even the division of the sexes. This was symbolized in the Egyptian Sphinx—Woman, Lion, Eagle, Bull.

Long after Atlantis, some humans started to develop a balanced use of the forces of the Group-Ego and become clear thinkers—abstract thinkers who could objectify the material world. Father Abraham was an example of that type of new and independent thinker. The Hebrew people, in general, identified with Abraham and the Hebrew forefathers through their blood memory and respect for the hereditary chain of the tribe. The saying was:—'I and Father Abraham are one.'

The ultimate intent of spiritual evolution is to let the tribes, caste systems, races, and nations go to the wayside as the Personal-Ego developed during the Consciousness Soul Period (1,414 A.D.-3,574 A.D.) that did not need a religious leader, doctrine, or dogma to tell the Individual-Ego what is right or wrong. Christ's gift of a budding Spiritual-Ego would eventually lead to a sufficiently developed Ego with the capacity to ascend as an Individual-I.

Unification is the term Rudolf Steiner used for denoting the concept of Christ as the future Group-Soul of humanity helping redeem the astral, etheric, and physical body of each human being. In a way, this can be seen as the concept of the Second Adam, Christ the Redeemer, and the underlying principle of love that is born from the Wisdom of Sophia, what Rudolf Steiner called 'the Sophia of Christ, the Wisdom of the Cosmic Christ.' The developed Higher-Ego of the human being helps create this Unification of the soul to the spirit, the Virgin Soul (Sophia or Wisdom) with the Lamb of God (Christ or Love).

These various perspectives are like different images that describe the same reality: the human phantom (the redeemed astral and etheric joining the phantom physical body) lies at the basis for the resurrection process, and since all human phantoms will link to the Macrocosmic-Ego of Christ as a Christened-Group-Soul, a new kind of Group-Soul for humanity will establish itself and provide the transition to the next incarnation of Earth, the Future Jupiter Planetary Condition, and there form the basis for humanity's living environment of love. This is made clearer by Rudolf Steiner in the following.

From Jesus to Christ, **Rudolf Steiner, Lecture VI,** *St. John and St. Paul, First Adam and Second Adam*, **Karlsruhe, October 10, 1911, GA 131**

"If you think more deeply, can you believe that all the work of the great Divine Spirits though the Old Saturn, Sun, and Moon periods has merely created something which is handed over at death to the elements of the Earth? No—that which was developed during the Old Saturn, Sun, and Moon periods is not the physical body that is laid aside at death. It is the Phantom, the Form, of the physical body. We must be quite clear that to understand the physical body is not an easy thing. Above all, this understanding must not be sought for in the world of illusion, the world of Maya. We know that the foundation, the germ, of this Phantom of the physical body was laid down by the Thrones during the Old Saturn period [1st Planetary Condition]; during the Old Sun period [2nd Planetary Condition] the Spirits of Wisdom worked further upon it, the Spirits of Movement during the Old Moon period [3rd Planetary Condition], and the Spirits of Form during the Earth period [4th Planetary Condition]. And it is only in this period that the physical body received the Phantom. We call these Spirits the Spirits of Form, because they really live in the Phantom of the physical body.

"Let us suppose that to this Phantom of the physical body the etheric body is added; will the Phantom then become visible? Certainly not; for the etheric body is invisible for ordinary sight. Thus the physical body as Phantom, plus etheric body, is still invisible to external physical sense. And the astral body even more so; hence the combination of physical body as Phantom with the etheric and astral bodies is still invisible."

From Jesus to Christ, **Rudolf Steiner, Lecture VII,** *The Mystery of Golgotha, Greek, Hebrew and Buddhist Thought,* **Karlsruhe, October 11, 1911, GA 131**

"Just as man, through his place in the stream of physical evolution, inherits the physical body in which the destruction of the Phantom, the force-bearer, is gradually taking place, so from the pure Phantom that rose out of the grave he can inherit what he has lost.

"No one, having gone through death, had ever overcome death as a human Phantom. Similar things had certainly occurred, but never this—*that a man had gone through a complete human death and that the complete Phantom had then gained victory over death.* Just as it is true that only this Phantom can give rise to a complete humanity in the course of human evolution, so is it true that this Phantom took its beginning from the grave of Golgotha."

In the *Bible* we have a picture of the human being's biography in a nutshell:—

'And so it is written, the first man Adam was made a living soul; the last Adam was made a life-giving spirit.' *Corinthians* (15:45)

This First Adam is the label used for the spiritual-seed of humanity, in which the Ego ("I Am"), consisting of the higher components of soul and spirit, could incarnate and go through the 'Fall'—the luciferic temptation/infection. The Second Adam is Christ's Resurrection-Body serving as the prototype for the Macrocosmic Life-Spirit in which in the Future Venus or 6th Planetary Condition—the spiritualized humanity will integrate

with the World or Macrocosmic 'I' of Christ; into what Rudolf
Steiner called the Christened-Group-Soul of Humanity.

The Biblical concept of the Second Adam indicates the Group-
Soul evolution of the souls who, during the developmental stage
of the Earth (the 4th Planetary Condition), have ennobled and
redeemed their lower bodies. When a person uses his "I Am" to
consciously work toward the improvement and spiritualization of
his lower bodies; this, in turn, affects his higher components in
the Spiritual World. As each individual is purifying this 'second
man' in their soul (Second Adam) they are building the Future
Jupiter incarnation of the Earth where they will incarnate as
Angel/Humans. This Second Adam could be seen as an after-
effect of Christ's resurrection, following the Mystery of Golgotha,
when the resurrected ether bodies of Christ and humanity formed
the basis for what will create this Unification between Christ and
humanity's Higher-Ego or 'I Am.'

Ultimately, all future human beings who will freely join their
purified ether bodies with other Christened souls, in the Future
Venus or 6th Planetary Condition, as Archangels within the realm
of Macrocosmic-Life-Spirit of Christ, will as a result conjoin with
the World or Macrocosmic-I (Christ-Ego), as the Christened-
Group-Soul of Humanity.

The mysteries of the human Group-Soul are profound and
far-reaching and must be contemplated thoroughly so as to begin
to understand their importance. The ramifications of the effects
of either 'falling' again into a lower Group-Soul consciousness
or evolving upwards into Christ-consciousness are critical for
human spiritual development.

It is a key factor of initiation to join together with the higher
forces of consciousness emanating from the Christened-Group-
Soul (Life-Spirit/Love) to transform the lower bodies into suitable

vehicles into the future to serve as prototypes for the higher three *Microcosmic I Principles* (3. Spirit-Self / Manas; 2. Life-Spirit / Budhi; 1. Atman / Spirit-Human) that will arise as individuated principles in the three following Planetary Conditions in alignment with Christ taking up the three *Macrocosmic Principles* in the three following Planetary Conditions. For, until the end of Earth evolution these will ray into mankind from outside as *Microcosmic Principles* from Higher Beings in service to Christ, in anticipation of them becoming our individual *Macrocosmic Principles* on Future Jupiter (Spirit-Self), Future Venus (Life-Spirit), Future Vulcan (Spirit-Human).

Spiritual Science provides us with the necessary Language of the Spirit; the 'Christ Language' that is needed to communicate regarding these higher realms as made clear by Rudolf Steiner in the following entry from the *Michael Letters*.

The Michael Mystery, Rudolf Steiner, Pt. VI, *Mankind's Future and the Work of Michael*, GA 26

"But one must also learn to speak—*which means, to feel*—about the world of Nature too in a manner befitting the Christ. Not only about redemption from Nature, not only about the soul and things divine; but about the Cosmos—*we must learn the Christ-language*. That our human link with our first divine-spiritual origin may be so preserved, that we may know how rightly to speak the Christ-language about the Cosmos—this is something to which we shall in the end attain, if with inward sincerity of heart we learn to feel and ever more fully enter into all that Michael and Michael's Company are amongst us—in their mission, in all that they perform.

"Anthroposophy would speak the Christ-Michael language. For if both languages are spoken, then the continuity will remain unbroken, and evolution will not pass over to Ahriman, before finding again its first, divine, spiritual origin."

Once we have learned to enter these realms and communicate with these Supersensible Beings, we will find that the Group-Egos of the kingdoms of nature are also directed by ranks of spiritual hierarchies above the Spirits of Form (Exusiai/Elohim). These Higher-Egos of the animals, plants, and minerals dwell within realms of being where parts of our own higher nature also dwell; and are tended with love by the higher spiritual hierarchies. Over time, we find that we are an 'Ego within an Ego within an Ego' dwelling amongst the ranks of higher spiritual beings who generously help maintain our astral, etheric, and physical bodies. For knowing our Threefold Higher-Egos, and the true nature and history of the evolving human Group-Soul (Group-Ego), can open direct communication with higher beings working through our own bodies.

Hierarchical Rank of the Group-Souls of Kingdoms

Human	Elohim	Spirits of Form
Animal	Dynamis	Spirits of Motion
Plant	Kyriotetes	Spirits of Wisdom
Mineral	Thrones	Spirits of Will

Rudolf Steiner's Indications Concerning Group-Souls

The edited quotes below can be found in their original complete form in the individual selections from Rudolf Steiner's lectures and books found throughout this article.

- All animals of the same type formation share a Group-Soul, a Group-Ego moving in a continual circular movement around the Earth.

- The plant kingdom has just one Group-Ego located in the center of the Earth.
- All minerals have their Group-Egos in the higher worlds, on the Higher Devachanic plane.
- All-embracing Group-Souls were the basis of the human races on the Old Moon.
- One individual human being is, in himself, the equivalent of whole animal species.
- The Human-Ego originated from a Group-Ego that descended from the astral plane to the physical plane, and thereby, over time, separated into Individual-Egos.
- There were present on the Old Moon all-embracing Group-Souls filled with wisdom.
- The tribe was like a single organism in that a group of people who were related by blood had one 'I-Soul' in common.
- The present 'I' has developed from such a group-consciousness; for a Group-Ego became many separate individuated 'I's.
- These [human] Group-Souls were originally in the astral world and then descended to live in the physical body.
- There are four chief types of human Group-Souls; these four prototypes are traditionally represented in Christian cathedrals in zodiacal art works known as the *Tetramorph*:
  - 1. The image of a Bull/Taurus (metabolic system/*Gospel of Luke*).
  - 2. The image of a Lion/Leo (rhythmic system/*Gospel of Mark*).
  - 3. The image of an Eagle/Scorpio (nervous system/ *Gospel of John*).

- ○ 4. The image of a Man/Aquarius (synthesis/*Gospel of Matthew*).
- From out of the shared Divine-Human entelechy that was donated for the whole of humanity, there descended the four Group-Souls.
- The Group-Souls of the minerals are to be found in the sphere of the Thrones, those of the plants in the sphere of the Spirits of Wisdom (Kyriotetes), and the animals in the sphere of the Spirits of Motion (Dynamis).
- Man has so received his Group-Soul that with the inflowing of his 'I' or Ego, a Group-Soul was originally given him, as an emanation from the Spirits of Form.
- The Group-Soul of mankind was originally allotted by the Spirits of Form to be a unitary soul for the whole of humanity.
- Man was created to be 'one,' all the world over; in this unity, the primeval Ego of man was to assert itself as a Group-Soul dwelling in all men, a Group-Soul which had descended to the physical plane.
- The four apocalyptic animals are the four classes of the Group-Souls which live in the astral world alongside the human beings with their Individual-Souls.
- A whole species of animals is a being on the astral plane, a being with whom conversations can be held as with an individual here on Earth.
- The individuation of mankind through the 'luciferic fall' torn them away from their Group-Soul; for only thus can true love freely develop—by going beyond the ties of family and tribe through one individual freely drawing close to another.

- Where Egos are united within the Group-Soul, there is no true love—beings must be separated from each other so that love may be offered as a free gift.
- In the Fifth Post-Atlantean Epoch, Christ comes in an etheric body, in the Sixth Epoch in an astral body, and in the Seventh as a mighty *Macrocosmic-I or Ego* that is like a great Group-Soul of humanity.
- Starting from a physical man on Earth, the Christ gradually evolves as Etheric Christ, as Astral Christ, as Ego-Christ, in order, as the *Macrocosmic-I* of Christ, to be the Spirit of the Earth who then rises to even higher stages together with all mankind on Future Jupiter (*Macrocosmic-Spirit-Self*), Venus (*Macrocosmic-Life-Spirit*) and Vulcan evolution (*Macrocosmic-Spirit-Human*).
- Two origins of mankind were formed for the Ego to develop: a lower man, consisting of physical body, ether body, and astral body; and a higher man, consisting of Spirit-Human (Atman), Life-Spirit (Budhi), and Spirit-Self (Manas).
- The Life-Spirit (Budhi) was formed with the assistance of the Cherubim on Old Sun.
- The 'higher man' (Spirit-Human, Life-Spirit, Spirit-Self) also exists as a higher unity within the consciousness of the Spirits of Form.
- When man has evolved the Spiritual-Soul, the upper triad, Spirit-Self, Life-Spirit, and Spirit-Human will gradually come to meet him over time, so that the opening flower of his being can receive into it this upper triad streaming in from above.

- The gift from above that is indicative of the nature of humanity in the far future is He who lives, the Life-Spirit, the Son of the Living God.
- The Son of Man evolves upwards from below; while the Son of the living God, comes down to meet him from above.
- In the ancient Mysteries there were three stages of initiation into the *Macrocosm*—Spirit-Self, Life-Spirit and Spirit-Human.
- As we evolve, the Spirit-Self as a *Microcosmic Principle* rays into us as a gift from the hierarchy of the Angels; this is in preparation for what is to come to us through Christ as a *Macrocosmic Principle* in the future—*as our own Spirit-Self* in the Future Jupiter Planetary Condition.
- As we evolve, the Life-Spirit as a *Microcosmic Principle* rays into us as a gift from the hierarchy of the Archangels; this is in preparation for what is to come to us through Christ as a *Macrocosmic Principle* in the future—*as our own Life-Spirit* in the Future Venus Planetary Condition.
- As we evolve further, the Spirit-Human as a *Microcosmic Principle* rays into us as a gift from the hierarchy of the Archai; this is in preparation for what is to come to us through Christ as a *Macrocosmic Principle* in the future—*as our own Spirit-Human* in the Future Vulcan Planetary Condition).
- Man can experience in the middle of a long sleep, what may be called an inner union with the Spirit-Self—he can have a meeting with his genius (Paraclete/Paráklētos/good daemon) in the form of an Angel (Holy Spirit).

- This second meeting with the Life-Spirit depends on the nearness of Christ Jesus who reveals Himself by working through the Archangelic realm of the Life-Spirit (the Son).
- A third meeting with the Spirit-Human is brought near to him through a being belonging to the hierarchy of the Archai (the Father).
- The daily course of universal world processes includes our meeting with our genius (Holy Spirit/3rd Logos): the yearly course includes our meeting with Christ Jesus (Son/2nd Logos): and the course of a whole human life, includes the meeting with the Father Principle (Father/1st Logos).
- Out of the purified astral body there arises the Spirit-Self (Manas). Out of the transformed etheric body arises Budhi (Life-Spirit). Out of the transformed physical-body arises Atman (Spirit-Human).
- For at a higher level, it is the activity of the Christened-Ego that will refashion and transmute the etheric, or life body, into Life-Spirit or Budhi.
- The Intellectual or Mind-Soul (Higher-Feeling-Soul) is a foreshadowing of what the Life-Spirit or Budhi will become.
- There is a Group-Soul for the higher manifestation of humanity, which is represented in Christian art by the lamb in the center of the seal, the Mystical Lamb, the sign of the Redeemer.
- Some people will experience a new 'Fall' of mankind; which will consist of unconsciously falling back by a connection with the old outmoded types of Group-Souls of humanity.

- Those who do not develop their individual 'I,' will be obliged to join on to a certain group from which they will be directed as to how they should think, feel, will, and act.
- The Group-Egos of the animal species travel in a continual circular movement around the Earth at all heights and in all directions.
- The Group-Egos of animals are in possession of wisdom; but they have no real knowledge of the love that can arise from a free individual.
- All that connects men, through folk, race, and family, will be ever more completely severed; while everything in man will evolve more and more into individual personhood—*so that love that can arise from the free individual.*
- When men unite together within the higher wisdom of Sophia, then out of higher worlds through Christ there descends a transcendental Universally-Human Group-Soul as a manifestation of love.
- As together we turn our hearts towards a higher wisdom (Theotokos), we provide a dwelling-place (Christophorus) for the Group-Soul that is a gift of Christ—'the Lamb of God that taketh away the sins of the world.'
- That is expressed when it is said that the Holy Spirit, the Group-Soul, sank down as it were into incarnation to become the dwelling-place for the Being who descends out of higher worlds.
- If his individual soul keeps itself aloof too long on the Earth it could come about that it lets the chance of *union* go by; it would then become a sort of elemental being and the elemental beings originating from man would be of quite an evil nature.

- There is actually active within the human being two modalities operating from below and above. From below the ancient feminine principle as Group-Soul (Theotokos; 'God-bearer'); and from above a new masculine principle as the individualizing element (Christophorus; 'bearer of Christ'); which together provide the conjoined vehicles (Mysterium Coniunctionis) to serve the unfolding of a higher understanding (Theodidaktos; 'God-taught').

- For what lives in the 'I,' is the same spiritual substance that weaves and lives through the world as Spirit.

Sergei O. Prokofieff on the Three Human-Egos

Rudolf Steiner's Path of Initiation and the Mystery of the Ego, **Sergei O. Prokofieff, A lecture in Bologna, March 2011, Temple Lodge Press**

"The real being of man lives outside of the body. Ego-consciousness, otherwise experienced as the everyday Ego, is only a mirror image of the Higher-Ego in the body. We must seek the path to the transcendental Human-Ego by dropping the prior developed symbolic pictures and voluntarily extinguish them and concentrate on the pure power within us that creates the pictures within us. We must direct our attention to the inner-activity itself and not the pictures. This is how we create a free space inside our soul into which the spirit world can flow. One can then perceive one's essential nature and find one's own consciousness outside of the body. This is designated as the higher Human-Ego."

Group-Souls of the Animals, Plants, and Minerals

Nature and Spirit Beings Their Effects in Our Visible World,
Pt. II, Rudolf Steiner, Lecture V, *The Group-Souls of Animals,*
Plants, and Minerals, **Pt. I, Frankfurt, February 2, 1908, GA 98**

"When looking at the other beings, one could at first believe that the animal beings do not have a soul like human beings. The Ego of man, man's soul, is certainly different from an animal's Ego, in that the Ego of man lives on the physical plane. When we look at an animal as such, then each individual animal has a physical body, an etheric body and an astral body. Human beings have in addition to these three bodies an Ego. During his waking state man's Ego is contained in him. The animal, however, does not have an Ego on the physical plane. For this, we have to go a bit deeper into the so called astral world. On the astral plane we will find a population of animal Egos, just like we have a human population here on the physical plane. Just as one man meets another here, a clairvoyant is able to meet self-contained personalities on the astral plane—these are the animal Egos.

"One has to imagine it thus—imagine the ten fingers of a human being stretched through a wall. They are moving. We can see the ten fingers moving, but not the human being himself. He is hidden behind the wall. We are not able to explain to ourselves how the ten fingers can get through the wall and move. We have to assume that there is some being to which they belong. It is the same with animals in the physical world. All animals of similar shape have one Group-Ego. Here in the physical world we see the animals roam about, and what we are seeing has a physical body, an etheric body and an astral body. If we see here in the physical world, for example, lions, then these lions are externalized organs of those lion-Egos that live in the astral world. The lion-Ego, the Group-Ego of physical lions, is a similarly self-contained being on the astral plane as we are self-contained beings here. Thus each group of animals has an Ego on the astral plane: a lion-Ego, a tiger-Ego, a vulture-Ego are on the astral plane. The single animals exist here in the physical world like fingers stretched through a wall.

"When we observe the individual animals here, many of them appear to be extraordinarily smart. These animals are being managed from the astral plane where the animal-Egos, the Group-Egos, are located. The population of the astral plane is much more clever than human beings. The animal Group-Egos on the astral plane are very wise beings. Observe the bird-migration, whereby the birds migrate through the various regions, how their flight is arranged, how during autumn they move to warmer regions and how they gather together again in spring. If we deeply look into these wise arrangements, we have to ask ourselves: who is hidden behind the wall, who arranges all of this?—These are the Group-Egos. When we watch a beaver building, then we will see that the beaver built more wisely than the greatest engineering art.

"One has observed the intelligence of bees at work by giving sugar instead of honey to them. Then they were watched. They cannot take along the sugar, so they go and fetch other bees. First they fly to a source of water, from which each bee carries a drop of water, drenches the sugar with it and transforms it into a kind of syrup. This is then carried to the hive. The spirit of the beehive is behind the work of the bees. The individual bees belong to a single bee personality, just like our limbs belong to us. Only it is the case that each bee is more separate from the others, and as individuals our limbs are closer together, more compact. We walk everywhere through entities invisible for us, through the animal Group-Egos, who evade physical observation.

"As we begin to empathize with beings of which man has not the slightest idea, we can also empathize with the plant souls. The plant-Egos live in an even higher world than the animal-Egos. The plant-Egos, those self-contained Group-Egos, to each of which a series of plant belongs, are on the so-called Devachanic Plane. We can also tell the place where these plant-Egos actually are—all plant-Egos are at the center of the Earth. The animal Group-Egos are circumventing the Earth like the trade-winds, while the plant-Ego's are in the center of the Earth. They are beings that all penetrate each other. In the Spiritual World the law of permeability holds sway—one being passes through another. We see the animal Group-Egos pass across the Earth like the trade-winds and observe how they, out of their wisdom, perform what we consider to be the deeds of the animals. When we observe the plants, then we see the head of the plant, the root, is extended to the center of the Earth, because there, at the center of the Earth, is their Group-Ego.

"The Earth itself is an expression of soul-spiritual entities. The plants appear to us, from a spiritual viewpoint, to be something like the nails on our fingers. The plants belong to the Earth. One who observes the individual plants, can never see them completely. Each plant belongs to the sum of entities that make up the plant-Egos. Thus we can immerse ourselves into the feelings and emotion of the plants themselves. The part of the plant that grows out of the Earth, that strives from within the Earth to the surface, has a different nature from what grows under the Earth. If you cut off the bloom, stalk and leaves of a plant, then that is something different from pulling out the root. If you cut off a plant this will create a certain type of well-being, like a pleasure for the plant soul. This pleasure it similar to what is felt, for example, by a cow whose young calf suckles at its udder. The plant part that grows out of the Earth really is something similar to the milk of animals.

"When we walk through the fields in autumns and the stalks are falling under the scythe of the reaper, when the scythe strikes the sheaves, then feelings of well-being, akin to ecstasy, breathe across the fields. It is something immensely significant when the reaper goes through the field with his scythe, and we not only can watch the falling sheaves with our physical eyes, but we can see feelings of pleasure stroking the Earth.

"However, when you rip out a plant by its root, this causes pain for the plant soul. The laws that apply in the physical world are not the same as those in the higher worlds. We will gain different insights when we ascend to the Spiritual Worlds. Sometimes also here in the physical world the principle of beauty contradicts the principle of pain or joy. It is possible that someone, driven by beauty concepts, rips out a few white hairs, although it will hurt him. This applies to plants too. It might look more tidy to rip out a plant by its root, it might be more beautiful; but it will still hurt the plant.

"The stones are also lifeless only in the physical world—in the higher worlds they too have their Group-Egos. In the upper areas of Devachan, the Group-Egos of the minerals exist. They too experience joy and pain. We will not find out anything about this by way of speculation, but only through the Science of the Spirit.

"If we observe a worker in a quarry breaking up stone-by-stone, we could believe that this would cause pain to the stone soul. But this is not so. Just when a stone is blasted, then feelings of pleasure burst forth from the stone in all directions. Out of the quarry, where rock is blasted apart, strong feelings of well-being stream out on all sides. When we have a glass of water and add salt to it, and the salt dissolves, then feelings of desire and pleasure will stream through the water. Joy streams through the water when the dissolution of salt is being observed from a spiritual viewpoint. But if we allow the dissolved salt to settle and harden again, then this happens under pain. Likewise, it would cause pain to the stone soul if we could amalgamate the rock again that was blasted apart."

The Influence of Spiritual Beings Upon Man, Rudolf Steiner, Lecture I, Berlin, January 6, 1908, GA 102

"You will have gathered from the lectures given here recently that when we ascend with clairvoyance into the higher worlds, we there meet with beings who, it is true, do not belong to our physical world; but who are in themselves so independent that we can describe them as 'persons' for those worlds, just as we call men here on the physical plane 'persons.' You have seen that groups of animals of the same species together belong to a Group-Soul or Group-Ego and that on the astral plane we come upon the lion-soul, the tiger-soul, and so on, as independent personalities whom we can meet there as we meet the human being on the physical plane. In the same way we find in still higher regions, on the Devachanic Plane, the Egos of quite large plant groups, and in the highest parts of Devachan we find the Egos of the minerals, personalities as distinct as men are here on the physical plane. We saw in this way that in these higher worlds we meet with certain beings who, so to speak, extend part of their organism, their separate members, down into the physical plane. If a man were to extend his fingers through openings in a curtain or partition, we should only see the ten fingers, the man himself would be behind the partition. So, it is with the Group-Egos of the animals.

Here with the physical eye, we see what is extended down below as members by higher beings of the astral world, and the actual Ego is behind the partition, behind that wall which separates the physical world from the astral world. And in a corresponding way this holds good for the other Group-Egos, the Group-Egos of the plant or the mineral world. When we raise ourselves from the physical world into higher worlds, we meet not only these beings who have been described as extending their members down below here, but we meet a whole number of other beings who may equally well be considered personalities for those worlds, but whose physical members are not so directly visible and evident as those of the group Egos of animals, plants, and minerals."

Human Group-Souls

The Influence of Spiritual Beings Upon Man, **Rudolf Steiner, Lecture VI, Berlin, March 24, 1908, GA 102**

"On our Earth therefore, man had a kind of group-consciousness connected with his Group-Soul. If we were to go back to the Old Moon where the human being had not a restricted Ego of this sort embedded in the group-consciousness; but where he had no Ego at all, where he still consisted of physical body, etheric body, astral body, we should find that this Old Moon-consciousness was not a smaller one but embraced immensely great groups—that in fact all-embracing Group-Souls were the basis of the human race on the Old Moon. These Group-Souls who, so to speak, set individual Old Moon-men on to the Old Moon merely as their limbs, were wise souls. We have, as you know, also described the animal Group-Souls on the Earth and have also found wisdom as their out-standing characteristic. These Moon Group-Souls have implanted in our planet's previous embodiment the wisdom which we know today and which we so much wonder at and admire. And when today we are amazed how every bone, how heart and brain, how every plant leaf, is permeated and imbued with wisdom, then we know that the wisdom of the Group-Souls trickled down from the atmosphere of the Old Moon—as clouds today let the rain trickle down—and membered itself into all the beings. These received it as a propensity and brought it out again when they appeared on the Earth after the Pralaya [cosmic-rest]. Thus, there were present on the Old Moon all-embracing Group-Souls filled with wisdom."

The Common 'I-Soul'

The Apocalypse of St. John, Rudolf Steiner, Lecture II, Nuremberg, June 19, 1908, GA 104

"We have now to describe more exactly what the initiate then began to see. When he had been led to illumination it was clear to him when he was awakened, that he had seen something which he had previously never been able consciously to grasp. What then had he seen? What was he able to call up in a certain sense before his soul as an important memory-picture of his vision? If we wish to understand what he had seen we must cast a glance at the evolution of man. We must remember that man has only gradually gained the degree of individual consciousness he now possesses. He could not always say 'I' to himself as he does today. We need only go back to the time when the Cherusci, the Heruli, etc., lived in the parts now inhabited by the Germans. The different human beings did not then feel themselves as separate Human-Egos, but as members of the tribe. Just as a finger does not feel itself to be something existing independently, so each Cheruscan did not feel that he could unconditionally say 'I' to himself; his 'I' was the 'I' of the whole tribe. The tribe represented a single organism and a group of men who were related by blood had one 'I-soul' in common. In those days you yourselves were members of a great community, just as today your two arms belong to your 'I.' This may be clearly seen in the case of the people dealt with in the *Old Testament*. Each single member felt himself to be a member of the race. The individual did not speak of himself in the highest sense when he uttered the ordinary 'I'; but he felt something deeper when he said, 'I and the Father Abraham are one.' For he felt a certain 'I-consciousness' which descended from Abraham through all the generations to each member of the race. That which was related by blood was included in one 'I.' It was like a common 'Group-Soul-I' which included the whole race and those that understood the matter said: That which really forms our inmost immortal being dwells not in the separate members but in the entire race. All of the several members belong to this common 'I.' Hence one who understood the matter knew that when he died, he united himself with an invisible being which reached back to Father Abraham. The individual really felt that he returned into Abraham's bosom. He felt that his immortal part found refuge, as it were, in the Group-Soul of the race. This Group-Soul of the entire race could not descend to the physical plane. The people themselves saw only the separate human forms; but these were to them not the reality—*for this was in the Spiritual World*. They dimly felt that that which flowed through the blood was the Divine. And because they had to see God in Jehovah, they called this Divinity 'Jahve' or also his Countenance, 'Michael.' They considered Jahve as the spiritual Group-Soul of the people.

"The individual human being on the physical plane could not see these spiritual beings. The initiate, on the other hand, who experienced the great moment when the astral body was imprinted in the etheric body, was able to see first of all the most important Group-Souls. When we look back into ancient periods of humanity, we everywhere find that the present 'I' has developed from such a group-consciousness, a Group-Ego; so that when the seer looks back, he finds that the individual human beings flow together more and more into the Group-Souls. Now there are four chief types of [human] Group-Souls, four prototypes. If we observe all the various Group-Souls of the different souls, we notice a certain similarity—*but there are also differences.* If we classify them there are four groups, four types. The spiritual observer sees them clearly when he looks back to the time when man was not yet in the flesh, when he had not descended to the Earth. We must now consider more exactly the moment when from the spiritual regions man descended into flesh. This can only be represented in great symbols.

"There was a time when our Earth was composed of very much softer material than it is now, when rock and stone were not so solid, when the forms of the plants were quite different, when the whole was as if embedded like a primeval ocean in water-caves, when air and water were not separated, when all the beings now dwelling on the Earth, the animals and plants, were developed in water. When the minerals began to assume their present form, man emerged from invisibility. The neophyte saw it in this way: Surrounded by a kind of shell, man descended from the regions which are now the regions of air. He was not yet as physically condensed when the animals already existed in the flesh. He was a delicate airy being even in the Lemurian Epoch and he so developed that the spiritual picture presents the four Group-Souls: On one side something like the image of a Lion, on the other the likeness of a Bull, up above something like an Eagle and below something similar to Man. Such is the spiritual picture. Thus, man moves forth from the darkness of the spirit-land. And the force which formed him appears as a kind of rainbow. The more physical powers surround the entire structure of this human being like a rainbow (*Revelation* 4). We have to describe this development of man in various realms and in various ways. The above description represents the way it appears to the investigator when he looks back and sees how these four Group-Souls have developed out of the common Divine-human which descends. From time immemorial this stage has been symbolized in the form represented in the second of the so-called seven seals. That is the symbolic representation; but it is more than a mere symbol.

"There you see these four Group-Souls emerging from an indefinite background, the rainbow surrounding it and the number twelve. Now we must understand what this number twelve signifies. When that which has just been described is seen coming forth, there is a clairvoyant feeling that it is surrounded by something of an entirely different nature from that which emerges from the indeterminate spiritual. In ancient times, that by which it is surrounded was symbolized by the Zodiac, by the twelve signs of the Zodiac. The moment of entering into spiritual vision is connected with many other experiences. The first thing perceived by one whose etheric body goes forth is that it seems to him as if he grew larger and larger and extended himself over what he then perceives. The moment comes when the initiate says: 'I do not merely see these four forms; but I am within them, I have expanded my being over them.' He identifies himself with them. He perceives that which is symbolized by the constellations, by the number twelve. We shall best understand that which spreads itself around, that which reveals itself, if we remember that our earth has passed through previous incarnations. We know that before the Earth became Earth it went through the condition of [Old] Saturn, then through that of [Old] Sun, then through that of [Old] Moon, and only then did it become our present Earth. This was necessary, for only in this way was it possible for the beings we see on the Earth around us to come forth as they have done. They had gradually to work through those changing forms."

Cosmic Ego and Human-Ego, Rudolf Steiner, Munich, January 9, 1912, GA 130

"The Christ is quite radically different from other beings who share in the Earth evolution. He is a Being of quite another order; He is a Being who remained behind, not only during the [Old] Moon evolution, as the Luciferic spirits did; but who, foreseeing the Moon evolution, actually remained behind still earlier, namely, during the Old Sun evolution; and it was from a certain assured wisdom far above the human that He remained behind during the Old Sun evolution. We cannot regard this Being as microcosmic in the sense which applies to the other beings we have been considering; for we have to regard as microcosmic beings those who were connected with this Earth evolution from its beginning. The Christ was not directly connected with the Earth evolution—*but with the Sun evolution*. He was a *macrocosmic* Being from the beginning of the Earth evolution on, a Being who was exposed to entirely different conditions of evolution from those of the *microcosmic* beings. And His evolutionary conditions were of a special sort; they were such that this macrocosmic Christ Being evolved the Macrocosmic-Ego ['I'] outside earthly conditions. For this Christ evolution it was normal to bring to Ego-perfection, outside the Earth, an Ego of a macrocosmic sort—*and then to descend to Earth*. And so, for the evolution of the Christ Being it was normal, when He descended from the macrocosm to our Earth, to bring into it the great impulse of the Macrocosmic-Ego, in order that the microcosmic Ego, the Human-Ego, might take up this impulse, and be able to go forward in its evolution. It was normal for the Christ to have the Macrocosmic Ego-impulse—not the microcosmic Ego-impulse—just as much evolved as man upon the Earth had developed the microcosmic. Thus, the Christ Being is a Being Who in a certain sense is like the human being, only that man is *microcosmic* and has brought his four principles to expression microcosmically, and hence has his Ego ['I'] also microcosmically as *Earth-Ego*—but the Christ as *Cosmic-Ego*. His evolution was such that He was great and significant because of the perfect development of this Cosmic Ego [Macrocosmic-I], which He brought down to Earth; furthermore, He did not have the fifth Macrocosmic Principle [Manas; Spirit-Self], and not the sixth [Budhi; Life-Spirit]; for He will evolve these on [Future] Jupiter and on [Future] Venus—*in order that He may give them to man.*

"The Christ, then, is a four-membered Being, including His Macrocosmic-Ego [Macrocosmic-I], just as man himself is *microcosmically* a four-membered being. And as, man during Earth evolution, has as his mission the development of his Ego [I], in order to be able to *receive*, so the Christ had to develop His Ego, in order to be able to *give*. When He descended to Earth His whole being was employed in bringing His fourth principle to expression in the most perfect possible form. Now each *macrocosmic principle* has an inner relationship to the corresponding *microcosmic principle*; the fourth macrocosmic principle in the Christ corresponds to the fourth microcosmic principle in man, and the fifth in the Christ will correspond to the Spirit-Self in man [in the Future-Jupiter Planetary Condition].

"Thus, the Christ entered upon His earthly course in that He brought down to man out of the *macrocosm* what man was to evolve *microcosmically*—only the Christ brought it as a *macrocosmic* principle. He entered the Earth evolution in such a way that during its course He would not have a fifth, sixth and seventh principle as His personal possession, just as man in his way does not possess them.

"The Christ is a Being Who had evolved *macrocosmically* up to the fourth principle, and the evolution of His fourth principle during the Earth course consists in His bestowing upon man everything which will enable him to evolve his Ego.

"If we take a complete survey, we have at the beginning of Earth evolution three classes of beings: human beings who were to bring their fourth principle to full development on Earth; a class of Luciferic beings who were to evolve their sixth principle; and a class of Luciferic beings who were to develop their seventh principle:—beings who, because they were ready to develop their sixth and seventh principles, stood higher than man,—in fact, ranged far above man in this respect. But they also ranged above Christ in this regard; for the Christ was to bring His fourth principle to expression on the Earth, in devotion to humanity. It will not be the Christ, let us say, that will quicken man in the future to bring to expression something other than the True-Ego [True-I], the innermost human being—to reach ever higher and higher stages. It will be the Luciferic spirits who will lead man out beyond himself in a certain sense.

"Anyone who looks at the matter superficially can say: 'Of course then the Christ stands lower than, for example, the Luciferic spirits.' ... because the Christ came to Earth with something which is fully related to man's fourth principle. For that reason He is not at all fitted to lead man above himself;

but only more deeply into his own soul being. He is fitted
to lead the individual soul-being of man more-and-more
to itself. The Luciferic beings have evolved the fourth, fifth
and sixth principles, and hence in a certain way stand higher
than the Christ. Practically, that will work out in the future
so that through the admission of the Christ principle into
human nature, this human nature will become more and more
deepened, will take up more and more light and love into its
own being; so that the human being will have to feel *Light and
Love* as belonging to his very self. *The immeasurable deepening
of the human soul—that will be the gift of the Christ-Impulse,
which will work on and on forever.* And when the Christ shall
come, as that coming has been represented in many lectures—
then He will work only upon the deepening of human souls. The
other spirits who have higher principles than the Christ, *though
only microcosmic principles*, will in a certain sense lead man out
beyond himself. The Christ will deepen the inner-life of man—
but also make him humble. The Luciferic spirits, on the other
hand, will lead man out beyond himself, and make him wise,
clever, talented—*but also in a certain sense haughty; will teach
him that he might become something superhuman even during the
Earth evolution.* Everything, therefore, which in the future shall
lead man to rise above himself, as it were, which will make him
proud of his own human nature even here upon Earth—*that
will be a Luciferic impulse*; but what makes a man more deeply
sincere, what brings his inner-life to such depths as can come
only through the complete development of the fourth principle—
that comes from the Christ.

"People who look at the matter superficially will say that
Christ really stands lower than the Luciferic beings; for He has
developed only the fourth principle, and the others, higher

principles. Only the difference is that these other beings bring
the higher principles as something parasitic, grafted upon
human nature; *but the Christ brings the fourth principle in such
a way that it penetrates human nature, takes root within it, and
fills it with power.* As the fleshly body of Jesus of Nazareth was
once permeated and empowered by the Fourth Macrocosmic-
Principle ['I-Am'], so will the bodies of those who take the Christ
into themselves be permeated by the Fourth Macrocosmic-
Principle. Just as the Fourth Macrocosmic-Principle is the gift
of Christ, so will the sixth and the seventh principles be the
gifts of the Luciferic spirits. So that in the future—and such
time is now being prepared for—we may experience that people
lacking in understanding will say: If we examine the *Gospels,* or
otherwise allow to work upon us what Christ gave to humanity,
we see that in regard to His teaching He does not at all rank as
high as perhaps do other spiritual beings who are connected
with humanity ... They are higher than man in a certain way.
They cannot penetrate the entire man; but they take root in his
intellect, they make him a genius! And one who observes only
outwardly says that these beings stand higher than the Christ
... And the time will come when the most powerful, the most
significant of these Luciferic spirits, who will wish to lead the
people out beyond themselves, so to speak, will be extolled, and
looked upon as a great human leader; and it will be said that
what the Christ was able to furnish was really only a bridge. Now
already there are people who say: 'What do the teachings of the
Gospels amount to! We have outgrown them.'—As has been said,
men will point to a lofty, versatile spirit, a spirit of genius, who
will take possession of a human fleshly nature, which he will
permeate with his genius. It will be said that he surpasses even the
Christ! For the Christ was one who gave opportunity to develop

the fourth principle; but this one gives opportunity during the Earth evolution to attain to the seventh principle.

"Thus, will the Christ Spirit and the spirit of this being face one another—the Christ Spirit, from whom humanity may hope to receive the mighty macrocosmic impulse of its fourth principle, and the *Luciferic Spirit*, who will wish in a certain way to lead humanity beyond this.

"If people would agree that we must acquire from the Luciferic spirits only that to which we can look up in the same way that we look down to our lower nature ... then they would be doing right. But if people should come to say:—

> You see the Christ gives only the fourth principle, while these spirits give the sixth and seventh ... people who think thus concerning Christ will worship and extol ... *the Antichrist*.

"Thus, will the position of the Antichrist towards the Christ make itself felt in the future. And with the outer intellect, with the outer wisdom, one will not be able to challenge such things; for it will be possible to produce much which from the point-of-view of the intellect and talent will be more clever in the Antichrist than that which will more and more flow into the soul from the Christ, as the highest human principle. Because Christ brings to man the Fourth Macrocosmic Principle—*since it is macrocosmic, it is infinitely more important than all microcosmic principles*; it is stronger than they, even though it is related to the Human-Ego, stronger than all others which can be gained during Earth evolution—still, because it is only the fourth principle, it will be thought of as lower than the fifth, sixth and seventh, which come from the Luciferic spirits; *and especially lower than that which comes from Antichrist.*"

Cosmic Christianity and the Impulse of Michael, Rudolf Steiner,
Lecture VI, Dornach, August 27, 1924, GA 240

"And so, before the Mystery of Golgotha, the Knights of King
Arthur received into themselves the Sun-Spirit, that is to say,
the Christ as He was in pre-Christian times. And they sent their
messengers out into all Europe to subdue the wild savagery of the
astral bodies of the peoples of Europe, to purify and to civilize—
for such was their mission. We see such men as these Knights of
King Arthur's Round Table starting from this point in the West
of England to bear to the peoples of Europe as they were at that
time, what they had received from the Sun, purifying the astral
forces of the then barbarous European population—barbarous at
all events in Central and Northern Europe.

"Then came the Mystery of Golgotha. What happened in
Asia? Over yonder in Asia, the sublime Sun Being, Who was
later known as the Christ, left the Sun. This betokened a kind
of death for the Christ Being. He went forth from the Sun as we
human beings go forth from the Earth when we die. And as a
man who dies leaves his physical body behind on the Earth and
his etheric body which is laid aside after three days is visible to
the seer, so Christ left behind Him in the Sun that which in my
book *Theosophy* is called 'Spirit-Man' [Spirit-Human] the seventh
member of the human being.

"Christ died to the Sun. He died cosmically, from the Sun
to the Earth. He came down to the Earth. From the moment
of Golgotha onwards His Life-Spirit was to be seen around the
Earth. We ourselves leave behind at death the Life-Ether, the
etheric body, the life-body. After this Cosmic Death, Christ left
His Spirit-Man on the Sun; and around the Earth, His Life-Spirit.
So that after the Mystery of Golgotha the Earth was swathed as it
were by the Life-Spirit of the Christ.

"Now the connections between places are not the same in the spiritual life as they are in physical life. The Life-Spirit of the Christ was perceived in the Irish Mysteries, in the Mysteries of Hibernia; and above all by the Knights of King Arthur's Round Table. So, up to the time of the Mystery of Golgotha, the Christ-Impulse belonging to the Sun actually went out from this place where the impulses were received from the Sun. Afterwards the power of the Knights diminished; but they lived at the time within this Life-Spirit which encircled the Earth and in which there was this constant interplay of light and air, of the Spirits in the Elements from above and from below.

"Try to picture to yourselves the cliff with King Arthur's castle upon it and from above the Sun-forces playing down in the light and air and pouring upwards from below the elementary beings of the Earth. There is a living interplay between Sun and Earth.

"In the centuries which followed the Mystery of Golgotha this all took place within the Life-Spirit of the Christ. So that in the play of nature between sea and rock, air and light, there was revealed, as it were in spiritual light—*the Event of Golgotha*.

"Understand me rightly, my dear friends. If in the first five centuries of our era men looked out over the sea, and had been prepared by the exercises practiced by the twelve who were around King Arthur and who were concerned above all with the Mysteries of the Zodiac, if they looked out over the sea they could see not merely the play of nature; but they could begin to read a meaning in it just as one reads a book instead of merely staring at it. And as they looked and saw, here a gleam of light, there a curling wave, here the Sun mirrored on a rocky cliff, there the sea dashing against the rocks, it all became a flowing, weaving picture—a truth whose meaning could be deciphered. And when

they deciphered it, they knew of the spiritual Fact of the Mystery
of Golgotha. The Mystery of Golgotha was revealed to them
because the picture was all irradiated by the Life-Spirit of Christ
presented to them by nature.

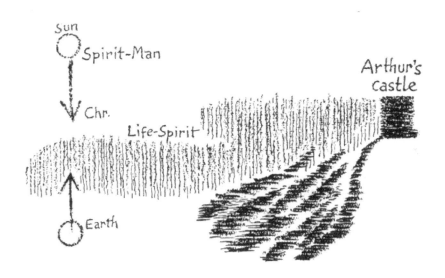

"Yonder in Asia the Mystery of Golgotha had taken place
and its impulse had penetrated deeply into the hearts and souls
of men. We need only think of those who became the first
Christians to realize what a change had come about in their souls.
While all this of which I have been telling you was happening in
the West, the Christ Himself, the Christ Who had come down to
Earth leaving His Spirit-Man on the Sun and His Life-Spirit in the
atmosphere around the Earth, bringing down His Ego ['I'] and
His Spirit-Self to the Earth—*the Christ was moving from East to
West in the hearts of men, through Greece, Northern Africa, Italy,
Spain, across Europe. The Christ worked here in the hearts of
men—while over in the West He was working through nature.*"

Earthly and Cosmic Man, **Rudolf Steiner, Lecture VI,**
The Mission of the Earth. Wonder, Compassion and Conscience.
The Christ-Impulse, **Berlin, May 14, 1912, GA 133**

"We know that what we actually see in the kingdoms of Nature around us is not reality, but 'Maya,' the 'Great Illusion.' In the kingdom of the animals we see the individual forms coming into being and passing away; the Group-Soul alone endures. In the plant kingdom, the individual plants appear and disappear, but behind them there is the Earth-Spirit which does not pass away. So it is, too, in the kingdom of the minerals. The Spiritual endures, but the Physical, whether in the animal, plant or mineral kingdom, is transient, impermanent. Even the outer senses discern that the planet Earth is involved in a process of pulverization and will at some future time disintegrate into dust. We have spoken of how the Earth-body will be cast off by the Spirit of the Earth, as the human body is cast off by the individual human Spirit. What will remain as the highest substance of the Earth when its goal has been reached? *The Christ-Impulse was present on the Earth, so to say as 'spiritual Substance.' That Impulse endures and will be received into men during the course of Earth-evolution.* But how does it live on? When the Christ-Impulse was upon the Earth for three years, it had no physical body, no Etheric-Body, no astral body of its own; but was enveloped in the three sheaths of Jesus of Nazareth. When the goal has been reached, the Earth, like man, will be a fully developed being, a meet and fitting vehicle for the Christ-Impulse.

"But from whence are the three sheaths of the Christ-Impulse derived? From forces that can be unfolded only on the Earth. Beginning with the Mystery of Golgotha, whatever has unfolded on the Earth since the Fourth Post-Atlantean period as the *Power of Wonder*, whatever comes to life in us as wonder—passes, finally, to the Christ, weaving the Astral Body of the Christ-Impulse. *Love or Compassion* in the souls of men weaves the Etheric-Body of the Christ-Impulse; and the *Power of Conscience* which from the time of the Mystery of Golgotha until the goal of the Earth is attained, lives in and inspires the souls of men, weaves the Physical Body—or what corresponds with the physical body—for the Christ-Impulse.[1]

"The true meaning of words from the *Gospel* can only now be discerned:—

'Whatsoever ye have done to one of the least of these My Brethren, ye have done it unto Me.' (*Matthew* 25:40).

"The forces streaming from man to man are the units integrating the Etheric-Body of Christ: love, or compassion, weaves the Etheric-Body of Christ. Thus when the goal of Earth-evolution is attained, He will be enveloped in the threefold vesture woven from the *powers* that have lived in men—and which, when the limitations of the 'I,' have been transcended, become the sheaths of Christ.

"And now think of how men live in communion with Christ. From the time of the Mystery of Golgotha to the attainment of the goal of Earth-evolution, man grows more perfect in that he develops to the stature that is within his reach as a being endowed with the power of the 'I.' But men are united with the Christ Who has come among them, in that they transcend their own 'I'—and through *Wonder*, build the Astral Body of Christ. Christ does not build His own Astral Body, but in the wonder that arises in their souls, men share in the forming of the Astral Body of Christ. His Etheric-Body will be fashioned through the *Compassion and Love* flowing from man to man; and His 'physical body' through the *Power of Conscience* unfolding in human beings. Whatever wrongs are committed in these three realms deprive the Christ of the possibility of full development on the Earth—that is to say, Earth-evolution is left imperfect. Those who go about the Earth with indifference and unconcern, who have no urge to understand what the Earth can reveal to them—deprive the Astral Body of Christ of the possibility of full development; those who live without unfolding compassion and love—hinder the Etheric-Body of Christ from full development; and those who lack conscience—hinder the development of what corresponds with the Physical Body of Christ ... but this means that the Earth cannot reach the goal of its evolution.

"The principle of Egotism has to be overcome in Earth-evolution. The Christ-Impulse penetrates more and more deeply into the life and culture of humanity and the conviction that this Impulse has lived its way into mankind, free from every trace of denominationalism—as, for example, in the paintings of Raphael.[2] this conviction will bear its fruit."

Notes:

1. See also: *Turning Points of Spiritual History, Rudolf Steiner, Lecture VI, Christ and the 20th Century, Berlin, January 25,1912, GA 61*

2. Raphael: Raffaello Sanzio da Urbino (March 28 or April 6, 1483–April 6, 1520), an Italian painter and architect. One of the traditional trinity of great masters of the High Renaissance, along with Michelangelo, and Leonardo da Vinci. It is widely considered that Raphael's works embody the Neoplatonic ideals of the 'Good, the True and the Beautiful' through their visual grandeur, purity of form, and harmonious composition.

The History of Art as an Image of an Inner Spiritual Impulse,
Rudolf Steiner, Lecture VIII, *Raphael and the Northern Artists,*
Dornach, Jan 17, 1917, GA 292

"Anyone who lets Raphael's creations work upon his soul,
will admit that in Raphael—with respect to certain artistic
intentions—the highest ideal has been attained."

The Influence of Spiritual Beings Upon Man, **Rudolf Steiner,**
Lecture II, Berlin, January 27, 1908, Berlin, GA 102

"Let us think for a moment of what was said at the beginning
of the lecture, namely that there are ascending and descending
forces—forces that are ascending to the Zodiac and forces that
are descending from the Zodiac. How has man reached a position
which makes it possible for something to stream from within
him? What has happened to man that enables something to
stream forth from him? He has reached this position because
his Ego, after long, long preparation, has steadily unfolded and
developed. This I, this Ego, has been in a course of preparation
for long, long ages. For truth to tell, the object of all existence in
the Old Saturn-condition, the Old Sun-condition and the Old
Moon-condition when the sheaths into which the I was to be
received were produced—was to prepare for the I. In those earlier
conditions, other beings created the dwelling-place for the I.
Now, on the Earth, the dwelling-place was at the stage where the
I could take root in man and from then onwards the I began to
work upon the outer, bodily sheaths from within. The fact that the
Ego is able to work from within has also brought about a surplus,
a surplus of ascending forces—*there was no longer a state of
parity.* Before the Ego was able to work within man, the ascending
forces gradually evolved until the middle-point had been reached;

and when the Ego actually entered into man the ascending
and the descending forces had reached the stage where they
were in 'balance.' At the entry of the Ego, the ascending and the
descending forces were in balance, and it rests with man to turn
the scales in the right direction. That is why the occultists have
called the constellation which was entered at the time when the
Ego itself began to operate, the 'Balance' (Libra). Up to the end
of Virgo, preparation was being made for the deeds of the Ego in
our planetary evolution—*but the Ego had not itself begun to work.*
When Libra had been reached the Ego itself began to participate
and this was a most important moment in its evolution.

"Just think what it means that the Ego had reached this
stage of evolution: From then on it was possible for the Ego to
participate in the work of the forces belonging to the Zodiac, to
reach into the Zodiac. The more the Ego strives for the highest
point of its evolution, the more it works into the Zodiac. There
is nothing that happens in the innermost core of the Ego that
does not have its consequences right up to the very Zodiac.
And inasmuch as man with his Ego lays the foundations for his
development to Atman, or Spirit-Man, he develops, stage-by-
stage, the forces which enable him to work upwards into the
sphere of Libra, the Balance, in the Zodiac. He will attain full
power over Libra in the Zodiac when his Ego has developed to
Atman, or Spirit-Human. He will then be a being from whom
something streams out—*a being who has passed out of the Sphere
of Time into the Sphere of Duration, of Eternity.*

"Such is the path of man. But there are other beings whose
lowest sphere of operation is man's highest. Let us try to
conceive of these beings whose lowest sphere of operation is
man's highest (Libra in the Zodiac). When we relate man to the
Zodiac, he reaches to Libra. The Being whose innermost nature

belongs wholly to the Zodiac, whose forces belong wholly to the Zodiac, who only manifests in planetary life through his lowest member, which corresponds to Libra (just as man's lowest member corresponds to Pisces)—*this is the Being who spreads life throughout the whole of our Universe*:

Human Being						
			Aries	12th	member	
			Taurus	11th	member	
			Gemini	10th	member	
			Cancer	9th	member	'Mystical Lamb'
			Leo	8th	member	
	7th	Spirit-Man	Virgo	7th	member	
	6th	Life-Spirit	Libra	6th	member	
	5th	Spirit-Self	Scorpio			
	4th	Ego 'I'	Sagittarius			
	3rd	Astral Body	Capricorn			
	2nd	Etheric Body	Aquarius			
	1st	Physical Body	Pisces			

"Just as man receives life into himself, so does this Being radiate life through the whole of our Universe. This is the Being Who has the power to make the great sacrifice and Who is inscribed in the Zodiac as the Being Who—*for the sake of our world*—offers Himself in sacrifice. Just as man strives upwards into the Zodiac, so does this Being send us His sacrificial gift from Aries—which is related to Him as Libra is related to man. And just as man turns his Ego upwards to Libra, so does this Being radiate His very Self over our sphere in sacrifice. This Being is called the 'Mystical Lamb,' for Lamb and Aries are the same; therefore, the description 'Sacrificial Lamb' or 'Ram' is given to Christ. Christ belongs to the Cosmos as a whole. His I, his Ego, reaches to Aries and thus He becomes Himself the 'Great Sacrifice,' and is related with the whole of mankind; for in a certain sense the beings and forces present on the Earth are His creations. The configuration of forces is such that He could become the Creator of these beings in the constellation of Aries, or the Lamb. The designation 'Sacrificial Lamb' or 'Mystical Lamb' is drawn from the heavens themselves.

"This is one of the aspects revealed to us when from our circumscribed existence we look up into the heavens and perceive the interworking of heavenly forces and beings in Cosmic Space. Gradually we begin to realize that the forces streaming from heavenly body to heavenly body are akin to those forces which stream from one human soul to another as love and hate. We perceive soul-forces streaming from star to star and learn to recognize the heavenly script which records for us what is wrought and effected by those forces in Cosmic Space."

The Elohim Donate the Group-Soul of Humanity

Beyond the everyday Earthly-Ego and the Higher-Ego there is another facet of the Ego, or 'I' that can only be found by eliminating from his consciousness all the inner experiences of his own self that he has achieved with so much effort. This third Ego leads to intuition. This Ego is called the 'Zodiacal Ego' or the third or 'True-Ego'. In accordance with the concept of the threefold Egos of humanity, this means that a person must initially come to a conscious connection with the second, Christened-Ego. It is the intermediate station on the path leading from the Earthly-Ego via the Higher-Ego to the True-Ego (Zodiacal-Ego). The third Ego embodies the mystery of the Human-Ego in connection with the whole world, with the Cosmos.

The path leads from Earthly-Ego to the Higher-Ego, the Christened-Ego, and then to the True-Ego—it is the 'Royal Road' leading beyond maya or illusion to true supersensible knowledge: Moral Imagination (Angelic realm), Moral Inspiration, (Archangelic realm), and Moral Intuition (Archai realm). For the more the soul develops supersensible cognitive powers, the nearer it comes to the Christ Being. Christ is related to the Human-Ego; for in the Spiritual World, Christ represents the principle of the Ego or 'I' as its highest example and also its eternal archetype. Here they converge: the human soul developing upward from below and downward Christ mercifully inclines towards us from the heights. With mankind, we are only concerned with the *microcosmic Human-Ego*. On the other hand, with Christ we have to do with the World Ego, the *Macrocosmic Divine Ego*.

The True-Ego is inseparably connected with the Christ Being, the understanding of it leads at the same time to the new Christ Consciousness within man. Christ is the only one in the Spiritual World who possesses the consciousness that pervades everything in Heaven and on Earth. A complete union with Christ is only possible at the level of Moral Intuition (Spirit-Man) but begins with the level of Moral Inspiration (Life-Spirit). This happens with the help of the etheric body, which in this process assumes the role of a mirror in which the reflection of the Higher-Ego appears, thus enabling a person to become selflessly conscious through being 'Christened.' The True-Ego (True-I), however remains in the Spiritual World and can only be found there.

Three Egos

Reincarnating-Ego	Higher-Ego	Spirit-Self	Manas	Holy Spirit
Christened-Ego	World-Ego	Life-Spirit	Budhi	Christened-Group-Soul
True-Ego	Zodiacal-Ego	Spirit-Man	Atman	Father God

The Earthly-Ego examines the physical world of the senses while the Spiritual-Egos examine the supersensible worlds. These two currents must be supplemented by a 'third current' coming to meet them which is capable of beholding the synthesis of the sensible and the supersensible. The confluence of the two currents may be conceived as given through a possible further development of the life of the mind up to intuitive cognition. Only within this third current is that polarity superseded. It is the Stage of Moral Intuition where the True-Ego which is so deeply connected with the Christ Being can be grasped. There it is possible to unite the threefold Ego in a synthesis which becomes a new Heaven and a new Earth lighting the conscious path from Earth back to Heaven.

Spiritual Beings in the Heavenly Bodies and in the Kingdoms of Nature, **Rudolf Steiner, Lecture X, Helsinki, April 14, 1912, GA 136**

"We have seen that in man everything is compressed into the physical plane which as it were, for the mineral, is distributed over the world. We have found Group-Souls for minerals, plants, and animals. Is there also a sort of Group-Soul for the human being? Oh, yes, there is. The Group-Souls of the minerals are to be found in the sphere of the Thrones, those of the plants in the sphere of the Spirits of Wisdom, and the animals in the sphere of the Spirits of Motion; but man has so received his Group-Soul that with the inflowing of his Ego ['I'], a Group-Soul was originally given him, as an emanation from the Spirits of Form. This Group-Soul of man was originally allotted by the Spirits of Form to be a unitary soul for the whole of humanity. What differentiated this Group-Soul into such variety that differences of race, differences of tribe arose? This was brought about through the action of other spirits. Man was created to be one all the world over; in this unity the primeval Ego of man was to assert itself as a Group-Soul dwelling in all men, a Group-Soul which had descended to the physical plane. Just as the external form only of the minerals can be brought into being by the Spirits of Form, so by these same Spirits of Form was the Group-Ego created for humanity, which was then differentiated by the activity of other beings of the various hierarchies."

Theosophy of the Rosicrucian, **Rudolf Steiner, Lecture II,**
The Ninefold Constitution of Man, **Munich, May 25, 1907, GA 99**

"Just as the human being has an Individual-Ego, so in every
astral body there lives something of a Group-Ego; this animal-
ego lives in the human astral body and the human being does
not become independent of this animal-ego until he develops
astral sight and becomes a companion of astral beings, when the
Group-Souls of the animals confront him on the astral plane as
individual animals confront him here. In the astral world there
are beings who can only come down in fragments, as it were, to
the physical plane as so-and-so many animals. When the life of
these animals comes to an end, they unite in the astral world with
the rest of this astral being. A whole species of animals is a being
on the astral plane, a being with whom conversations can be held
as with an individual here on Earth. Although there is not exact
similarity, the Group-Souls are not incorrectly characterized in
the second seal of the *Apocalypse* where they are divided into
four classes: Lion, Eagle, Bull, Man (i.e., man who has not yet
descended to the physical plane). These four apocalyptic animals
are the four classes of the Group-Souls which live in the astral
world by the side of the human being with his individual soul."

The Group-Soul and Love

Universe, Earth and Man, **Rudolf Steiner, Lecture VIII,** *Man's
Connection with the Various Planetary Bodies—The Earth's
Mission*, **August 12, 1908, Stuttgart, GA 105**

"What is to be implanted in a similar way in the beings of our
Earth? Just as wisdom was implanted in our predecessors on
the ancient Moon, so love has to be implanted on our planet.
Our planet (the Earth) is the planet of love. The development

of this, the first instilling of love, had to be in its lowest form. This happened during the Lemurian Epoch, when the Ego ['I'] of man took shape; at that time the development of love in its lowest form began through the separation of the sexes. All further development consists in the continual refinement, the spiritualizing, of this love-principle. Just as in the [Old] Moon-period wisdom was instilled into Moon-beings, so one day, when our Earth shall have attained its goal, all earthly beings will be filled with love.

"Let us now turn for a moment to the next planetary existence, that which is to succeed our Earth—the Jupiter planet. When the beings reappear who will inhabit Jupiter they will regard all those in their environment with their own spiritual powers of perception; and just as with our intellect we admire the wisdom contained in stones, plants, and animals, and indeed in everything that surrounds us—just as we draw wisdom from them that we also may have it—the Jupiter-beings will direct their forces to all that surrounds them, and the love which had been implanted in them during the Earth evolution will be wafted to those who now surround them. In the same way that we analyze objects and learn from the wisdom contained in them, so the Jupiter-beings will edify themselves with the outpourings of love that proceed from the beings about them. This love which is to develop on Earth can only develop through the Earthly-Ego being related one to another in the way described. Development in this direction can only take place through men being torn away from Group-Soul qualities; through one man drawing close to another; only thus can true love develop. Where Egos are united within the Group-Soul there is no true love. Beings must be separated from each other so that love may be offered as a free gift. Only by such a separation as has come about in the human kingdom, where

Ego meets Ego as independent individual, has love as a free gift become possible. This is why an increasing individualism and a uniting of separate individuals had to come about on Earth.

"Think of the various beings that are united within a Group-Soul; the Group-Soul directs them as to how they shall act. Can it be said that the heart loves the stomach? No, the heart is united to the stomach by the being within who holds them together. In the same way the several animals in a group are united one with the other within the Group-Soul nature, and what they have to do is regulated by the wise Group-Soul.

"Only when the group-nature is overcome, and individual confronts Individual-Ego, can the sympathy of love be offered as a free gift from one being to another.

"Man could only be prepared for this mission gradually, and we see how he passes through a kind of preparatory school for love before he is fully individualized. We see how, before he possessed a complete Ego ['I'] of his own, he was gathered into groups that were related by blood by guiding beings, and the members of these groups loved each other because of the blood tie. This was a great time of preparation for humanity."

Christ's Macrocosmic Ego is the Group-Soul of Humanity

Buddha and Christ: The Sphere of the Bodhisattvas, Rudolf Steiner, Lecture III, Milan, September 21, 1911, GA 130

"In the age when Christ works in the world of men as the etheric Christ it matters not whether we are living in a physical body or between death and a new birth, if on the physical plane we have acquired the power to behold Him. Let us suppose, for example, that because of his earlier death a man had no opportunity of beholding Christ in his present etheric Form. Nevertheless, if during his life in the physical world such a man had acquired the necessary understanding, vision of the Christ would be possible for him between death and rebirth. A man who keeps aloof from spiritual life and acquires no understanding of Christ will remain without such knowledge until he can acquire it in his next incarnation.

"What has just been said will indicate to you that as humanity lives on through the fifth, sixth and seventh epochs of civilization the Christ-Impulse will gain increasing power on the Earth. We have heard that in the sixth epoch, intellectuality will be impaired through immorality. The other aspect is that a man who has paralyzed his intellectual faculty as a result of immorality must turn to Christ with all the greater strength in order that Christ may lead him to morality and imbue him with moral strength.

"What I have told you has been investigated particularly closely by Rosicrucians since the 13th century but it is a truth that has at all times been known to many occultists.

"If it were to be asserted that there could be a second appearance of Christ on Earth in a physical body, according to occultism that would be equivalent to stating that a balance works more efficiently if it is supported at two points instead of at one. In very truth the three years' duration of Christ's life on Earth in the body of Jesus of Nazareth constitutes the fulcrum of Earth evolution; and just as there can be only one point at which the beam of a balance is attached, so too there can be only one fulcrum of Earth evolution:—

The *teaching* of moral development is not the same as the *impulse* for such development.

"Before the Event of Golgotha the Bodhisattva who was the successor of Buddha was present on the Earth in order to prepare for that Event and give teaching to those around him. He incarnated in the personality of Jeshu ben Pandira, 1. one century before the birth of Jesus of Nazareth. Thus we must distinguish between the Jeshu ben Pandira-incarnation of the Bodhisattva who was the successor of Gautama Buddha, and the incarnation at the beginning of our era of Jesus of Nazareth who for three years of his life was permeated by the Cosmic Being we call the Christ. The Bodhisattva who incarnated in Jeshu ben Pandira and in other personalities too, returns again and again, until in about three thousand years from now, he will attain Buddhahood and as Maitreya Buddha live through his final incarnation. The Christ-Individuality was on the Earth in the body of Jesus of Nazareth for three years only and does not come again in a physical body; in the Fifth Post-Atlantean Epoch He comes in an etheric body, in the Sixth Epoch in an astral body, and in the Seventh in a mighty Cosmic Ego that is like a great Group-Soul of Humanity.

"When a human being dies, his physical, etheric, and astral bodies fall away from him, and his Ego passes over to the next incarnation. It is exactly the same with planet Earth. What is physical in our Earth falls away at the end of the Earth-period and human souls in their totality pass over into the Future Jupiter condition, the next planetary embodiment of the Earth. And just as in the case of an individual human being the Ego ['I'] is the center of his further evolution, so for the whole of future humanity the Christ-Ego in the astral and etheric bodies of men goes on to ensoul the Future Jupiter-existence. We therefore see how starting from a physical man on Earth, the Christ gradually evolves as Etheric Christ, as Astral Christ, as Ego-Christ, in order, as Ego-Christ, to be the Spirit of the Earth who then rises to even higher stages together with all mankind."

Note:

1. See *Jeshu ben Pandira*, two lectures given by Rudolf Steiner at Leipzig on November 4th and 5th, 1911, and references in his later cycle, *The Gospel of St. Matthew*.

Comic Memory, Rudolf Steiner, XVII, *The Life of Earth*, GA 11

"In the preceding chapters has been shown how the components were successively formed which make up the so-called 'lower nature of man'—the physical body, the ether body and the astral body. It has also been described how, with the appearance of a new body, the old ones must always be transformed so that they can become carriers and instruments of the one formed later. An advance of human consciousness is also associated with this progress. As long as the lower man has only a physical body, he possess merely an utterly dull consciousness, which is not equivalent even to that of dreamless sleep of the present, although for man of today this latter state-of-consciousness is in fact an 'unconscious' one. In the time when the ether body appears, man reaches the consciousness which is his today in dreamless sleep. With the formation of the astral body a dim image consciousness makes its appearance, similar to, but not identical with the one man at present ascribes to himself while he is dreaming. The fourth, the current condition of consciousness of Earth man, will now be described.

"This present condition of consciousness develops in the fourth great universal era, that of Earth which follows the preceding Old Saturn, Old Sun, and Old Moon eras.

"On Old Saturn the physical body of man was developed in several stages. At that time it could not have been the carrier of an ether body. And the latter was added only during the course of Old Sun. Simultaneously, the physical body was so transformed in the successive Sun cycles that it could become the carrier of this ether body, or in other words, that the ether body could work in the physical body. During the Old Moon development the astral body was added, and again the physical body and the ether body were transformed in such a way that they could provide suitable carriers and instruments for the then appearing astral body. Thus, on Old Moon, man is a being composed of physical body, ether body, and astral body. Through the ether body he is enabled to feel joy and pain; through the astral body he is a being with emotions, rage, hate, love and so forth.

"As has been shown, higher spirits actively work on the different members of his being. On Old Moon the ether body received the capacity for joy and pain through the Spirits of Twilight [Angels]; the emotions were implanted in the astral body by the Fire Spirits [Archangels].

"At the same time, something else was taking place during the three great cycles of Old Saturn, Old Sun, and Old Moon. During the last Saturn cycle the Spirit-Man (*Atman*) was formed with the help of the Spirits of Will (*Thrones*). During the penultimate Old Sun cycle, the life-spirit (*Budhi*) was joined to it with the assistance of the Cherubim. During the third from the last Old Moon cycle, the Spirit-Self (*Manas*) united with the two others through the help of the Seraphim. Thus actually two origins of man were formed during these three great cycles: a lower man, consisting of physical body, ether body, and astral body, and a higher man, consisting of Spirit-Man (*Atman*), Life-Spirit

(*Budhi*), and Spirit-Self (*Manas*). The lower and the higher nature of man followed separate paths at first.

"The Earth development serves to bring the two separate origins of man together.

"But first, after the seventh small cycle, all of Old Moon existence enters a kind of sleeping state (*Pralaya*). Thereby everything becomes mixed together, so to speak, in a homogeneous mass. The Sun and the Moon too, which were separate in the last great cycle, again become fused during the last Old Moon cycles.

"When everything again emerges from the sleeping state there must first be repeated in their essentials the Old Saturn condition during a first small cycle, the Old Sun condition during a second, and the Old Moon cycle during a third. During this third cycle the beings on the Moon, which has again been split off from the Sun, resume approximately the same forms of existence which they already had on the Old Moon. There the lower man is a being intermediate between man of today and an animal; the plants stand midway between the animal and plant natures of today, and the minerals only half bear their lifeless character of today, while for the rest they are still half plants.

"During the second half of this third cycle something else is already in preparation. The minerals harden, the plants gradually lose the animal character of their sensibility, and out of the uniform species of animal man there develop two classes. One of these remains on the level of animality, while the other is subjected to a division of the astral body into two parts. The astral body splits into a lower part, which continues to be the carrier of the emotions, and a higher part, which attains to a certain independence, so that it can exercise a kind of mastery over the lower members, over the physical body, the ether body, and the lower astral body. Now the Spirits of Personality [Archai] seize upon this higher astral body and implant in it just that independence we have mentioned, and therewith also selfishness. Only in the lower human astral body do the Fire Spirits [Archangels] now accomplish their work, while in the ether body the Spirits of Twilight [Angels] are active, and in the physical body that power entity begins its work which one can describe as the real ancestor of man. It is the same power entity which formed the Spirit-Man (*Atman*) with the help of the Thrones on Old Saturn, the Life-Spirit (*Budhi*) with the assistance of the Cherubim on Old Sun, and the Spirit-Self (*Manas*) together with the Seraphim on Old Moon.

"But now this changes. Thrones, Cherubim, and Seraphim ascend to higher spheres, and the higher man now receives the assistance of the Spirits of Wisdom, of Motion, and of Form. These are now united with Spirit-Self, Life-Spirit, and Spirit-Man (with *Manas-Budhi-Atman*). With the assistance of these entities the human power being characterized above develops its physical body during the second half of the third Earth cycle. It is the Spirits of Form which act here in the most significant way. They already form the human physical body so that it becomes a kind of precursor of the later human body of the fourth cycle (the present one, or the fourth round).

"In the astral body of the animal beings which have been left behind, it is exclusively the Fire Spirits [Archangels] which remain active, while in the ether body of the plants it is the Spirits of Twilight [Angels]. On the other hand, the Spirits of Form [Exusiai; Elohim] participate in the transformation of the mineral realm. They make the latter hard, that is, implant rigid and fixed forms in it.

"One must not imagine, however, that the sphere of activity of the spirits we have mentioned was confined only to what has been characterized. Always it is only the Main directions of their activities which are meant, in a subordinate way all the spirit beings participate everywhere. Thus at the time indicated, the Spirits of Form also have certain functions to perform in the physical plant and animal bodies, and so forth.

"After all this has taken place, around the end of the third earth cycle all the entities—including Sun and Moon—again become fused and then pass through a shorter stage of sleep (a small *Pralaya*). At that time everything is again a uniform mass (a chaos), and at the end of this stage the fourth Earth cycle begins in which we are at present.

"At first, everything which already previously had had a being in the mineral, plant, animal, and human realms, begins to separate out of the uniform mass in germinal form. First there can re-emerge as *independent* germs only those human ancestors on whose higher astral bodies the Spirits of Personality [Archai] have worked in the preceding small cycle. All other beings of the mineral, plant, and animal realm do not yet lead an independent existence here. At this stage everything is still in that high spiritual condition which is called the 'formless' or *Arupa* condition. At the present stage of development, only the highest human thoughts—for example, mathematical and moral ideals— are woven of that substance which was proper to all beings at the stage we are describing. That which is lower than these human ancestors can only appear as an activity in a higher being. The animals exist only as states of consciousness of the Spirits of Fire [Archangels], the plants as states of consciousness of the Spirits of Twilight [Angels]. The minerals have a double existence in thought. First they exist as thought germs in the human ancestors mentioned above, then as thoughts in the consciousness of the Spirits of Form. The 'higher man' (Spirit-Man, Life-Spirit, Spirit-Self also exists in the consciousness of the Spirits of Form."

Three Meetings with the Spirit-Self, Life-Spirit, and Spirit-Human

The Gospel of Matthew, Rudolf Steiner, Lecture XI, *Advent of instructing and life-giving powers from the Cosmos through the Christ*, Bern, September 11, 1910, GA 123

"According to the elementary teachings of Anthroposophy, mankind is formed of different members; these we call the physical body, etheric body, and astral body. With the astral body is associated the Sentient-Soul; then the Rational or Intellectual-Soul; and then the Consciousness or Spiritual-Soul. Beyond these are the higher principles of human nature towards which mankind is evolving; they are Spirit-Self, Life-Spirit, and Spirit-Human. Now, in the course of each of the Post-Atlantean Periods, something definite was given for these different members of human nature. In the first Period, the Ancient Indian Period of civilization [Old Indian Period, 7,227 B.C.-5,067 B.C.], man had added to him an increase in the capacities of his etheric body whereby it became something more than it had been before. What was implanted in him in this respect as regards his physical body already had a beginning during the last part of the Atlantean Epoch; but he only received these enhanced powers into his etheric body during the Post-Atlantean Period. Thus it was during the Period, known as the ancient Indian that the etheric body received these gifts. Then during the Persian civilization [Old Persian Period, 5,067 B.C.-2,907 B.C.] similar forces were implanted in his astral or Sentient-Body; and during the Egypto-

Chaldean Period [2,907 B.C.-747 B.C.] he received those suited to his Sentient-Soul; during the Greco-Latin Period [747 B.C.-1,414 A.D.]—the fourth Period of post-Atlantean culture—the forces of the Rational-Soul [Intellectual-Soul] were imprinted in man; and now, in the fifth Period [Anglo-Germanic Period, 1,414 A.D.-3,574 A.D.], we are living in an age in which the forces belonging to these lines of progress are gradually to be impressed on the Spiritual-Soul [Consciousness-Soul]. As yet humanity has made but little progress with this.

"Following on this age [Fifth Cultural Period] will come the Sixth Post-Atlantean Period [Slavic Period, 3,574 A.D.-5,734 A.D.], which is to witness the impressing of the forces of the Spirit-Self on human nature; and the Seventh Period [American Period, 5,734 A.D.-7,894 A.D.], will see that of Life-Spirit. Beyond this our vision reaches out to a far distant future, in which the Spirit-Human or Atman will be impressed on normal humanity.

"Let us now consider human evolution in relation to the individual man—*for this is how it was viewed in the Mysteries*; man was always considered from this aspect by those who knew somewhat of the true relationship of things. It was thus the disciples had gradually to learn to know him, in the light of the life-giving, illuminating force that streamed into them from Christ Jesus. When we observe mankind—either at the present time, or at the time of Christ Jesus—we must recognize that rudiments lie in men just as plants contain seeds, even when only in leaf and before the blossom and fruit is formed. In looking at such a plant we can say:—

'As surely as this plant which so far only possesses green leaves has within it the germ of both flower and fruit, so man, who at the time of Christ Jesus possessed only Sentient and

Intellectual-Soul, holds within him the germ of the Spiritual-Soul [Consciousness-Soul]; which then opens itself to the Spirit-Self [Manas], in order that the higher triad, as a new spiritual gift from God, may flow into him from above.'

"Thus we can say:—

'Man unfolds through the content and qualities of his soul in the same way as a plant unfolds in turn green leaves, blossoms, and fruit. In developing his Sentient-Soul, Intellectual-Soul, and Spiritual-Soul man develops something that corresponds to the flower of his being, and lifts this up to receive the inpouring of the Divine Spirit from above, so that by receiving the Spirit-Self he may rise to ever further heights of human evolution.'

"At the time Christ Jesus walked on Earth the normal man had developed the Rational-Soul [Intellectual-Soul/Higher-Feeling-Soul] as his highest principle; this was not as yet capable of receiving into it the Spirit-Self [Manas]; but out of the same man as now had developed to the Rational-Soul, the Spiritual-Soul [Consciousness-Soul] would evolve as his child—as the consummation of his being, which later would become the receptacle for the Spirit-Self.

"What is to unfold out of the whole nature of man, and come forth from him like a blossom? How was this described in the Mysteries, and in the circle where Christ Jesus spoke to His disciples of their further development? Translated into our language it was called the 'Son of Man.' [Greek: υἱὸς τοῦ ἀνθρώπου; yiós toú anthrópou] The Greek has a less restricted meaning than our word 'son,' meaning 'son of a father,' and signifies rather the offspring of a living organism, something that evolves out of such an organism, as a blossom evolves from a plant which at first possessed only green leaves. So it was said of the ordinary man, whose being had not yet blossomed into the Spiritual-Soul [Consciousness-Soul], that the 'Son of Man' had not yet evolved in him. But there are always some who are in advance of their contemporaries, who bear within them the life and knowledge of a future age. So in the fourth Period [Greco-Roman Period, 747 B.C.-1,414 A.D.], that in which the Rational-Soul [Intellectual-Soul] was normally developed, there were some among the leaders of mankind who, though appearing outwardly as other men, had developed inwardly the possibility of the Spiritual-Soul, out of which the Spirit-Self [Manas] was to dawn. These were the 'Sons of Men.'

"The disciples had to grow to an understanding of the nature of these leaders of humanity. It was to test their understanding of this that Christ asked His more intimate disciples:—

'Tell me, of what beings, of what men in this generation, can it be said that they are "Sons of Men?"'

"So runs the question according to the Aramaic Script—for though the Greek translation from the Aramaic Script when read aright is certainly better, yet something has been lost in it also. We have to picture Christ Jesus standing thoughtfully before His disciples and saying:—

'What is the general opinion concerning the men who, in previous generations of this Greco-Latin Period, were called "Sons of Men"? Who were they?'

And the disciples spoke to Him of Elias, of John the Baptist, of Jeremiah, and other prophets. They were able to answer thus through the illuminating forces that came to them from Christ. They knew that these leaders of men had developed powers by which they had given birth within themselves to the 'Son of Man.'

"On the same occasion, the disciple who is usually called Peter gave a different answer. In order to understand this answer we must allow what we have heard in recent lectures concerning the mission of Christ Jesus, according to the *Gospel of Matthew*, to sink deeply into our souls. It was there explained that through the Impulse of Christ it has become possible for men to develop full Ego-consciousness [I-consciousness]—*that what lies within the "I Am" can blossom fully through His Impulse*. In other words Men will be able in time to enter the higher worlds—*may even attain to initiation*—while retaining their Ego-consciousness, the only state-of-consciousness considered normal for men in the physical world today. This has become possible through the life of Christ Jesus on Earth. He is the representative of the force that gives complete consciousness of the "I Am" to man…

"Forgive me if I now refer to something of great importance to our day by employing a rather trivial example. We must learn to use the Greek word 'Auton' (Αυτών; the same as appears in the modern word automobile; but not so that we apply it exclusively to machines, or understand it only in its external sense); we must learn to associate it as a 'self-starting' activity within the realm of spirit where it belongs. This advice might well be taken by our contemporaries. Men love a self-starting action in connection with machines; but they must learn to employ it also in connection with all they used to experience unconsciously in the Mysteries before the coming of Christ. This must now be learnt through 'a setting of themselves in action,' so that they gradually become creative from within themselves. *The men of today will come to understand this when they fill themselves with the impulse brought to them by Christ.*

"Keeping this in mind we can see how important the second question was that Christ put to His disciples. After asking them: Who among the leaders of former generations could be described as 'Sons of Men,' He questioned them further, and wished gradually to bring them to an understanding of His own nature, to an understanding of that Ego-nature [I-nature] of which He was the representative. Hence He asked, 'And what think ye that I am?' On every occasion you see how special stress is laid on the "I Am" in the *Gospel of Matthew*. Then Peter answered Him, and showed by his answer that he now recognized the Christ not only as a 'Son of Man,' but as the 'Son of the living God.' This brings us to a consideration of the difference between these two phrases, 'Son of Man' and 'Son of the living God.' In order to understand them, we must enter more fully into some facts already dealt with.

"In the course of his development man evolves the Spiritual-Soul [the higher aspect of the Consciousness-Soul] so that in it the Spirit-Self may appear. When he has evolved the Spiritual-Soul, the upper triad, Spirit-Self, Life-Spirit, and Spirit-Human come to meet him, so that the opening flower of his being can receive into it this upper triad from above...

"When a man has made himself receptive by developing his Spiritual-Soul, the higher triad, Spirit-Self or Manas, Life-Spirit or Budhi, and Spirit-Human or Atman, draw near; this may be likened to a spiritual fructification coming towards him from on high. While with the other principles of his being he grows upwards from below, unfolding the blossom of the 'Son of Man,' there must come to meet him from on high, so that he may gain his 'Ego-consciousness,' [I-consciousness], that which brings with it Spirit-Self, Life-Spirit, and Spirit-Human.

"Who is the representative of the gift which comes down to man from above and is indicative of the nature of humanity in the far future? *It is the Son of God, He who lives, the Life-Spirit, the Son of the Living God!*

"So, in the scene to which we have just referred Christ Jesus asked the question, 'What is to come to men through My impulse?' The answer is, 'The life-giving Spirit-Principle from on high!'

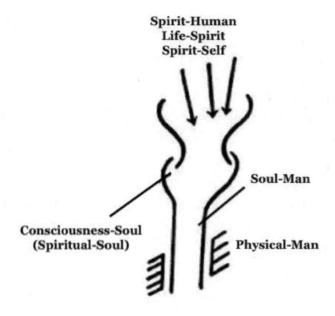

"So, we have to distinguish the *Son of Man* who evolves upwards from below, and the *Son of God*, the Son of the living God, who comes down to meet him from above. These must be distinguished. We can understand what a difficult question this was for the disciples. Especially so because they were receiving for the first time those things which the simplest of mankind have had implanted in them through the *Gospels* from the beginning of the Christian era; things which first reached the disciples through the living, instructing forces of Christ Jesus. Through powers such as had previously been developed by them, no answer could be given to the question: 'Whose representative am I Myself?' To this question one of the disciples—Peter—answered: 'Thou art the Christ, the Son of the living God.' This was an answer which—if we may say so—*did not spring from the normal spiritual powers of Peter at that moment.*

"Let us try to picture this scene vividly. Christ Jesus, looking at Peter, said to Himself: 'It means much that such an answer should have come from this mouth; for it is an answer that points to the distant future.' Then having gazed into Peter's consciousness, and seen how far he had progressed, seen that through his intellect, or the powers that initiation had evoked in him, he was able to give such an answer, the Christ was bound to say:—

> 'This answer has not sprung from Peter's conscious knowledge here spoken, those deeper forces that are inherent in all men; but which will only gradually become conscious forces in them.'

"We bear within us physical body, etheric body, astral body, and Ego ['I']; we are rising towards Spirit-Self, Life-Spirit, and Spirit-Human through transmutation of the powers of the lower bodies. This is an elementary lesson of Spiritual Science. The forces that we shall one day evolve in our astral body as Spirit-Self are already there—*only they have been put there by Divine Spiritual Powers and have not been evolved by us.* It is the same as regards our etheric body, which already contains within it a divine Life-Spirit. Therefore, looking at Peter, Christ said:—

'What spoke to me is not what is within thy consciousness at the present time, thou hast spoken from out of something that will certainly be evolved within thee at a future time; but of which at present thou knowest nothing. What at the present time is within thy flesh and blood could not have spoken, so that the words: "Thou art the Christ, the Son of the living God" could have sprung from it. In these words divine spiritual forces spoke, forces lying deep below the threshold of consciousness, in the profoundest depths of human nature.'

"The mysterious Higher Powers that at this moment spoke through Peter, Christ calls the 'Father in Heaven.' These were the forces out of which he was born; but of which he was not as yet conscious. Hence Christ's words:—

'The man of flesh and blood thou art at present did not reveal this unto thee; but the Father which is in Heaven revealed it.'

"But Christ had something further to say to Peter. He had to say to Himself:—

'In Peter I have a disciple before me, whose nature is so constituted, that through the forces that have already evolved consciousness in him, and through the whole manner in which spiritual forces have worked in him the Father-force has remained intact; this subconscious, human force has remained so strong in him that when he surrenders himself to it he can build thereon. This is the most important thing in Peter.'

"And Christ might have gone on to say:—

'What is present in Peter is present in all men, but they are not sufficiently advanced either to be aware of it or to make conscious use of it; the power to do so will only be developed in the future. If that which I am to give to man, if that for which I am the impulse, is to develop further and become a part of him, it must be founded on the consciousness which spoke through the mouth of Peter in the words: "Thou art the Christ, the Son of the living God"; on this rock in human nature which the surging waves of consciousness as at present evolved have not yet destroyed, and which, as Father-force has just made itself heard, I will build that which will emerge with ever-increasing strength as the result of my impulse.'

"When men have constructed this foundation, what the Christ-Impulse can become for humanity will be revealed. This is contained in the words: *'Thou art Peter, and on this rock I will build what a certain number of men, a community, can reveal when they confess the Impulse of Christ.'*

"Such words must not be passed over as lightly as are the discussions which at this moment are the subject of violent controversy. They can only be understood when reconstructed out of the depth of that wisdom which is the same as the wisdom met with in the Mysteries.

"The sentence that follows shows clearly that Christ Jesus built on this deep subconscious force in Peter. For immediately afterwards He speaks of the events that are about to take place, and of the Mystery of Golgotha. The moment, however, had already passed when the more deeply lying forces spoke in Peter.

It is the conscious Peter who now speaks, who fails to understand Christ, and cannot believe that suffering and death are to follow. So when the conscious Peter speaks (he who had already developed conscious powers within himself) Christ has to correct him, saying:—

'It is not God Who now speaks in thee but that which thou hast evolved within thee as man; the source from which it comes is of no value, but is a vain deception, for it comes from Ahriman—that is Satan!'

"This is contained in the words:—

'Remove thyself from Me, Satan, thou offendest Me, for thou considerest not the things that are divine; but those that are human.'

"Christ compares Peter to Satan, employing the word used to designate Ahriman. Whereas in other parts of the *Bible* the word 'devil' stands for everything Luciferic, Christ here makes deliberate use of the word 'Satan'; for it was to the Ahrimanic form of deception that Peter had succumbed.

"These are the facts. What do modern critics of the *Bible* make of them? They say: It is most unlikely that Christ Jesus would stand before Peter one minute saying, 'Thou alone hast grasped the fact that a God confronts thee,' and immediately afterwards call him 'Satan.' So the critics conclude that the word 'Satan' must have been interpolated by someone later, and is therefore incorrect. The truth is that current opinions concerning the deeper meaning of these words when gained only through philological research are worthless, unless preceded by an actual understanding of the Biblical records. An understanding of the actual facts of the *Bible* is necessary before anyone can speak of the historical origin of corresponding documents...

"The story of the Passover that follows is nothing else than the actual living inflow of that magic force, which first, in the form of teaching, and later as the outcome of the Mystery of Golgotha, was to enter humanity. With this in mind it becomes clear why the writer of this *Gospel* always felt it necessary to emphasize the contrast between the living teaching heard by the disciples coming to them from the heights of cosmic existence, a teaching suited to them; and the other teaching given to those who stood outside, who were not sufficiently ripe to receive the Christ-force itself. This difference will be dealt with in the next lecture in connection with the conversation of the Scribes and Pharisees. Just now we would remind you that Christ Jesus, having led the disciples to the point of initiation, showed them that by following this path they would themselves be able to experience expansion into the Spiritual World of the Macrocosm. He explained that they had already experienced the preliminaries of initiation, that the way was open, to where they could become more and more able to recognize the true nature of Christ as the Being Who fills all spiritual spaces, Whose reflection had been in Jesus of Nazareth. Christ Jesus told His disciples that they must progress in ripeness for initiation so that they might become initiates for humanity. He taught them further that they could only attain individual initiation if with patience and perseverance they furthered this inner ripeness.

"What had to increase in strength in man's inner being, if his inner nature was to evolve clairvoyant higher forces? The as yet undeveloped attributes of his being had to ripen, so that he could become capable of receiving into himself the forces of Spirit-Self, Life-Spirit, and Spirit-Human. As to when this would happen, when the power from above which leads to initiation and makes of a man a participator in the Kingdoms of the Heavens dawns in him, depends on the degree of ripeness he has attained; it depends on the karma of the individual. Who can tell when this moment is at hand? Only the highest Initiates. It is not known to those on lower stages of initiation. The hour of man's attainment comes to those who are ripe for entry into the Spiritual World. It must surely come—*but it comes like a thief in the night.*

"But how does this expansion into the Spiritual World come to pass? In the ancient Mysteries, and to a certain extent in the new, there were three stages of initiation into the Macrocosm. The first stage brought knowledge of all that could be perceived through the Spirit-Self. The initiate was then not only a man in the new sense; but he had attained to what, in the language of the hierarchies, is called 'Angel Nature' the nature of the hierarchy next above man. Thus, in the Persian Mysteries a man who had advanced to this stage at which he had expanded to the Macrocosm, when the Spirit-Self was active in him was called either a Persian (since he was no longer an isolated being but belonged to the Angel of the Persian nation) or he was simply called an Angel, one whose nature was divine. The second stage is that in which the Life-Spirit had awaked in like manner; at this stage a man was called a 'Sun Hero' in the Old Persian Mysteries; for he had then advanced to the point where he could draw into himself the spiritual forces of the Sun, when these forces had approached the Earth. Such a man might also be called 'Son of the Father.' And he who had won to the heights of the third stage, the stage of Atman (Spirit-Human), was called in the ancient

Mysteries 'the Father.' *These were the three stages of initiation—* 'Angel,' 'Son or Sun Hero,' and 'Father.'

"Only the highest initiates can judge when initiation is about to awaken in man. Hence Christ said:—

'Initiation will come when you have travelled further along the way on which I have led you; you will then ascend to the Kingdom of Heaven; but the hour of your arrival is known neither to the Angels [those initiated with the Spirit-Self], nor to the Son [those initiated with Life-Spirit]; but only to the highest initiates [those initiated with the Father].'

"Here once more the language of the *Gospel of Matthew* conforms absolutely with the tradition of the Mysteries.

"And we shall see as the *Gospel* continues how all that Christ tells His disciples concerning the Kingdom of Heaven is merely a prediction of what they are to experience in initiation. Examining carefully the sentences dealing with this subject, it is easily seen that Christ is referring to a certain teaching common at that time—concerning the way in which the Kingdom of Heaven was to be attained. People had accepted this attainment of the Kingdom of Heaven in a material sense, believing it applied to the whole Earth; whereas they ought to have known that this was only possible to certain individuals, those who had passed through initiation. Some people really expected that the Earth would be transformed into Heaven in a material way. Christ refers directly to this when He says that certain people who will appear and announce this teaching are lying prophets and false Messiahs. It is amazing to find expounders of the *Gospels* who even today spread this false doctrine of the material heavenly kingdom, and declare it to be the teaching of Christ Himself. Anyone who really knows how to read the *Gospel of Matthew* knows that Christ refers to a spiritual event, towards which those seeking initiation grow. In the course of earthly evolution it will, however, be possible for all humanity—*for all who follow Christ*—to grow to this condition—inasmuch as the Earth itself is spiritualized.

"When from this side also we have looked more deeply into the whole form and content of the *Gospel of Matthew*, our reverence for it deepens enormously. This is more especially the case in respect of the teaching Christ gave to His disciples from the standpoint of the Ego—the 'I.' In none of the other *Gospels* is this given so clearly. We can picture the Christ, with His disciples gathered round Him, and can see how cosmic forces work through the agency of His human body; we can see the disciples learning of initiation as He leads them by the hand, and we catch a glimpse of the human conditions of His environment. All this makes the *Gospel of Matthew* a most human production. Through it we really learn to know the man Jesus of Nazareth, the bearer of the Christ; we recognize all that came to pass through the descent of Christ into human nature. Yes, in the *Matthew Gospel* even heavenly events are clothed in garments that are truly human."

Cosmic and Human Metamorphoses, **Rudolf Steiner, Lecture III,** *The Human Soul and the Universe*, **Berlin, February 20, 1917, GA 175**

"Now, as I indicated in the last lecture, we are in connection with the universe, with the whole Cosmos; and this connection is such that—as I merely hinted in the last lecture—it can even be reckoned and expressed in numbers. This connection of ours with the Universe can of course be expressed and shown in many other ways; but, I might say, to our great astonishment it can be expressed by the fact that the number of breaths a man draws in a day equals the number of years required for the Vernal Point to return to its original point of departure.[1] These discoveries in the realm of numbers can, if we permeate them with feeling, fill us with awe, with a holy awe; if we reflect that we too belong to the Divine Spiritual Universe which is manifested in all external phenomena.

"The fact that we are the Microcosm, the 'little-world' formed and manifested out of the Macrocosm, the 'great-world,' is felt as still more profound when we visualize such facts as will be brought before our minds today, and which I may enumerate as follows: the three meetings of the Human Soul with the Being of the Universe: and this is the subject I shall speak about today. We all know that as Earth-men we bear within us the physical body and etheric body, the astral body and Ego ['I']. Each of the two beings I have referred to bears within him what I might call two sub-beings. The more external man—the physical and etheric body; the more inner man—the Ego and astral body. Now we know moreover that man is to undergo further development. The Earth as such will someday come to an end. It will then evolve further, through a Jupiter, Venus, and a Vulcan planetary evolution. Man during this time will rise stage-by-stage; and to his Ego will, as we know, be added a higher being—the Spirit-Self [Manas] which will manifest within him. This will reach full manifestation during the Jupiter evolution—which will follow that of our Earth. The Life-Spirit [Budhi] will attain full manifestation in man during the Venus period; and the actual Spirit-Human [Atman] during the Vulcan period. When, therefore, we look forward to the great cosmic future of man, to these three stages of evolution, we look forward to the Spirit-Self, Life-Spirit, and Spirit-Human. But these three which in a sense await us in our future evolution are even now in a certain respect related to us, although they are as yet not in the least developed; for they are still enclosed in the bosom of the Divine-Spiritual Beings whom we have learnt to know as the Higher Hierarchies. They will come forth to us from out of the Higher Hierarchies; and we today are already in relation with these Higher Hierarchies, who will endow us with the Spirit-Self, Life-Spirit, and Spirit-Human. So that today, instead of using the more complicated expression and saying: 'We are in connection with the Hierarchy of the Angeloi'; we can simply say: 'We are in connection with that which is to come to us in the future—our Spirit-Self.' And instead of saying that we are in connection with the Archangels, we can say: 'We are in connection with what is to come to us in the future, as our Life-Spirit,' and so on.

"Indeed we human beings are already in a certain respect, though at present only in rudiment—(and in the Spiritual World rudiments are something much higher than they are in the physical world); more than merely four-principled beings consisting of physical body, etheric body, astral body and Ego ['I']. We already bear the seed of the Spirit-Self within us, as well as that of the Life-Spirit and Spirit-Human—*for they will evolve out of us in the future*—though at present we only have them in seed-form within us. This is no mere abstract saying, it has quite a concrete significance; for we have meetings, real meetings with these higher principles of our being. These meetings take place in the following way. We, as human beings, would as time went on feel ourselves increasingly estranged from everything Spiritual—a state of things very difficult to endure—did we not from time-to-time encounter our Spirit-Self. Our Ego must meet that Higher Self—the Spirit-Self which we have yet to develop, and which in a Spiritual respect is of like nature to the Hierarchy of Angels.

So therefore we may say in simple language, and speaking in the Christian sense: we must from time-to-time meet with a being of the Hierarchy of the Angels, a being closely related to ourselves; and when it comes to us, it brings about in us a Spiritual change, which will enable us someday to take in a Spirit-Self. We must also meet with a being of the Hierarchy of the Archangels; for this being then so affects us that something is prepared which will someday lead to our developing the Life-Spirit.

"Whether in the Christian sense we place this being in the Hierarchy of Angels, or whether we refer to it in the older sense understood by the ancients when they spoke of their *genius* [daimon] as the guiding genius of man, makes no difference. We know that we are living at a time when but few people—though this will soon alter—few can gaze into the Spiritual World and perceive the things and the beings therein. The time has now gone by when the beings and even the various processes of evolution in the Spiritual-world could be perceived in a much wider and more comprehensive sense; for at the time when one spoke of the genius of a man, there was a direct, concrete perception of that being.[2]

"In a not very distant past this vision was still so strong that men were able to describe it quite concretely and objectively; describing it in terms now looked upon as poetic fancies, although they were not intended as such. Thus Plutarch describes the relation of man to his genius, as follows (I should like to quote the passage literally). Plutarch, the Roman writer, says that besides the portion of the soul embedded in the earthly body, there is a purer part outside, soaring above man's head, in appearance like a star, and which is rightly called a man's daimon, who guides him, and whom the wise man willingly follows, In this concrete way does Plutarch describe what he does not wish to be taken as a poetic fancy; but as a concrete external reality. Indeed so concretely does he describe it that he expressly states:—

'The rest of the Spiritual part of man can to a certain extent be perceived at the same time as the physical body, inasmuch as it normally fills the same space; but the genius, the leading and guiding genius of man is something apart and can be seen outside the head of every man.'

"Paracelsus too, one of the last who, without special training, or without special gifts, was able to give forceful information about these things, said very much the same from his own knowledge of this phenomenon. Many others also said the same.

"This genius is none other than the Spirit-Self in process of evolution, though borne by a being belonging to the Hierarchy of Angels. It is of great importance that one should enter somewhat deeply into these things; for when this genius becomes perceptible it has its own special conditions. This subject can be considered from another very different point-of-view, but we will now consider it from the following one.

"Let us take the subject of the mutual intercourse between man and man, for we can learn much from that; it teaches us what is by no means without significance in the perception of the Spiritual principles of the human being.

"If a man is only capable of observing the meeting of two persons with his physical-sense vision, he merely notices that they come together, greet one another, and so on. But when he becomes able to observe such an event Spiritually, he will find that each time two human beings meet a Spiritual process is established, which, among other things, is also expressed outwardly in the fact that the part of their etheric bodies which forms the head becomes the expression of every feeling of sympathy and antipathy which the two persons feel for each other; and this continues as long as they are together. Suppose two people were to meet who could not bear each other (an extreme case; but there are such in life). Suppose two persons meet who dislike each other, and that this feeling of antipathy is mutual. It can then be seen that that part of the etheric body which forms the head projects beyond the head in both cases, and that both the etheric heads incline towards each other. A mutual antipathy between persons meeting is expressed as a continual bowing and inclining of the etheric head of each towards the other. When two persons come together who love each other, a similar process can be observed; but then the etheric head inclines back, it bends backwards. Now whether the etheric head bends forward as though in greeting when antipathy is felt, or bends backward where love is felt, in both cases the physical head then becomes freer than it is wont to be. This is of course always relative; the etheric body does not entirely emerge but extends in length, so that a continuation can be observed. A more rarified etheric body then fills the physical body than is normally the case, and the result of this, by reason of the exceptional transparency of the etheric body, is that the astral body remaining inside the head becomes more clearly visible to clairvoyant vision. So that not only is there a movement of the etheric body but also an alteration in the astral light of the head. This then, my dear friends,—*which is no poetic imagination but an actual fact*—is the reason that in places where such things are understood, persons who are capable of selfless love are represented with an aura round their heads, which is known as a halo. When two people meet, with simply a strong tinge of Egotism in their love, this phenomenon is not so apparent; but if a man comes in contact with humanity at certain times when he is not concerned with himself and his own personal relation to another; but is filled with a universal human love for all humanity, such phenomena appear. At such times the astral body in the vicinity of the head becomes clearly visible. If there are persons then present who are able to see this in a man clairvoyantly, they can see the halo and cannot do otherwise than paint or represent it as a reality. These things are absolutely in connection with the objective facts of the Spiritual World; but that which is thus objectively present, and which is a lasting reality in the evolution of humanity, is connected with something else.

"Man must necessarily from time-to-time enter into inner communion with his Spirit-Self, with the Spirit-Self which is visible in the astral aura in rudimentary form as I have described; but it still has to be developed; it will be rayed down, as it were, from above, and stream in from the future. Man must from time-to-time be brought into touch with his Spirit-Self. When does this occur?

"We now come to the first meeting of which we have to speak. When does it take place? It takes place quite simply in normal sleep, on almost every occasion, between sleeping and waking. With simple country people, who are nearer to the life of nature, and who go to bed with the setting Sun and get up at sunrise, this meeting takes place in the middle of their sleeping time, which as a rule is the middle of the night. With people who have detached themselves from their connections with nature, this is not so much the case. But this depends on man's free will. A man of modern culture can regulate his life as he pleases, and though this fact is bound to affect his life, still he can regulate it as he likes, within certain limits. None the less he too can experience in the middle of a long sleep, what may be called an inner-union with the Spirit-Self—that is, with the Spiritual qualities from which the Spirit-Self will be extracted; he can have a meeting with his genius. Thus this meeting with one's genius takes place every night, that is, during every period of sleep—though this must not be taken too literally. This meeting is important for man. For all the feelings that gladden the soul with respect to its connection with the Spiritual World proceed from this meeting with one's genius during sleep. The feeling, which we may have in our waking state, of our connection with the Spiritual World, is an after-effect of this meeting with our genius. That is the first meeting with the higher world; and it may be said that most people are at first unconscious of it, though they will become more and more conscious the more they realize its after-effects by refining their waking conscious life, through absorbing the ideas and conceptions of Spiritual Science, until their souls become refined enough to observe carefully these after-effects. It all depends on whether the soul is refined enough, sufficiently acquainted with its inner-life, to be able to observe these. This meeting with the genius is brought to the consciousness of every man in some form or other; but the materialistic surroundings of the present day which fill the mind with ideas coming from the materialistic view of the world and especially the life of today, permeated as it is by materialistic opinions, prevent the soul from paying attention to what comes as the result of the meeting. As people gradually fill their minds with more Spiritual ideas than those set forth by materialism, the perception of the nightly meeting with the genius will become more and more self-evident to them.

"The second meeting of which we now have to speak is higher. From the indications already given it may be gathered that the first meeting with the genius is in connection with the course of the day. If we had not, through modern civilization, become free to adjust our lives according to our own convenience, this meeting would take place at the hour of midnight. A man would meet his genius every night at midnight. But on account of man's exercise of free will the time of this meeting has become movable; the hour when the Ego meets the genius is now not fixed. The second meeting is however not so movable; for that which is more connected with the astral body and etheric body is not so apt to get out of its place in the cosmic order. That which is connected with the Ego ['I'] and the physical body is very greatly displaced in present-day man. The second meeting is already more in connection with the great Macrocosmic Order. Even as the first meeting is connected with the course of the day, the second meeting is connected with the course of the year. I must here call attention to various things I have already indicated in this connection from another point-of-view. The life of man in its entirety does not run its course quite evenly through the year. When the sun develops its greatest heat, man is much more dependent upon his own physical life and the physical life around him than in the winter when, in a sense, he has to struggle with the external phenomena of the elements, and is more thrown back on himself; but then his Spiritual nature is more freed, and he is more in connection with the Spiritual World—both his own and that of the Earth—*with the whole Spiritual environment.*

"Thus the peculiar sentiment we connect with the Mystery of Christmas and with its Festival is by no means arbitrary; but hangs together with the fixing of the Festival of Christmas. At that time in winter which is appointed for the Festival, man, as does indeed the whole Earth, gives himself up to the Spirit. He then passes, as it were, through a realm in which the Spirit is near him. The consequence is that at about Christmas-time and on to our present New Year, man goes through a meeting of his astral body with the Life-Spirit, in the same way as he goes through the first meeting, that of his Ego ['I'] with the Spirit-Self. Upon this meeting with the Life-Spirit depends the nearness of Christ Jesus. *For Christ Jesus reveals Himself through the Life-Spirit. He reveals Himself through a being of the Realm of the Archangels.* He is, of course, an immeasurably higher Being than they; but that is not the point with which we are concerned at the moment; what we have to consider is that He reveals Himself through a Being of the order of the Archangeloi. Thus through this meeting we draw specially near to Christ Jesus at the present stage of development—which has existed since the Mystery of Golgotha—and in a certain respect we may call the meeting with the Life-Spirit: the meeting with Christ Jesus in the very depths of our soul.

"Now when a man either through developing Spiritual Consciousness in the domain of religious meditation or exercises, or, to supplement these, has accepted the concepts and ideas of Spiritual Science, when he has thus deepened and spiritualized his life of impression and feeling, then, just as he can experience in his waking life the after-effects of the meeting with his Spirit-Self, so he will also experience the after-effects of the meeting with the Life-Spirit, or Christ. It is actually a fact, my dear friends, that in the time following immediately on Christmas and up to Easter the conditions are particularly favorable for bringing to a man's consciousness this meeting with Christ Jesus. In a profound sense and this should not be blotted out by the abstract materialistic culture of today—the season of Christmas is connected with processes taking place in the Earth; for man, together with the Earth, takes part in the Christmas changes in the Earth. The season of Easter is determined by processes in the heavens. Easter

Sunday is fixed for the first Sunday after the first full-moon after the Vernal Equinox. Thus, whereas Christmas is fixed by the conditions of the Earth, Easter is determined from above. Just as we, through all that has just been described, are connected with the conditions of the Earth, so are we connected, through what I shall now describe, with the conditions of the heavens— *with the great Cosmic Conditions.* For Easter is that season in the concrete course of the year, in which all that is aroused in us by the meeting with Christ at Christmas, really unites itself with our physical Earth humanhood. The great Mystery that now brings home to the individual the Mystery of Golgotha at the Easter Season—*the Good Friday Mystery*—signifies among other things, that the Christ, who, as it were, has been moving beside us, at this season comes still closer to us. Indeed, roughly speaking, in a sense He disappears into us and permeates us, so that He can remain with us during the season that follows the Mystery of Golgotha—the season of summer—during which, in the ancient Mysteries, men tried to unite themselves to John in a way not possible after the Mystery of Golgotha.

"In that respect we are, as we see, the Microcosm, and we are attached to the Macrocosm in a profoundly significant way. There is a continual union with the Macrocosm in the seasons of the year, and this union, being a more inner-process in man, is connected with the year's course. Thus does Spiritual Science endeavor gradually to reveal the ideas, the spiritually scientific conceptions, that man may acquire as to the way in which Christ is now able to penetrate and permeate our Earth-life, since the Mystery of Golgotha.

"At this point I feel obliged to make an interpolation which is of importance and which ought to be thoroughly understood, particularly by the friends of Spiritual Science. It ought never to be represented that our attempts at Spiritual Science are a substitute for the life and exercise of religion. Spiritual Science may in the highest sense, and particularly as regards the Mystery of Christ, be taken as a support, as a foundation for the life and exercise of religion; *but it should not be made a religion—for we ought to be clear that religion in its living form and living practice enkindles the Spiritual consciousness of the human community.* If this Spiritual consciousness is to become a living thing in man, he cannot possibly remain at a standstill, stopping at the merely abstract ideas of God or Christ; but must stand renewed amidst the religious practices and activities (which in different people may take various forms) as something which provides him with a religious center and appeals to him as such. If this religious sentiment is only deep enough, and finds means of stimulating the soul, it will soon feel a longing—a real longing— for the very ideas that can be developed in Spiritual Science. If Spiritual Science may be said to be a support for a religious life, as, objectively speaking, it certainly is—subjectively the time has come today when we may say that a man with true religious feelings is driven by these feelings to seek knowledge. For Spiritual Consciousness is acquired through Religious Feeling and Spiritual knowledge by Spiritual Science, just as knowledge of nature is acquired by Natural Science. Spiritual Consciousness leads to the impulse to acquire Spiritual Knowledge. It may be said that an inner religious life may today subjectively drive a man to Spiritual Science.

"A third meeting is that in which a man approaches the Spirit-Man, which will only be developed in the far future and which is brought near to him by a being belonging to the Hierarchy of the Archai. We may say that the ancients were sensitive to this, as are even the people of the present day, although the latter, in speaking of such things, no longer have a consciousness of the deeper truth of the subject. The ancients felt this meeting as a meeting with that which permeates the world, and which we can now hardly distinguish in ourselves or in the world; but in which we merge in the world as in a unity. Just as we can speak of the second as a meeting with Christ Jesus, so can we speak of the third as a meeting with the Father-Principle, with the Father, with that which lies at the foundation of the world, and which we experience when we have the right feeling for what the various religions mean by 'the Father.' This meeting is of such a nature that it reveals our intimate connection with the Macrocosm, with the Divine-Spiritual Universe. The daily course of universal processes, of world processes, includes our meeting with our genius [daimon]: the yearly course includes our meeting with Christ Jesus: and the course of a whole human life, of this human life of ours, my dear friends—which can normally be described as the patriarchal life of seventy years—includes the meeting with the Father-Principle. For a certain time, our physical Earth-life is prepared—and rightly so—by education—at the present day to a great extent unconsciously, yet it is prepared; and most people experience unconsciously, between the ages of twenty-eight and forty-two—and though unconsciously, yet fully appreciated in the intimate depths of the soul—the meeting with the Father-Principle. The after-effects of this may extend into later life, if we develop sufficiently fine perceptions to note that which thus comes into our life from within ourselves, as the after-effects of our meeting with the Father-Principle.

"During a certain period of our life—the period of preparation—education ought, in the many different ways this can be done, to make the meeting with the Father-Principle as profound an experience as possible. One way is to arouse in a man, during his years of education, a strong feeling of the glory of the world, of its greatness, and of the sublimity of the world-processes. We are withholding a great deal from the growing boy and girl if we fail to draw their attention to all the revelations of beauty and greatness in the world; for then, instead of having a devoted reverence and respect for these, they may pass them by unobserved. If we fill the minds of the young with thoughts connecting the feelings of their hearts with the beauty and greatness of the world, we are then preparing them for the right meeting with the Father-Principle. For this meeting is of great significance for the life spent between death and a new birth. This meeting with the Father Principle, which normally occurs between the above-mentioned ages, can be a strong force and support to a man, when he has, as we know, to recapitulate his life on Earth retrospectively after having passed through the portals of death, and while he passes through the soul-world. This retrospective journey, which as we know, lasts one-third as long as the time spent between birth and death, can be made strong and forceful; as indeed it ought to be, if a man can see himself at a certain point and place meeting with that Being, whom he can only dimly guess at and express in stammering words, when he speaks of the Father of the Cosmic Order. This is an important Picture, which after a man has passed through the gates of death, should always be present with him, together with the picture of death itself.

"Now it is natural that a certain question should arise in connection with this. There are people who die before they reach the middle-of-life, when they would normally have the meeting with the Father-Principle. We must consider the case of those whose death is brought about by some outer cause, such as illness (which is an outer cause) or weakness of some kind.

If then, through this early death, the meeting with the Father-Principle has not yet taken place in the subconscious depths of the soul—It will take place at the hour of death. At the moment of death this meeting occurs. Here we may express, somewhat differently, what has indeed already been expressed in another form in a like connection, in the book *Theosophy* in reference to the always deplorable phenomenon of a man bringing his life to an end by his own will. No man would do this if he could see the significance of his deed; and when once Spiritual Science has really been taken into people's feelings and thoughts, there will be no more suicides. For the meeting with the Father-Principle at the hour of death, when death occurs before middle-life, depends upon that death approaching a man from outside, not being brought about by himself. The difficulty then encountered by the soul and which is described from another standpoint in the book *Theosophy*, might be described from that from which we are speaking today, and we might say: Through his self-chosen death a man may eventually deprive himself of the meeting with the Father-Principle in this incarnation.

"Thus, my dear friends, since the truths which Spiritual Science has to tell us concerning human life as a whole, affect our life so deeply, they are indeed serious in cases of special importance. These truths can provide serious explanations of life, which man needs in an age when he must find his way out of the materialism which rules the present world ordering and the current point-of-view, in so far as these depend on man himself. Stronger forces will be required to overcome the strong connection with the purely material powers which rule over man today, and to give him once again the possibility of recognizing his connection with the Spiritual World from the immediate experiences of life.

"If we speak in a more abstract way of the Beings of the Higher Hierarchies we can speak in a more concrete way of the fact that man himself—in the experiences at first passed through unconsciously, but which even during his life between birth and death may be brought to his consciousness—may ascend in three stages: through the meeting with his genius, through the meeting with Christ Jesus, and through the meeting with the Father.

"Of course a great deal depends on our gaining as many concepts as possible which force themselves into our feelings, concepts that so refine our inner soul-life that we do not carelessly and inattentively pass things by, which in reality, if we are but attentive, play a part in our lives. In this respect education will have a very great deal to do in the near future. I should just like to bring forward one such concept. Just think how infinitely life would be deepened, if to the general knowledge concerning karma such details could be added, as the fact that when a man's life comes to an end in early youth the meeting with the Father-Principle occurs at the hour of death. This shows that the particular karma of this man made an early death necessary, so that an abnormal meeting with the Father-Principle should take place. For what actually occurs in such a case? The man is destroyed from without; his physical being is undermined from without. In illness, too, this is really the case. For the scene of action of the meeting with the Father-Principle is really here in the physical Earth-world. When it happens that this external physical Earth-world has destroyed a man, the meeting with the Father-Principle can be seen at that very place, and of course it is always to be seen again in the retrospect. This however makes it possible for a man throughout the whole of his life after death to hold firmly, the thought of the place on Earth where, descending from heavenly heights, the Father-Principle came to the meeting

which then took place. The recollection of this makes him want
to be as active as he possibly can to work down into the physical
Earth-world from the Spiritual World.

"Now if we consider our present time from this standpoint
and try to arouse the same feeling of solemnity as we have just
tried to do with respect to the meeting with the Father-Principle,
trying not merely to look upon the numerous premature deaths
now occurring in the light of feeling or abstract conception,
we shall be driven to admit that these were predestined in
preparation for the coming need for a great activity to be directed
from the Spiritual World to the physical Earth-world. This is
another aspect of what I have often said with reference to the
tragic events of the last few years: that those who today pass so
early through the portals of death will become special helpers in
the future development of humanity, which will indeed require
strong forces to disentangle itself from materialism. But all this
must be brought to men's consciousness; it must not take place
unconsciously. Therefore it is necessary that even now, souls here
on the Earth should make themselves receptive—I have already
mentioned this—otherwise the forces developed in the Spiritual
World may go in other directions. In order that these forces,
these predestined forces, may become fruitful to the Earth, it is
necessary that there should be souls on the Earth permeated with
the knowledge of the Spiritual World. And there must be more
and more of such souls on the Earth. Let us therefore try to make
fruitful the content of Spiritual Science, which must once be given
out in words. By the help of the language (I mentioned this in
the last lecture but one) the language we learn through Spiritual
Science—let us try to re-animate the old conceptions which are,
not without purpose, interwoven in our present life. Let us try to
quicken anew what we have heard from Plutarch: that man, even

as mere physical man, is permeated by the Spiritual man, and that in a peculiar but normal way a man has a higher Spiritual principle outside his head which represents his genius and which, if he be wise, he obeys. Let us try, as I have said, to take the feelings acquired by Spiritual Science to our assistance—so that the phenomena of life may not pass us by unnoticed.

"In conclusion, we will today take one feeling, one conception, which may be of great help to our souls. Unfortunately many people in our modern materialistic age find it very difficult to feel what I might call the holiness of sleep. (The materialistic life is being somewhat softened by this period of trial, and not only ought it to remain softened thereby—which can hardly be hoped if materialism remains at its present strength—but it ought even to be enormously and increasingly softened.) It is indeed a curious phenomenon of human intelligence today that it is entirely devoid of respect for the holiness of sleep. We need only consider how many people who spend the evening hours in purely materialistic ways, go to sleep without developing the realization—which indeed can never become a living thing in a materialistic mind—that sleep unites us with the Spiritual World, that sleep sends us across into the Spiritual World. (These things are not mentioned by way of blame, nor intended to drive people to asceticism: we must live with the world, but we must at the same time have our eyes open; for only thus can we wrench our bodily nature away from the lower and lift it higher.) People should at least become gradually able to develop a feeling which can be expressed somewhat as follows:—

'I am going to sleep; until I wake, my soul will be in the Spiritual World. There it will meet with the guiding-power of my Earth-life, who lives in the Spiritual World, and who soars round and surrounds my head. My soul will have the meeting with my genius. The wings of my genius will come in contact with my soul.'

"Yes, my dear friends, as regards the overcoming of the materialistic life, a great deal, a very great deal, depends on whether one can create a strong feeling of what this means, when one thinks over one's relation to sleep. The materialistic life can only be overcome by stimulating intimate feelings such as these—which are themselves in correspondence with the Spiritual World. Only when we intensify such feelings and make them active, will the life of sleep become so intense, that the contact with the Spiritual World will on the other hand be gradually able to strengthen our waking life too. We shall then have around us not merely the sense-world, but also the Spiritual World—*which is the true, the truly real world.* For this world that we generally call the real one, is, as I expounded in the last open lecture, nothing but a reflection, an image of the actual real one. The real world is the World of Spirit. The small community which is today devoted to Anthroposophy or Spiritual Science, will better be able to grasp the earnest signs of the times and undergo the severe trials of the times, if besides all the other trials to which man is subject today, it learns to consider this time as a time of trial, of testing and probation, whether we are able with sufficient strength of soul and warmth of heart to unite our whole being with the Spiritual Science which we must take in through our reason and our intellect.

"In these words, I wished once more to emphasize what I have often said here before: that Spiritual Science will only find its right place in the hearts of men, when it is not merely theory and knowledge; but when—symbolically speaking—it constantly permeates and penetrates the soul—*just as our physical blood, our heart's blood, constantly permeates and gives life to our bodily nature.*

Notes:

1. *Karma of Untruthfulness* **I, Rudolf Steiner, Lecture XXIV, Dornach, January 28, 1916, GA 173c**

   "What is important for us is the fact that the position of the Sun at the spring equinox moves backward, passing through the whole Zodiac little by little. It traverses the whole Zodiac until it finally returns to the original position, taking approximately 25,920 years. These 25,920 years are termed the Platonic Year, the Cosmic Year. The exact figure varies according to the various methods of calculation. However, we are not concerned with exact figures but with the rhythm this precession entails. You can imagine that a cosmic rhythm must lie in this movement which repeats itself every 25,920 years. We can say that these 25,920 years are very important for the life of the Sun, for during this time the life of the Sun passes through one unit, a proper unit. The next 25,920 years are then a repetition. We have a rhythm in which one unit measures 25,920 years....

   "On average, a human being takes eighteen breaths a minute. Not all breaths are equal, for those in youth differ from those in old age, but the average is eighteen breaths a minute. Eighteen times a minute we rhythmically renew our life. Multiply this by 60 and you have 1,080 times an hour. Now multiply by 24, and the number of breaths in twenty-four hours comes to 25,920!

   "A year has 365¼ days and if we divide 25,920 by 365.25 the answer is: nearly 71. Let us say 71 years, which is the average life-span of the human being. The human being is free, however, and often lives much longer; but you know that the patriarchal life-span is given as 70 years. The span of a human life is 25,920 days, 25,920 Great Breaths, and so we have another cycle wonderfully depicting the Macrocosm in the Microcosm. We could say that by living for one day, taking 25,920 breaths, we depict the Platonic Cosmic Year, and by living for 71 years, waking up and going to sleep 25,920 times—a breathing on a larger scale—we once again depict the Platonic Year."

2. *genius/daimon/daemon* (German: dämon):

"*Conversations of Goethe with Eckermann and Soret*, Vol. II," by John Oxenford, publ. Smith, Elder & Co.: London, 1850 (pg. 197, entry: Sunday December 6, 1829)

"When one is old one thinks of worldly matters otherwise than when one is young. Thus, I cannot but think that the demons, to tease and make sport with men, have placed among them single figures, which are so alluring that everyone strives after them, and so great that nobody reaches them. Thus they set up Raffaelle [Raphael], with whom thought and act were equally perfect; some distinguished followers have approached him, but none have equalled him. Thus, too, they set up Mozart as something unattainable in music; and thus Shakespeare in poetry. I know what you can say against this thought; but I only mean natural character, the great innate qualities. Thus, too. Napoleon is unattainable."

"*Conversations of Goethe with Eckermann and Soret*, Vol. II," by John Oxenford, publ. Smith, Elder & Co.: London, 1850 (pg. 344, entry: Friday February 18, 1831)

"…But now I can do reverence to all these hindrances; for during these delays things have ripened abroad among other excellent men, so that they now bring the best grist to my mill, advance me beyond all conception, and will bring my work to a conclusion which I could not have imagined a year ago. The like has often happened to me in life; and, in such cases, one is led to believe in a higher influence, in something daemonic (dämonisch), which we adore without trying to explain it further."

"*Conversations of Goethe with Eckermann and Soret*, Vol. II," by John Oxenford, publ. Smith, Elder & Co.: London, 1850 (pgs. 46-47, entry: Tuesday March 11th, 1828)

"Every Entelechia [a] is a piece of eternity, and the few years during which it is bound to the earthly body does not make it old. If this Entelechia is of a trivial kind, it will exercise but little sway during its bodily confinement; on the contrary, the body will predominate, and when this grows old the Entelechia will not hold and restrain it. But if the Entelechia is of a powerful kind, as is the case with all men of natural genius, then with its animating penetration of the body it will not only act with strengthening and ennobling power upon the organization, but it will also endeavour with its spiritual superiority to confer the privilege of perpetual youth. Thence it comes that in men of superior endowments, even during their old age, we constantly perceive fresh epochs of singular productiveness; they seem constantly to grow young again for a time, and that is what I call a repeated puberty. Still youth is youth, and however powerful an Entelechia may prove, it will never become quite master of the corporeal, and it makes a wonderful difference whether it finds in the body an ally or an adversary."

> a. Entelechia: Late Latin entelechia, from Ancient Greek ἐντελέχεια (entelékheia), coined by Aristotle. From ἐντελής (entelḗs, "complete, finished, perfect") (from τέλος (télos, "end, fruition, accomplishment") + ἔχω (ékhō, "to have"). *Aristotelian metaphysics*: The complete realization and final form of some potential concept or function; the conditions under which a potential thing becomes actualized. *Philosophy*: A particular type of motivation, need for self-determination, and inner strength directing life and growth to become all one is capable

of being; the need to actualize one's beliefs; having both a personal vision and the ability to actualize that vision from within. (Wiktionary)

"*Conversations of Goethe with Eckermann and Soret*, Vol. II,"
by John Oxenford, publ. Smith, Elder & Co.: London, 1850
(pgs. 351-352; Wednesday, March 2, 1831)

'I dined with Goethe to-day, and the conversation soon turning again on the Daemonic, he added the following remarks to define it more closely.

"The Daemonic," said **he, "is that which cannot be explained by Reason or Understanding; it li**es not in my nature, but I am subject to it."

"Napoleon," said I, "seems to have been of the daemonic sort."

"He was so thoroughly," said Goethe, "and in the highest degree, so that scarce any one is to be compared with him. Our late Grand-Duke, too, was a daemonic nature, full of unlimited power of action and unrest, so that his own dominion was too little for him, and the greatest would have been too little. Daemonic beings of such sort the Greeks reckoned among their demigods."

"Is not the Daemonic," said I, "perceptible in events also?"

"Particularly," said Goethe, "and, indeed, in all which we cannot explain by Reason and Understanding. It manifests itself in the most varied manner throughout all nature—in the invisible as in the visible. Many creatures are of a purely daemonic kind; in many parts of it are effective."

"Has not Mephistophiles," said I, "daemonic traits, too?"

"No," said Goethe, "Mephistophiles is much too negative a being. The Daemonic manifests itself in a thoroughly active power."

"Among artists," he continued, "it is found more among musicians—less among painters. In Paganini, it shows itself in a high degree; and it is thus he produces such great effects." I was much pleased at all these remarks, which made more clear to me what Goethe meant by the Daemonic.'

The Cosmic Year—Post-Atlantean Epochs

5th Post Atlantean Epoch 7,227 B.C.-7,894 A.D.

1. ♋ 2. ♊ 3. ♉ 4. ♈ 5. ♓ 6. ♒ 7. ♑

6th Post Atlantean Epoch 7,894 A.D.-23,014 A.D.

1. ♐ 2. ♏ 3. ♎ 4. ♍ 5. ♌ 6. ♋ 7. ♊

7th Post Atlantean Epoch 23,014 A.D.-38,134 A.D.

1. ♉ 2. ♈ 3. ♓ 4. ♒ 5. ♑ 6. ♐ 7. ♏

The Gospel of St. John, Rudolf Steiner, Lecture III, Basel, November 18, 1907, GA 100

Saturn	Sun	Moon	Earth
Spirit-Human	Spirit-Human	Spirit-Human	Spirit-Human
	Life-Spirit	Life-Spirit	Life-Spirit
		Spirit-Self	Spirit-Self
			Ego ('I')
		Astral body	Astral body
	Etheric body	Etheric body	Etheric body
Physical body	Physical body	Physical body	Physical body

The European Mysteries and their Initiates, Rudolf Steiner, Berlin, May 6, 1909, GA 57

"In the Mysteries of Wales and Britain the teachings of Dionysos *were* received and the influence of the Christ Mystery so permeated the [Celtic] Druid and [Nordic-Germanic] Trotten Mysteries that the Initiates realized in full clarity of consciousness that He whom they had sought as Hu and Baldur, had come to earth as Christ. But they said among themselves that mankind in general was not ripe to understand the mystery of the blood flowing from the Redeemer's wounds—*that men were not fit to receive into themselves the blood that runs through all creation.*

"It was only in small circles of Initiates that this sacred Christ Mystery was preserved. A man who was initiated into this Mystery experienced the overcoming of the Ego that functions in the world of sense. This is how he experienced it.—He asked himself:—

'What has been the manner of my life hitherto? In my quest for truth, I have turned to the things of the outer-world. The Initiates of the Christ-Mystery, however, demand that I shall not wait until outer things tell me what is true but that in my *soul*, without being stimulated by the outer-world, I shall seek the invisible.'

"This quest of the soul for the highest was called by the outer-world in later times: *The secret of the Holy Grail*. And the Parsifal or Grail legend is simply a form of the Christ Mystery. The Grail is the Holy Cup from which Christ drank at the Last Supper and in which Joseph of Arimathea caught the blood as it flowed on Golgotha. The Cup was then taken to a holy place and guarded. So long as a man does not ask about the invisible, his lot is that of Parsifal. Only when he asks, does he become an Initiate of the Christ Mystery.

"Wolfram von Eschenbach speaks in his poem of the three stages through which the soul of man passes. The first of these is the stage of outer, material perception. The soul is caught up in matter and allows matter to say *what is truth*. This is the 'stupor'

(Dumpfheit) of the soul, as Wolfram van Eschenbach expresses it. And then the soul begins to recognize that the outer-world offers only illusion. When the soul perceives that the results of science are not answers but only questions, there comes the stage of 'doubt' (Zwifel), according to Wolfram von Eschenbach. But then the soul rises to 'blessedness' (Saelde, Seligkeit)—*to life in the spiritual worlds.*—These are the three stages.

"The Mysteries which were illuminated by the Christ-Impulse have one quite definite feature in common whereby they are raised to a higher level than that of the more ancient Mysteries. Initiation always means that a man attains to a higher kind of sight and that his soul undergoes a higher development. Before he sets out on this path, three faculties live within his soul: *thinking, feeling, and willing.* He has these three soul-powers within him. In ordinary life in the modern world, these three soul-powers are intimately bound together. The Ego ['I'] of man is interwoven with thinking feeling and willing because before he attains initiation he has not worked with the powers of the Ego at the development of his higher members. The first step is to purify the feelings, impulses, and instincts in the astral body. Out of the purified astral body there rises the 'Spirit-Self' or 'Manas.' Then man begins to permeate every thought with a definite element of feeling so that each thought may be said to have something 'cold' or 'warm' about it. He is transforming his 'Etheric-Body' or 'life-body.' Out of the transformed Etheric-Body (it is a transformation of feeling), arises 'Budhi' or 'Life-Spirit.' And finally, he transforms his willing and therewith the physical body itself, into 'Atman' or 'Spirit-Human.'

"Thus, by transforming his thinking, feeling, and willing man changes his astral body into Spirit-Self or Manas, his etheric body into Life-Spirit or Budhi and finally his physical body into

Spirit-Human or Atman. This transformation is the result of the
initiate's systematic work upon his soul, whereby he rises to the
Spiritual Worlds. But something very definite happens when
the path to Initiation is trodden in full earnest and not light-
heartedly. In true Initiation it is as if a man's organization were
divided into three parts, and the Ego reigns as king over the three.
Whereas in ordinary circumstances the spheres of thinking,
feeling and willing are not clearly separated, when a man sets out
on the path of higher development thoughts begin to arise in him
which are not immediately tinged with feeling; but are permeated
with the element of sympathy or antipathy according to the free
choice of the Ego. Feeling does not immediately attach itself to a
thought—but the man divides, as it were, into three: he is a man
of feeling, a man of thinking, a man of will, and the Ego, as king,
rules over the three. At a definite stage of Initiation he becomes,
in this sense, three men. He feels that by way of his astral body he
experiences all those thoughts which are related to the spiritual
world; through his Etheric-Body he experiences everything that
pervades the spiritual world as the element of feeling; through
his physical body he experiences all the will-impulses which
flow through the spiritual world. And he realizes himself as king
within the sacred *Three*. A man who is not able or ripe enough
to bear this separation of his being, will not attain the fruits of
Initiation. The sufferings that crowd upon him in his immature
state will keep him back. A man who approaches the Holy Grail
but is not worthy, will suffer as Amfortas suffered. He can only be
redeemed by one who brings the forces of good.—*He is freed from
his sufferings by Parsifal.*

"And now let us return once more to what Initiation brings
in its train. The seeking soul finds the spiritual world; the soul
finds the Holy Grail which has now become the symbol of the

spiritual world. Individual Initiates have experienced what is here described. They have gone the way of Parsifal, have become as kings looking down on the three bodies. The Initiate says to himself: 'I am king over my purified astral body which can only be purified when I strive to emulate *Christ.*' He must not hold to any outer link, to anything in the external world; but unite himself in the innermost depths of his soul with the Christ Principle. *Everything that binds him with the world of sense must fall away in that supreme moment...*"

The Mission of the Individual Folk Souls, Rudolf Steiner, Lecture I, *Angels, Folk Spirits, Time Spirits: their Part in the Evolution of Mankind*, Oslo, June 7, 1910, GA 121

"The Ego will transmute the astral body into Manas or Spirit-Self, so that it becomes something different from what it is today. In the same way, at a higher level, the Ego will refashion and transmute the etheric or life-body into Life-Spirit or Budhi. Finally, the highest achievement of man that we can envisage at present is the spiritualization of the physical body, the most intractable member of his being. When our present physical body, the densest and most material member, is transmitted into Atman or Spirit-Human it will be the highest member of man's being. Thus, we are familiar with three members of the human organism which were developed in past Epochs, the organism in which we are at present incarnated and three others which the Ego will fashion into something new in the future."

"Between the initial development of the higher members in the past and their further development in the future there lies an intermediate stage. We know that we must think of the Ego itself as inwardly organized. The Ego works upon a kind of intermediate being. Therefore, between the astral body which

man has inherited from the past and the Spirit-Self or Manas
which he will fashion out of the astral body in the distant future,
there are the three preparatory members; the Sentient-Soul,
the lowest member in which the Ego has already worked, the
Intellectual or Mind-Soul and the Spiritual or Consciousness-
Soul. But very little of Spirit-Self or Manas that we are in the
process of developing is present in man today, at most only the
first indications. On the other hand, man has laid the foundations
of this future development by having learnt to control his three
lower members to some extent. He learned to control the astral
body by permeating it with his Ego and forming the Sentient-
Soul within it. Just as the Sentient-Soul stands in a certain
relationship to the sentient [astral] body, so does the Intellectual-
Soul or Mind-Soul to the etheric body, so that the Intellectual or
Mind-Soul is a feeble foreshadowing of what the Life-Spirit or
Budhi will be a feeble foreshadowing, it is true; but nonetheless
foreshadowing. And in the Spiritual-Soul (or Consciousness-
Soul) the 'I' has worked down into the physical body to a certain
extent. Therefore, the Spiritual-Soul is a feeble foreshadowing of
what will one day be Spirit-Human or Atman.

"Since we know that we continue our evolution into the future
and that we further develop our present astral body, etheric or life
body, and our physical body, the question arises:—

'Is it not equally natural that the Beings who have already
experienced the human stage have now reached the stage
when they are transmuting their astral body into Spirit-Self
or Manas?

"Just as during the next incarnation of the Earth, the Jupiter
stage, we shall complete the transmutation of our astral body into

Spirit-Self or Manas, so the Angels who underwent the human stage on Old Moon have completed the transmutation of their astral bodies into Spirit-Self or Manas, or will do so during our Earth evolution, a stage that we shall first have to undergo in the next incarnation of the Earth. If we look still further back to the Beings who underwent the human stage on Old Sun, we realize that they already experienced on Old Moon the stage we shall have to experience for the first time in the next incarnation of the Earth. They are performing the work which will be the prerogative of man when, in his Ego, he transmutes his etheric or life body into Life-Spirit or Budhi. These Archangels, therefore, are Beings who are two stages beyond man; they have reached the stage that will one day be ours when from within our Ego, we shall transform the life body into Life-Spirit or Budhi. When we contemplate these Beings, we recognize them as Beings who are two stages beyond ourselves, who foreshadow what we ourselves will experience in the future; they are Beings who are now working upon their etheric or life body and are transmuting it into Life-Spirit or Budhi. In the same way we are aware of yet higher Beings, the Spirits of Personality (Archai). They are at a still higher stage than the Archangels, a stage which man will reach in a still more distant future when he will be able to transmute his physical body into Atman or Spirit-Human.

"Just as the Group-Soul directs the regular migrations of birds, so will man, after he has developed Spirit-Self or Manas, command his physical and etheric bodies; he will control and direct them. He will do this in a still higher sense from without when he has so far perfected himself that he is still in the process of transmuting his etheric or life body. The Beings who can already do this today are the Archangels. They are Beings who can already do what man will be able to do some day, Beings who are able to compass what is called 'directing the physical and etheric bodies from without'; but who are able at the same time to work upon their own etheric body.

"Try to form an idea of Beings living and working as it were with their Ego in the spiritual atmosphere of our Earth, whose Ego has already transformed the astral body and who with their fully developed Spirit-Self or Manas continue to work on our Earth and into human beings, transforming our etheric or life body; Beings who are themselves at the stage of transmuting their etheric or life body into Budhi or Life-Spirit. If you imagine such Beings who are at the Archangel stage among the spiritual Hierarchies, you will then have an idea of what are called the 'Folk Spirits,' the directing Folk Spirits of the Earth. The Folk Spirits belong to the rank of the Archangels. We shall see how they, for their part, direct their own etheric or life-body, and how they thereby work down into mankind and thus draw mankind into the sphere of their own activity. If we survey the various peoples on Earth and select out individual examples, then we see in the life and activity of these peoples, in the characteristic attributes peculiar to these peoples, a reflection of what we regard as the mission of the Folk Spirits."

An Esoteric Cosmology, Rudolf Steiner, Lecture XI, The Devachanic World—Heaven, Paris, June 7, 1906, GA 94

"Devachan is the Sanskrit term for the long period of time lying between the death and rebirth of man. After death, in the astral world, the soul first learns to cast off the instincts that are connected with the body. After this, the soul passes into Devachan for the long period that lies between two incarnations.

"The Devachanic world is a state or condition of existence. It surrounds us even in earthly life, but we do not perceive it. In order, by way of analogy, to understand Devachanic existence and its functions in earthly and cosmic life, it will be best to take our start from a consideration of the state of sleep.

"For the vast majority of human beings, sleep is a condition full of enigmas. During sleep, man's etheric body remains with his physical body and continues its vegetative, restorative functions; but the astral body and Individual-Ego ['I'] leave the sleeping body and live an independent existence.

"The physical body is used up, consumed, as it were, by our conscious life. From morning till night man spends his forces; the astral body transmits sensations to the physical body which gradually exhaust it. At night, the astral body functions in quite a different way. It no longer transmits sensations which come from outside; it works upon them and brings order and harmony into what the waking life, with its chaotic perceptions, has thrown into disorder. By day, the function of the astral body is to receive and transmit; by night, during sleep, its function is to bring order, to build up and refresh the spent forces.

"In man's present stage of evolution, it is not possible for the astral body to do this work of restoration by night and at the same time to observe what is happening in the surrounding astral world. How, then, can man arrive at the point of being able to relieve his astral body of its work, in order to set it free for *conscious* existence in the astral world?

"The procedure adopted by the adept in order to release his astral body is, on the one hand, to train and develop such feelings and thoughts as possess, in themselves, a certain rhythm which can then be communicated to the physical body; and, on the other, to avoid those which give rise to physical disorder. Joy or suffering that runs to extremes is avoided. The adept teaches the necessity for equanimity of soul.

"Nature is governed by one sovereign law which is that rhythm must enter into all manifestation. When the twelve-petalled lotus-flower which constitutes man's organ of astral-spiritual perception has developed, he can begin to work upon his body and imbue it with a new rhythm whereby its fatigue is healed. Thanks to this rhythm and the restoration of harmony it is no longer necessary for the astral body to perform the restorative work on the sleeping physical body which alone prevents it from falling into ruin.

"The whole of waking life is a process destructive of the physical body. Illnesses are caused by excessive activity of the astral body. Eating to excess affords a stimulus to the astral body which reacts in a disturbing way on the physical body. That is why fasting is laid down in certain religions. The effect of fasting is that the astral body, having greater quiet and less to do, partially detaches itself from the physical body. Its vibrations are modulated and communicate a regular rhythm to the etheric body. Rhythm is thus set going in the etheric body by means of fasting. Harmony is brought into life (etheric body) and form (physical body). In other words, harmony reigns between the Universe and man.

"This gives us some idea of the function performed by the astral body during sleep. Where is the Self, the Ego of man? In the world of Devachan—*but he has no consciousness of it.* We must distinguish between sleep that is filled with dreams and the state of deep sleep. Sleep that is filled with dreams is an expression of astral consciousness. Deep, dreamless sleep—the sleep that follows the first dreams—corresponds to the Devachanic state. Nothing of it is remembered because it is a condition of unconsciousness for the physical being of ordinary man. Only after the attainment of higher initiation is man aware of his experiences in deep sleep. In the Initiate there is continuity of consciousness through waking life, dream life and dreamless sleep.

"Let us now consider the condition of man in Devachan, after death. At the end of a certain time, the etheric body disperses into the forces of the living ether.

"What is the next task of the astral body and Ego? A new etheric body has to be built for the incarnation that is to follow. Devachanic existence is devoted, in part, to this work. The substance of the etheric body, like that of the physical body, is not conserved. The substance of which the physical body is composed, is constantly changing—*to the point of being wholly renewed in the course of seven years.* Similarly, etheric substance is renewed, although its principles of form and inner structure remain the same under the influence of the Higher Self. At death, this substance is given completely over to the etheric-world and nothing remains from one incarnation to another, any more than the substance of the physical body remains. In each successive incarnation, therefore, the etheric body of man is entirely renewed. That is why there is such a change in the physiognomy and bodily form of man from one incarnation to another. The physiognomy and bodily form do not depend upon the will of the individual but upon his *karma*, his desires, passions and his involuntary actions.

"It is quite different in the case of an initiated disciple. He develops his etheric body in earthly existence in such a way that it is conserved and is fit to pass into Devachan after death. Here on Earth, he is able to awaken, within his etheric forces, a 'Life-Spirit' which constitutes one of the imperishable principles of his being. The Sanskrit term for the etheric body which has developed into Life-Spirit is *Budhi*. When this principle of Life-Spirit has developed in the disciple, it is no longer necessary for him entirely to re-mold his etheric body between two incarnations. His period of Devachanic existence is then much shorter and for this reason the same character, temperament and outstanding traits are carried forward from one incarnation to another. When the *master* in occultism has reached the point of conscious control not only of his etheric but of his *physical* body, another, higher spiritual principle comes into being—Spirit-Human (in Sanskrit, Atman). At this stage the Initiate preserves the characteristics of his physical body every time he incarnates on Earth. With unbroken consciousness, he passes from earthly to Heavenly life, from one incarnation to another. Here we have the origin of the legend referring to initiates who lived for a thousand or two thousand years. For them there is neither Kamaloka or Devachan—*but unbroken consciousness through deaths and births.*"

Occult Signs and Symbols, **Rudolf Steiner, Lecture IV,** *The Lion, the Cow, the Eagle, and Man—Man, the Most Significant Symbol,* **Stuttgart, September 16, 1907, GA 101**

"When you compare a man of today with the animals, the difference between them forces one to say that the man, as an individual, has within him what cannot be found in the single animal. The man has an individual-soul, the animal a Group-Soul. The individual human being is, in himself, a whole animal species. All lions together, for example, have only one soul. Such Group-Egos are like Human-Egos except that they have not descended into the physical world but are to be found only in the astral world. Here on Earth, one sees physical men, each of whom bears his Ego ['I']. In the astral world one finds beings like one's self; but in astral sheaths rather than physical. One can speak with them as to one's peers. These are the animal Group-Souls. In earlier times, men also had Group-Souls. Only gradually have they developed themselves to their present independence. These Group-Souls were originally in the astral world and then descended to live in the physical body. When one investigates the original human Group-Souls in the astral world, one finds four species from which humans have sprung. Were one to compare these four kinds of beings with the Group-Souls that belong to the present-day animal species, one would find that one of the four is comparable to the lion, another to the eagle, a third to the cow, and a fourth to the man of ancient times before his Ego ['I'] had descended. Thus, in the second picture, in the apocalyptic animals, lion, eagle, cow, and man, we are shown an evolutionary stage of mankind. There is, and always will be as long as the Earth shall exist, a Group-Soul for the higher manifestation of men, which is represented by the lamb in the center of the seal, the Mystical Lamb—*the sign of the Redeemer*. This grouping of the five Group-Souls, the four of man around the great Group-Soul, which still belongs to all men in common, is represented by the second seal [*Book of Revelation*]."

The Ego, Rudolf Steiner, Lecture I, *From Group-Soul to Individuality,* Munich, December 4, 1909, GA 117 (Also: *The Universal Human, Individuality, and the Group-Soul*)

"Now we can say:—

> 'Immediately after the great Atlantean catastrophe, there were numerous human beings who knew through their direct powers of perception: Around us is a spiritual world. We live in a spiritual world.'

"Fewer and fewer became the human beings who knew this; more and more were the powers of man limited to the perception of the senses. But if, on the one hand, today, the power of perception for the spiritual world is the least conceivable, yet, on the other hand, something is preparing in our age which is so significant that already for a great number of people, quite different faculties will exist in that incarnation which follows the present one. As the faculties of man have changed during the five epochs of culture, so they will also change into the sixth, and a great number of people today will clearly show already in their next incarnation through their whole mood-of-soul, that their faculties have essentially changed. Today, we will make clear to ourselves how different these souls of human beings will be in the future, with a great number already in the next incarnation, with others, in the incarnation following.

"We could also look back in another way into past epochs of human evolution. Then we would see that the farther we go back to the ancient clairvoyance, at the same time, the more we have united with the human soul, what one can call the character of Group-Soulness. It has often been pointed out to you that the consciousness of the Group-Soulness was existing in the ancient Hebrew people in an eminent degree. He who felt himself—really consciously felt himself as a member of the ancient Hebrew people—said to himself—especial attention has been drawn to this:—

'As an individual man I am a transitory phenomenon; but in me lives something that has an immediate connection with all the soul-being which has streamed down since the racial father Abraham.'

"A member of the old Hebrew people felt that. We can indeed esoterically admit as a spiritual phenomenon what was thus felt by the old Hebrew people. We understand better what then happened if we keep the following in mind.

"Let us consider an old Hebrew initiate. Although initiation was not so frequent among the ancient Hebrews as among other peoples, we could not characterize such a real initiate otherwise— not merely one initiated into the theories and the Law; but an initiate really seeing in the spiritual worlds—than by taking into consideration the entire racial peculiarity. It is the custom today in external science, which busies itself with documents without any misgiving, to take everywhere what stands in the *Old Testament*, to test it by all kinds of external records, and then find it unsubstantiated. We shall have occasion to point out that the *Old Testament* gives the facts more faithfully than external historical records. In any case, spiritual science shows that a blood relationship of the Hebrew people can really be demonstrated back to the racial father Abraham, and that the assumption of Abraham as racial father is fully justified. This was something especially known in the old Hebrew secret schools: Such an individuality, such a soul-being as that of Abraham, was not merely incarnated as Abraham; but is an eternal being, who remained existing in the spiritual world. And in truth a real initiate was inspired by the same spirit, as he who inspired Abraham, and he could testify for him of himself, that he was permeated by the same soul-nature as Abraham. There was a real connection between every initiate and the racial father Abraham. We must hold that fast—*that expressed itself in the feeling of membership of the old Hebrew people.* That was a kind of Group-Soulness. One felt what expressed itself in Abraham as the Group-Soul of the people. One felt Group-Souls similarly in the rest of humanity. Mankind in general goes back to Group-Souls. The farther we go back in human evolution, the less do we find expressed the single individuality. That which we still find today in the animal kingdom: that a whole group belongs together— that was existing among mankind, and appears ever clearer and clearer, the farther we go back to ancient times. Groups of human beings then belonged together, and the Group-Soul was essentially stronger than what constituted the individual soul in the single human being.

"We can now say: Today in our time, the Group-Soulness of people is still not yet overcome, and whoever believes that it is completely overcome does not keep in mind certain finer phenomena of life. Whoever keeps it in mind will very quickly see that certain human beings not only appear alike in their physiognomy; but that also the soul-qualities are similar in groups of human beings: that one can, as it were, divide human beings into categories. Each person can still today be reckoned into a certain category; with reference to this or the other quality, he will belong perhaps to different categories; but a certain Group-Soulness is not only valid because the races exist—but also in other connections. The boundaries drawn between the single nations fall away more and more; but other groupings are still perceptible. Certain basic characteristics stand so connected in some people, that he who will only look, can still today perceive the last relics of the Group-Soulness of man.

"Now we, in our present age [5th Post Atlantean Period 1,414 A.D.-3,574 A.D.], are living in the most eminent sense, in a transition. All Group-Soulness has gradually to be stripped off. Just as the gaps between single nations gradually disappear as the single parts of different nations understand each other better, so also will other Group-Soul qualities be shed, and the individual nature of each single person come to the foreground more and more.

"We have therewith characterized something quite essential in evolution. If we want to grasp it from another side, we can say:— That idea whereby the Group-Soulness chiefly expresses itself loses meaning ever more and more in the evolution of mankind, i.e., the idea of race. If we go back beyond the great Atlantean catastrophe, we see how the human races are prepared. In the old Atlantean Age human beings were grouped according to external characteristics in their bodily structure, far more strongly than today. What we call races today are only the relics of those important distinctions between human beings as were customary in old Atlantis. *The idea of race is only really applicable to old Atlantis.* Since we deal with a real evolution of mankind, we have never employed the idea of race in the most eminent sense for the Post-Atlantean Epoch [7,227 B.C.-7,894 A.D.]. We speak of an Ancient Indian Period of civilization [1st Post Atlantean Period 7,227 B.C.-5,067 B.C.], of an Ancient Persian Period of civilization [2nd Post Atlantean Period 5,067 B.C.-2,907 B.C.], etc. If relics of the old Atlantean distinctions, of their Group-Soulness, are still existing in our time, so that one can still say the racial division continues to work on—that which is preparing for the Sixth Period of time [6th Post Atlantean Period 3,574 A.D.-5,734 A.D.] consists just in the character of race being stripped off. *That is the essential.* Therefore, it is necessary that that movement which is called the anthroposophical movement, which should prepare the Sixth Period of time, adopts in its basic character this stripping off of the character of race—*that especially it seeks to unite people out of all 'races,' out of all nations, and in this way bridges over these differences, these distinctions, these gaps, which are existing between various groups of human beings.* For the old racial standpoint had in a certain connection a physical character; whereas what will fulfil itself in the future will have a much more spiritual character. Therefore, it is so urgently necessary to understand that our anthroposophical movement is a spiritual one, which looks to the spirit, and overcomes just that which arises from physical distinctions through the force of a spiritual movement. It is, of course, thoroughly comprehensible that any movement has, as it were, its childish illnesses, and that in the beginning of the Theosophical Movement, matters were so represented as if the Earth fell into seven periods of time—they were called root-races—and each of these root-races into seven sub-races. *But one must get beyond the illnesses of childhood and be clear that the idea of race ceases to have any meaning, especially in our age.*

"Something else, in addition, is being prepared—something connected with the individuality of man in a quite special way—in man becoming ever more and more individual. It is only a question of this occurring in the right sense, and the anthroposophical movement should serve to this end, that human beings become individualities—or we could also say personalities—in the right sense. How can it do this?

"Something else, in addition, is being prepared—something connected with the individuality of man in a quite special way—in man becoming ever more and more individual. It is only a question of this occurring in the right sense, and the anthroposophical movement should serve to this end, that human beings become individualities—or we could also say personalities—in the right sense. How can it do this?

"Here we must look to the most striking new quality of man's soul, which is preparing. The question is often put: Well, if reincarnation exists, why does a person not remember the former incarnations? That is a question which I have often answered. Such a question appears as when one brings along a four-year-old child, and because it is a human being, and cannot reckon, one would say: Man cannot reckon. But let the child become ten years old, and then it will reckon. It is thus with the human soul. If today it cannot remember, yet, the time will come in which it can remember—the time when it has the same powers as he possesses who is initiated today. But just today that transition is happening. There exist today a number of souls who are so far on in our time, who stand close to the moment where they will remember their former incarnations, or at least the last one. A whole number of human beings today are, as it were, before the self-opening of the door to that embracing memory, which comprises not only the life between birth and death, but the previous incarnations, or at least, the last, in the first place. And when, after the present incarnation, a number of human beings are reborn, then they will remember this present incarnation. It is merely a question of *how* they remember. Anthroposophical development should give help and direction to remember in the right way.

"In order to characterize this anthroposophical movement from this point-of-view, it must be said: Its character is that it leads man to realize in the right way what one calls the human 'I,' the innermost member of the human being. I have often pointed out that Fichte rightly said, most human beings would sooner regard themselves as a piece of lava on the moon, than as an 'I.' And if you consider how many people there are in our time who make any idea at all of what is in the 'I'; *i.e.*, of what they themselves are, then in general, you would come to a very dismal result.

"When this question arises, I have always to call to mind a friend I had more than thirty years ago, and who as a quite young student was completely inoculated at that time by the materialistic mood—today it is more modern to say 'monistic' mood. He was already injected by it, in spite of his youth. He always laughed when he heard something was contained in man which could be designated as spiritual being; for he was of the view, that what lives as thought in us, was produced by mechanical or chemical processes in the brain. I often said to him: 'Look, if you earnestly believe this as a content of life, why do you continually tell lies?' He really lied, continually, because he never said: 'My brain feels, my brain thinks, but: I think, I feel, I know this or that.' Thus, he built up a theory which he contradicted with every word— as every man does; for it is impossible to maintain what one imagines as a materialistic theory. *One cannot remain truthful, if one thinks materialistically.* If one would say: My brain loves you, then, one should not say 'you'; but, *my brain loves your brain.* People do not make this consequence clear. But it is something which is not merely humoristic, but something which shows what a deep basis of unconscious untruthfulness lies at the basis of our present education.

"Now, most people really would sooner regard themselves as a piece of lava in the moon; *i.e.,* as a piece of compact matter, than as that which can be called an 'I.' And today one naturally comes least of all to a grasp of the 'I' through external science, which indeed, as such, must think materialistically, according to its methods. How can one attain this grasp of the 'I'? How can one gradually get an idea, a concept of what he instinctively feels, when he says: I think? Solely and alone through this, that he knows by means of the anthroposophical view of the world, how this human being is constituted, how the physical body has a Saturn character, the etheric body a Sun character, the astral body a Moon character, and the Ego ['I'] an Earth character.

When we keep in mind everything we thus get as ideas out of the entire Cosmos, then we understand how the 'I', as the real Master-worker, labors at all the other members. And so we come gradually to an idea of what we profess with the word 'I'. We gradually struggle up to the highest ideas of this 'I', if we learn to understand such a word. We not merely feel ourselves as a spiritual being if we feel ourselves within an 'I', but when we can say—In our individuality lives something which was there before father Abraham. When we cannot merely say—I and father Abraham are one, but: I and the FATHER, *i.e.*, the *Spiritual*, weaving and living through the world. What lives in the 'I', is the same spiritual substance that weaves and lives through the world as Spirit. Thus we gradually work our way up to understand this 'I'; *i.e.*, the bearer of the human individuality, that which goes from incarnation to incarnation. In what way, however, do we grasp the 'I'? Do we grasp the world at all through the anthroposophical view?

"This anthroposophical view of the world arises in the most individual way, and is, at the same time, the most un-individual thing that can be conceived. It can only arise in the most individual way by the secrets of the Cosmos revealing themselves in a human soul, into which stream the great spiritual beings of the world. And so the content of the world must be experienced in the human individuality in the most individual way, but at the same time, it must be experienced with a character of complete impersonality. Whoever will experience the true character of Cosmic Mysteries must stand entirely on the standpoint from which he says—*Whoever still heeds his own opinion, cannot come to Truth.* That is indeed the peculiar nature of anthroposophical truth that the observer may have no opinion of his own, no preference for this or the other

theory, that he may not love this or the other view more than
any other because of his own especial individual qualities. As
long as he stands on this standpoint, it is impossible for the true
secrets of the world to reveal themselves to him. He must pursue
knowledge quite individually, but his individuality must develop
so far, that it no longer has anything personal, *i.e.*, anything
of his own peculiar sympathies and antipathies. This must be
taken strictly and earnestly. Whoever still has any preference
for these or the other ideas and views, whoever can incline to
this or the other because of his education or temperament, will
never recognize objective truth.

"We have attempted here, this summer, to grasp Oriental
wisdom from the standpoint of Western learning. We tried to
be just towards Oriental wisdom, and truly presented it in such
a way that it received its full rights. (See: *The East in the Light
of the West*, GA 113) One must strongly emphasize that in our
time it is impossible for independent spiritual knowledge to
decide through any special preference for either the Oriental
or the Occidental view of the world. Whoever says according
to his different temperament he prefers the nature, the laws of
the world as existing in the Oriental or correspondingly in the
Occidental view, has not yet a full understanding for what is here
essential. One should not decide, *e.g.*, for the greater significance
of, let us say, the Christ, as compared with what Oriental teaching
recognizes, because one inclines to the Christ through one's
Occidental education or one's temperament. One is only fitted
to answer the question 'How is the Christ related to the Orient?'
when from a personal standpoint the Christian is as indifferent to
one as the Oriental. As long as one has preference for this or the
other, so long is one unsuited to make a decision. One first begins
to be objective when one lets the facts alone speak, when one

heeds no reasons derived from personal opinion—*but let facts alone speak in this sphere.*

"Therefore something meets us in the anthroposophical world-view, if it meets us today in its true form, which is inwardly woven with the human individuality, because it must spring out of the 'I'-force of the individuality, and on the other hand, must be independent, so that this individuality is again quite indifferent. That person in whom anthroposophical wisdom appears must be unconcerned by it, must be independent of it. This is essential, that he has brought himself so far, that he forces nothing of his own coloring into these matters. Then they will indeed be individual, because the spiritual cannot appear in the light of the moon, or the stars, but only in the individuality, in the human soul; but then, on the other hand, this individuality must be so far on that it can exclude itself in the production of what constitutes the wisdom of the world. Thus that which appears to mankind through the anthroposophical movement will be something which concerns each human being, no matter from what race, nation, etc., he is born, because it applies itself only to the new humanity, to man as such, not to an abstract, general man, but to each single human being. This is the essential. As it proceeds out of the individuality, out of the kernel of man's being, so it speaks to the deepest kernel of man's being, so it grasps this kernel of man. As we usually speak from man to man, fundamentally it is only surface speaking to surface, something which we have not united with the innermost kernel of our being. Understanding between man and man, full understanding, is hardly possible today in any other sphere, than in that where what is produced comes from the center of man's being, and, when it is understood aright by another, speaks again to his center. Hence in a certain connection, it is a new speech that is spoken by Anthroposophy.

And if today we are still obliged to speak in the various national languages what has to be announced, the content is a new speech, which is spoken by anthroposophy.

"What is spoken today outside in the world is a speech which is only really valid for a very limited sphere. In ancient times, when people still looked into the spiritual world through their old, dreamy clairvoyance, their word then meant something which existed in the spiritual world. The word signified something which existed in the spiritual world. Even in Greece, things were still different from what they are today. The word 'idea' used by Plato signified something different from the word 'Idea,' as used by our modern philosophers. These modern philosophers can no longer understand Plato, because they have no perception of what he called 'Idea,' and they confuse it with abstract concepts. Plato still had something spiritual before him, even if already rarefied; it was still something quite real. Then also, one still had in the words the sap of the spiritual, if one may express it thus. You can trace that in the words. If anybody today uses the word 'wind,' 'air,' then he means something external, physical. The word wind here corresponds to something external, physical. If, *e.g.*, in old Hebrew, the word wind, 'Ruach,' was employed, one did not merely mean something external, physical, but something spiritual, which swept through space. When man breathes in today he is told by materialistic science that he simply inhales material air; in ancient times, one did not believe one inhaled material air, but then one was clear that one inspired something of spirit, or at least, of soul. Thus the words then were absolutely designations for spirit and soul. That has ceased today; today speech is limited to the external world, or at least, those who seek to stand at the peak of the age busy themselves seeing only a materialistic meaning, even behind those things where it is still obvious they are derived from soul and spirit. Physics speaks of an 'impact' of bodies. It has forgotten that the word 'impact' is derived from that which a living being performs out of its inner living nature, when it pushes another being. The original significance of words is forgotten in these simple things.

"And so today, our speech—and this is most of all the case with scientific speech—has become a speech which is only able to express what is material. Because of this, what is in our soul while we speak is only comprehensible to those faculties of our soul which are bound to the physical brain as their instrument. And then the soul understands nothing more of all that is designated with these words, when it is disembodied. When the soul has gone through the gate of death, and no longer employs the brain, then all scientific considerations of today are forms quite incomprehensible to the disembodied soul. It does not even hear or perceive what one expresses in the speech of the time. This has no longer any meaning for a disembodied soul, because it only has meaning for what is the physical world. That again is something which is still more important to consider in what one can call the mode of thinking, the method of representation. It is even more important to consider it there than in theory, because it is a question of life, not of theory, and it is characteristic that one can see in the theosophical movement itself how materialism has crept in. Because it is the mode of the time, it has often crept into the theosophical view, so that real materialism prevails even in theosophy itself; *e.g.*, when one describes the etheric or life-body. Whereas a person should exert himself to come to a grasp of the spirit, one mostly describes it as if it were a finer matter; and the astral body also. One starts as a rule from the physical body, goes further to the etheric or life-body, and says: that is built after the pattern of the physical body, only finer—

thus one progresses to Nirvana. Here one finds descriptions which take their images from nothing else than the physical. I have already experienced that when one wanted to express the good feeling present in a room among those present, one did not do so directly, but one said: Fine vibrations are existing in this room. One did not heed that one materializes what exists spiritually in a mood if one thinks the space filled with a kind of thin cloud, permeated with vibrations. That is what I should like to call the most material way of thinking possible. Materialism has even got by the neck those who want to think spiritually. That is only a characteristic of our time, but it is important that we are conscious of it. And therefore we must pay especial heed to what has been said: that our speech, which is always a kind of tyrant for human thinking, has implanted in the soul a tendency to materialism. And many, who today would so willingly be thorough idealists, express themselves entirely in a materialistic sense, misled by the tyranny of speech. That is a speech which can no longer be understood by the soul as soon as it no longer feels itself bound to the physical brain.

"There is, indeed, something else, you may believe it or not. For one who knows occult perception, real spiritual perception, the method of presentation often employed today in theosophical-scientific writings causes real pain—because it appears irrational to him, if he begins to think, no longer with the physical brain, but with the soul, which is no longer bound to the physical brain; *i.e.*, which really lives in the spiritual world. As long as one thinks with the physical brain, so long can he go on characterizing the world thus. As soon, however, as one begins to develop spiritual perception, then, to speak of things in this way ceases to have any meaning. Then indeed it even causes pain if one must hear the utterance: There are good vibrations in this room, instead of: A good feeling prevails here. That at once causes pain in anyone who can really see things spiritually, because thoughts are realities. Space then fills itself out with a dark cloud, if one forms the thought: Good vibrations are in this space, instead of: A good mood is prevailing.

"It is now the task of the anthroposophical way of thinking— and the method of thought is more important than the theories— that we learn to speak a language, which is really not merely understood by the human soul so long as it is in a physical body; but understood also when this soul is no longer bound to the instrument of the physical brain. For instance, either by a soul still in the body—*but able to perceive spiritually*—or by a soul gone through the gate of death. If we bring forward those ideas which explain the world, which explain the human being, then that is a speech which cannot merely be understood here in the physical world; but also by those who are no longer incarnated in physical bodies but live between death and a new birth. Yes, what is spoken on our anthroposophical basis, is heard and understood by the so-called dead. There they are fully one with us on a basis where the same speech is spoken. There we speak to all human beings. And because we penetrate to the soul of man, we liberate man from all Group-Soulness; i.e., man becomes in this way more-and-more capable of really grasping himself in his Ego, his 'I.' And that is the characteristic, that those who come to anthroposophy today, who really take up anthroposophy, appear in comparison with others who remain far from it, as if through anthroposophical thoughts, their Ego would crystallize as a spiritual being, which is then carried through the gate of death. With the others, in that place where the I-being is, which remains there—which is now there in the body, and which remains after death—*there is a hollow space, a nothingness.* The central-point of man's being is grasped through what we take up as anthroposophical thoughts.

"That crystallizes a spiritual substance in man; he takes that with him after death, and with that he perceives in the Spiritual World. He sees and hears with it in the Spiritual World, with it he penetrates that darkness which otherwise exists for man in the Spiritual World. And thereby it is brought about that when through these anthroposophical thoughts and way of thinking man develops this 'I' in him today, which now stands in connection with all the world wisdom we can acquire—if he develops it—he carries it over also into hi next incarnation. Then he is born with this now developed 'I,' and he remembers himself in this developed 'I.' That is the deeper task of the anthroposophical movement today, to send over to their next incarnation a number of human beings with an Ego in which they remember themselves as an Individual-Ego. They will be the human beings who form the kernel of the next period of civilization. These people who have been well prepared through the anthroposophical spiritual movement, to remember their individual 'I,' will be spread over the whole Earth. For the essential in the next period of culture will be that these people will not be limited by single localities—*but spread over the entire Earth.* These individual people will be scattered over the whole Earth, and within the whole Earth sphere will be the kernel of humanity, who will be essential for the Sixth period of civilization. And so, it will be the case among these people, that they will know themselves as those who in their previous incarnation strove together for the individual 'I.'

"More and more human beings will have this memory of their former incarnation—in spite of their not having developed the 'I.' But they will not remember an individual 'I,' because they have not developed it; but rather, they will remember the Group-Ego, in which they have remained. Thus, people will exist, who in this incarnation have cared for the development of their individual 'I'—they will remember themselves as independent individualities, they will look back and say: You were this or the other. Those who have not developed the individuality will be unable to remember this individuality.

"If one has not cultivated the 'I,' it is not there as an inner human being; one looks back, and remembers as a Group-Ego, what one had in common. So that these people will say: Yes, I was there; but I have not freed myself. These people will then experience that as their 'Fall,' as a new Fall of Mankind, as a falling back into conscious connection with the Group-Soul. That will be something terrible for the Sixth Period of time [6th Post Atlantean Period 3,574 A.D.-5,734 A.D.]; to be unable to look back to oneself as an individuality, to be hemmed in by not being able to transcend the Group-Soulness. If one will express it strongly, one could say: The whole Earth with all it produces will belong to those who now cultivate their individuality; those, however, who do not develop their individual 'I,' will be obliged to join on to a certain group, from which they will be directed as to how they should think, feel, will, and act. That will be felt as a 'Fall'—*a falling back, in the future humanity.*

"Now the time is come where man begins to develop the human faculty of remembering backwards. It is only a question of our developing it aright; i.e., that we train in us an individual 'I.' *For only what we have created in our own soul can we remember.* If we have not created it, then there only remains to us a fettering memory of a Group-Ego, and we feel it as a kind of falling down into a group of higher-animality. Even if the human Group-Souls are finer and higher than the animal—*yet, they are but Group-Souls.* Humanity of an early age did not feel that as a 'Fall'; because they were intended to develop from Group-Soulness to the individual soul. If they are now held back, they fall consciously into it, and that will be the oppressive feeling in the future of those who do not take this step aright, either now or in a later incarnation. *They will experience the 'Fall' into Group-Soulness.*

"The real task of Anthroposophy is to give the right impulse. We must thus grasp it within human life. If we keep in mind that the Sixth Period of time is that of the first, complete conquest of the racial idea. It is a question of seeing that the word 'race' is a term only having validity for a certain time. This idea no longer has any meaning for the Sixth Period. Races have only in themselves the elements which have remained from the Atlantean age.

"In the future, that which speaks to the depths of man's soul will express itself more-and-more in the external nature of man; and that which man on the one side as a quite individual being has acquired, and yet, again experiences un-individually, will express itself by working out even to the human countenance; so that the individuality of man—*not the Group-Soulness*—will be inscribed for him on his countenance. That will constitute human manifoldness. Everything will be acquired individually, in spite of its being there through the overcoming of individuality. And we will not meet groups among those who are seized of the Ego; but the individual will express itself externally. That will form the distinction between human beings. There will be such as have acquired their Ego*ity*; they will indeed be there over the whole Earth with the most manifold countenances; but one will recognize through their variety how the Individual-Ego expresses itself even into the gesture. Whereas among those who have not developed the individuality, the Group-Soulness will come to expression by their countenance receiving the imprint of the Group-Soulness; i.e., they will fall into categories similar to each other. That will be the external physiognomy of our Earth: a possibility will be prepared for the individuality to carry in itself an external sign, and for the Group-Soulness to carry in itself its external sign. This is the meaning of earthly evolution, that man acquires more and more the power of expressing externally his inner being. There exists an ancient script in which the greatest ideal for the evolution of the 'I,' the Christ Jesus, is characterized by the saying: When the two become one, when the external becomes like the inner, then man has attained the Christ nature in himself..."

The Psychology of the Human Ego

Rudolf Steiner often spoke of the Mystery of Golgotha and its central place for understanding the Christ-Impulse. But a more in-depth study of his works reveals a unique facet of his Christology. That is what we might call the 'Three Egos of the Human Being' and how they occupy an important place in developing a more comprehensive understanding of the Fourth Human Principle the "I Am" or 'I'; sometimes referenced in English translations as the 'Ego.' In light of this, the best way is to let Rudolf Steiner explain this in his own words. To do this it was thought best to include a complete lecture; therefore it won't be surrounded by quotation marks; but rather it will be preceded and followed by a triangle.

$$\Delta$$

Esoteric Development, **Rudolf Steiner, II, *The Psychological Foundations of Anthroposophy*, Bologna, April 8, 1911, GA 35**

A Spiritual Scientific Mode of Approach
Based upon Potential Psychological Facts

The task which I should like to undertake in the following exposition is that of discussing the scientific character and value of a spiritual trend to which a widespread inclination would still deny the designation 'scientific.' This spiritual trend bears—in allusion to various endeavors of its kind in the present period—

the name theosophy. In the history of philosophy, this name has been applied to certain spiritual trends which have emerged again and again in the course of the cultural life of humanity, with which, however, what is to be presented here does not at all coincide, although it bears many reminders of them. For this reason we shall limit our consideration here to what can be described in the course of our exposition as a special condition of the mind, and we shall disregard opinions which may be held in reference to much of what is customarily called theosophy. Only by adhering to this point-of-view will it be possible to give precise expression to the manner in which one may view the relationship between the spiritual trend we have in mind and the types of conception characterizing contemporary science and philosophy.

Let it be admitted without reservation that, even regarding the very concept of knowledge, it is difficult to establish a relationship between what is customarily called theosophy and everything that seems to be firmly established at present as constituting the idea of 'science' and 'knowledge,' and which has brought and surely will continue to bring such great benefits to human culture. The last few centuries have led to the practice of recognizing as 'scientific' only what can be tested readily by anyone at any time through observation, experiment, and the elaboration of these by the human intellect. Everything that possesses significance only within the subjective experiences of the human mind must be excluded from the category of what is scientifically established. Now, it will scarcely be denied that the philosophical concept of knowledge has for a long time adjusted itself to the scientific type of conception just described. This can best be recognized from the investigations which have been carried out in our time as to what can constitute a possible object of human knowledge, and at what point this knowledge has to admit its limits. It would be superfluous for me to support this statement by an outline of contemporary inquiries in the field of the theory of knowledge. I should like to emphasize only the objective aimed at in those inquiries. In connection with them, it is presupposed that the relationship of man to the external world affords a determinable concept of the nature of the process of cognition, and that this concept of knowledge provides a basis for characterizing what lies within the reach of cognition. However greatly the trends in theories of knowledge may diverge from one another, if the above characterization is taken in a sufficiently broad sense, there will be found within it that which characterizes a common element in the decisive philosophical trends.

Now, the concept of knowledge belonging to what is here called anthroposophy is such that it apparently contradicts the concept just described. It conceives knowledge to be something the character of which cannot be deduced directly from the observation of the nature of the human being and his relationship to the external world. On the basis of established facts of the life of the mind, anthroposophy believes itself justified in asserting that knowledge is not something finished, complete in itself, but something fluid, capable of evolution. It believes itself justified in pointing out that, beyond the horizon of the normally conscious life of the mind, there is another into which the human being can penetrate. And it is necessary to emphasize that the life of the mind here referred to is not to be understood as that which is at present customarily designated as the 'subconscious.' This 'subconscious' may be the object of scientific research; from the point-of-view of the usual methods in research, it can be made an object of inquiry, as are other facts of the life of nature and of the mind. But this has nothing to do with that condition of the mind to which we are referring, within which the human being is as completely conscious, possesses as complete logical watchfulness over himself, as within the limits of the ordinary consciousness. But this condition of the mind must first be created by means of certain exercises, certain experiences of the soul. It cannot be presupposed as a given fact in the nature of man. This condition of mind represents something which may be designated as a further development of the life of the human mind without the cessation, during the course of this further development, of self-possession and other evidences of the mind's conscious life.

I wish to characterize this condition of mind and then to show how what is acquired through it may be included under the scientific concepts of knowledge belonging to our age. My present task shall be, therefore, to describe the method employed within this spiritual trend on the basis of a possible development of the mind. This first part of my exposition may be called: *A Spiritual Scientific Mode of Approach Based upon Potential Psychological Facts.*

What is here described is to be regarded as experiences of the mind of which one may become aware if certain prerequisite conditions are first brought about in the mind. The epistemological value of these experiences shall be tested only after they have first been simply described.

What is to be undertaken may be designated as a 'mental exercise.' The initial step consists in considering from a different point-of-view contents of the mind which are ordinarily evaluated to their worth as copies of an external item of reality. In the concepts and ideas which the human being forms he wishes to have at first what may be a copy, or at least a token, of something existing outside of the concepts or ideas. The spiritual researcher, in the sense here intended, seeks for mental contents which are similar to the concept and ideas of ordinary life or of scientific research; but he does not consider their cognitional value in relation to an objective entity, but lets them exist in his mind as operative forces. He plants them as spiritual seed, so to speak, in the soil of the mind's life, and awaits in complete serenity of spirit their effect upon this life of the mind. He can then observe that, with the repeated employment of such an exercise, the condition of the mind undergoes a change. It must be expressly emphasized, however, that what really counts is the repetition. For the fact in question is not that the content of the concepts in the ordinary sense brings something about in the mind after the manner of a process of cognition; on the contrary, we have to do with an actual process in the life of the mind itself. In this process, concepts do not play the role of cognitional elements but that of real forces; and their effect depends upon having the same forces lay hold in frequent repetition upon the mind's life. The effect achieved in the mind depends preeminently upon the requirement that the same force shall again and again seize upon the experience connected with the concept. For this reason the greatest results can be attained through meditations upon the same content which are repeated at definite intervals through relatively long periods of time. The duration of such a meditation is, in this connection, of little importance. It may be very brief, provided only that it is accompanied by absolute serenity of soul and the complete exclusion from the mind of all external sense impressions and all ordinary activity of the intellect. What is essential is the seclusion of the mind's life with the content indicated. This must be mentioned because it needs to be clearly understood that undertaking these exercises of the mind need not disturb anyone in his ordinary life. The time required is available, as a rule, to everyone. And, if the exercises are rightly carried out, the change which they bring about in the mind does not produce the slightest effect upon the constitution of consciousness necessary for the normal human life. (The fact that—because of what the human being actually is in his present status—undesirable excesses and peculiarities sometimes occur cannot alter in any way one's judgment of the essential nature of the practice.)

For the discipline of the mind which has been described, most concepts in human life are scarcely at all usable. All contents of the mind which relate in marked degree to objective elements outside of themselves have little effect if used for the exercises we have characterized. In far greater measure are mental pictures suitable which can be designated as emblems, as symbols.

Most fruitful of all are those which relate in a living way comprehensively to a manifold content. Let us take as an example, proven by experience to be good, what Goethe designated as his idea of the 'archetypal plant.' It may be permissible to refer to the fact that, during a conversation with Schiller, he once drew with a few strokes a symbolic picture of this 'archetypal plant.' Moreover, he said that one who makes this picture alive in his mind possesses in it something out of which it would be possible to devise, through modification in conformity with law, all possible forms capable of existence. Whatever one may think about the objective cognitional value of such a 'symbolic archetypal plant,' if it is made to live in the mind in the manner indicated, if one awaits in serenity its effects upon the mind's life, there comes about something which can be called a changed constitution of mind.

The mental pictures which are said by spiritual scientists to be usable in this connection may at times seem decidedly strange. This feeling of strangeness can be eliminated if one reflects that such representations must not be considered for their value as truths in the ordinary sense, but should be viewed with respect to the manner in which they are effective as real forces in the mind's life. The spiritual scientist does not attribute value to the significance of the pictures which are used for the mental exercises, but to what is experienced in the mind under their influence.

Here we can give, naturally, only a few examples of effective symbolic representations. Let one conceive the being of man in a mental image in such a way that the lower human nature, related to the animal organization, shall appear in its relation to man as a spiritual being, through the symbolic union of an animal shape and the most highly idealized human form superimposed upon this—somewhat, let us say, like a centaur. The more pictorially alive the symbol appears, the more saturated with content, the better it is. Under the conditions described, this symbol acts in such a way on the mind that, after the passage of a certain time— of course, somewhat long—the inner-life-processes are felt to be strengthened in themselves, mobile, reciprocally illuminating one another. An old symbol which may be used with good result is the so-called staff of Mercury—that is, the mental image of a straight line around which a spiral curves. Of course, one must picture this figure as emblematic of a force-system—in such a way, let us say, that along the straight line there runs one force system, to which there corresponds another of lower velocity passing through the spiral. (Concretely expressed, one may conceive in connection with this figure the growth of the stem of a plant and the corresponding sprouting of leaves along its length. Or one may take it as an image of an electro-magnet. Still further, there can emerge in this way a picture of the development of a human being, the enhancing capacities being symbolized by the straight line, the manifold impressions corresponding with the course of the spiral.)

Mathematical forms may become especially significant, to the extent that symbols of cosmic processes can be seen in them. A good example is the so-called 'Cassini curve,' with its three figures—the form resembling an ellipse, the *lemniscate*, and that which consists of two corresponding branches. In such a case the important thing is to experience the mental image in such a way that certain appropriate impressions in the mind shall accompany the transition of one curve form into the other in accordance with mathematical principles.

Other exercises may then be added to these. They consist also in symbols, but such as correspond with representations which may be expressed in words. Let one think, through the symbol of light, of the wisdom which may be pictured as living and weaving in the orderly processes of the cosmic phenomena. Wisdom which expresses itself in sacrificial love may be thought of as symbolized by warmth which comes about in the presence of light. One may think of sentences—which, therefore, have only a symbolic character—fashioned out of such concepts. The mind can be absorbed in meditating upon such sentences. The result depends essentially upon the degree of serenity and seclusion of soul within the symbol to which one attains in the meditation. If success is achieved, it consists in the fact that the soul feels as if lifted out of the corporeal organization. It experiences something like a change in its sense of existence. If we agree that, in normal life, the feeling of the human being is such that his conscious life, proceeding from a unity, takes on a specific character in harmony with the representations which are derived from the percepts brought by the individual senses, then the result of the exercises is that the mind feels itself permeated by an experience of itself not so sharply differentiated in transition from one part of the experience to another as, for example, color and tone representations are differentiated within the horizon of the ordinary consciousness. The mind has the experience that it can withdraw into a region of inner being which it owes to the success of the exercises and which was something empty, something which could not be perceived, before the exercises were undertaken.

Before such an inner experience is reached, there occur many transitional stages in the condition of the mind. One of these manifests itself in an attentive observation—to be acquired through the exercise—of the moment of awaking out of sleep. It is possible then to feel clearly how, out of something not hitherto known to one, forces lay hold systematically upon the structure of the bodily organization. One feels, as if in a remembered concept, an after-effect of influences from this something, which have been at work upon the corporeal organization during sleep. And if the person has acquired, in addition, the capacity to experience within his corporeal organization the something here described, he will perceive clearly the difference between the relationship of this something to the body in the waking and in the sleeping state. He cannot then do otherwise than to say that during the waking state this something is inside the body and during the sleeping state it is outside. One must not, however, associate ordinary spatial conception with this 'inside' and 'outside,' but must use these terms only to designate the specific experiences of a mind which has carried out the exercises described.

These exercises are of an intimate soul-character. They take for each person an individual form. When the beginning is once made, the individual element results from a particular use of the soul to be brought about in the course of the exercises. But what follows with utter necessity is the positive consciousness of living within a reality independent of the external corporeal organization and super-sensible in character. For the sake of simplicity, let us call such a person seeking for the described soul experiences a 'spiritual researcher' (*Geistesforscher*). For such a spiritual researcher, there exists the definite consciousness—kept under complete self-possession—that, behind the bodily organization perceptible to the senses, there is a super-sensible organization, and that it is possible to experience oneself within this as the normal consciousness experiences itself within the physical bodily organization. (The exercises referred to can be indicated here only in principle. A detailed presentation may be found in my book, *Knowledge of the Higher Worlds and Its Attainment*.)

Through appropriate continuation of the exercises, the 'something' we have described passes over into a sort of spiritually organized condition. The consciousness becomes clearly aware that it is in relationship with a super-sensible world in a cognitional way, in a manner similar to that in which it is related through the senses to the sense world. It is quite natural that serious doubt at once arises, regarding the assertion of such a cognitional relationship of the super-sensible part of the being of man to the surrounding world. There may be an inclination to relegate everything which is thus experienced to the realm of illusion, hallucination, autosuggestion, and the like. A theoretical refutation of such doubt is, from the very nature of things, impossible. For the question here cannot be that of a theoretical exposition regarding the existence of a super-sensible world, but only that of possible experiences and observations which are presented to the consciousness in precisely the same way in which observations are mediated through the external sense organs. For the corresponding super-sensible world, therefore, no other sort of recognition can be demanded than that which the human being offers to the world of colors, tones, etc. Yet consideration must be given to the fact that, when the exercises are carried out in the right way—and, most important, with never relaxed self-possession—the spiritual researcher can discern through immediate experience the difference between the imagined super-sensible and that which is actually experienced; just as certainly as in the sense world once can discern the difference between imagining the feel of a piece of hot iron and actually touching it. Precisely concerning the differences among hallucination, illusion, and super-sensible reality, the spiritual researcher acquires through his exercises a practice more and more unerring. But it is also natural that the prudent spiritual researcher must be extremely critical regarding individual super-sensible observations made by him. He will never speak otherwise about positive findings of super-sensible research than with the reservation that one thing or another has been observed and that the critical caution practiced in connection with this justifies the assumption that anyone will make the same observations who, by means of the appropriate exercises, can establish a relationship with the super-sensible world. Differences among the pronouncements of individual spiritual researchers cannot really be viewed in any other light than the different pronouncements of various travelers who have visited the same region and who describe it.

In my book, *Knowledge of the Higher Worlds and Its Attainment,* that world which, in the manner described, appears above the horizon of consciousness has been called—in accordance with the practice of those who have been occupied as spiritual researchers in the same field—'the imaginative world.' But one must dissociate from this expression, used in a purely technical sense, anything suggesting a world created by mere 'fancy.' Imag-

inative is intended merely to suggest the qualitative character
of the content of the mind. This mental content resembles in its
form the 'imaginations' of ordinary consciousness, except that an
imagination in the physical world is not directly related to something real, whereas the imaginations of the spiritual researcher are
just as unmistakably to be ascribed to a super-sensibly real entity
as the mental picture of a color in the sense world, for instance, is
ascribed to an objectively real entity.

But the 'imaginative world' and the knowledge of it mark
only the first step for the spiritual researcher, and very little more
is to be learned through it about the super-sensible world than
its external side. A further step is required. This consists in a
further deepening of the life of the soul than that which has been
considered in connection with the first step. Through intense
concentration upon the soul life, brought about by the exercises,
the spiritual researcher must render himself capable of completely
eliminating the content of the symbols from his consciousness.
What he then still has to hold firmly within his consciousness is
only the process to which his inner-life was subjected while he
was absorbed in the symbols. The content of the symbols pictured
must be cast out in a sort of real abstraction and only the form of
the experience in connection with the symbols must remain in
the consciousness. The unreal symbolic character of the forming
of mental images—which was significant only for a transitional
stage of the soul's development—is thereby eliminated, and
the consciousness uses as the object of its meditation the inner
weaving of the mind's content. What can be described of such a
process actually compares with the real experience of the mind as
a feeble shadow compares with the object which casts the shadow.
What appears simple in the description derives its very significant
effect from the psychic energy which is exerted.

The living and moving within the content of the soul, thus rendered possible, can be called a real beholding of oneself. The inner being of man thus learns to know itself not merely through reflecting about itself as the bearer of the sense impressions and the elaborator of these sense impressions through thinking; on the contrary, it learns to know itself as it is, without relationship to a content coming from the senses; it experiences itself in itself, as super-sensible reality. This experience is not like that of the Ego when in ordinary self-observation, attention is withdrawn from the things cognized in the environment and is directed back to the cognizing self. In this case, the content of consciousness shrinks more and more down to the point of the 'ego.' ['I'] Such is not the case in the real beholding of the self by the spiritual researcher. In this, the soul content becomes continuously richer in the course of the exercises. It consists in one's living within law-conforming interrelationships; and the self does not feel, as in the case of the laws of nature, which are abstracted from the phenomena of the external world, that it is outside the web of laws; but, on the contrary, it is aware of itself as within this web; it experiences itself as one with these laws.

The danger which may come about at this stage of the exercises lies in the fact that the person concerned may believe too early—because of deficiency in true self-possession—that he has arrived at the right result, and may then feel the mere after-effects of the symbolic inner pictures to be an inner-life. Such an inner-life is obviously valueless, and must not be mistaken for the inner-life which appears at the right moment, making itself known to true circumspection through the fact that, although it manifests complete reality, yet it resembles no reality hitherto known.

To an inner-life thus attained, there is now the possibility of a super-sensible knowledge characterized by a higher degree of certitude than that of mere imaginative cognition. At this point in the soul's development, the following manifestation occurs. The inner experience gradually becomes filled with a content which enters the mind from without in a manner similar to that in which the content of sense perception enters through the senses from the outer-world. Only, the filling of the mind with the super-sensible content consists in an actual living within this content. If one wishes to employ a comparison with a fact taken from ordinary life, it may be said that the entering of the Ego into union with a spiritual content is now experienced as one experiences the entering of the Ego into union with a mental picture retained in memory. Yet there is the distinction that the content of that with which one enters into union cannot be compared in any respect with something previously experienced and that it cannot be related to something past but only to something present. Knowledge of this character may well be called knowledge 'through inspiration,' provided nothing except what has been described is associated in thought with this term. I have used the expression thus as a technical term in my book, *Knowledge of the Higher Worlds and Its Attainment*.

In connection with this 'knowledge through inspiration,' a new experience now appears. That is, the manner in which one becomes aware of the content of the mind is entirely subjective. At first, this content does not manifest itself as objective. One knows it as something experienced; but one does not feel that one confronts it. This comes about only after one has through soul-energy condensed it, in a sense, within itself. Only thus does it become something which can be looked at objectively. But, in this process of the psyche, one becomes aware that, between the physical bodily organization and that something which has been separated from this by the exercises, there is still another entity.

If one desires names for these things, one may employ those which have become customary in so-called theosophy—provided one does not connect with these names all sorts of fantastic associations; but designates by them solely what has been described. That 'something' in which the self lives as in an entity free from the bodily organization is called the astral body; and that which is discovered between this astral body and the physical organism is called the etheric body. (One is, of course, not to connect this in thought with the 'ether' of modern physics.)

Now, it is from the etheric body that the forces come, through which the self is enabled to make an objective perception of the subjective content of inspired knowledge. By what right, it may be asked with good reason, does the spiritual researcher come to the standpoint of ascribing this perception to a super-sensible world instead of considering it a mere creation of his own self? He would have no right to do this if the etheric body, which he experiences in connection with his psychic process, did not in its inner conformity to law compel him to do so with objective necessity. But such is the case, for the etheric body is experienced as a confluence of the all-encompassing complex of laws of the macrocosm. The important point is not how much of this complex of laws becomes the actual content of the spiritual researcher's consciousness. The peculiar fact is that direct cognition sees clearly that the etheric body is nothing else than a compacted image reflecting in itself the cosmic web of laws. Knowledge of the etheric body by the spiritual researcher does not at first extend to showing what content from the sum total of the universal cosmic web of laws is reflected by this formation; but to showing what this content is.

Other justifiable doubts which the ordinary consciousness must raise against spiritual research, together with much besides,

are the following. One may take note of the findings of this
research (as they appear in contemporary literature) and may
say:—

'Actually, what you there describe as the content of super-
sensible knowledge proves upon closer scrutiny to be nothing
more, after all, than combinations of ordinary conceptions
taken from the sense world.'

"And, in fact, this is what is said. (Likewise, the descriptions
of the higher worlds which I myself felt justified in giving in the
volumes, *Theosophy* and *Occult Science: An Outline,* are found to
be, so it seems, nothing but combinations of conceptions taken
from the sense world—as, for instance, when the evolution of the
Earth through combinations of entities of warmth, light, etc., is
described.)

Against this view, however, the following must be said.
When the spiritual researcher wishes to give expression to his
experiences, he is compelled to employ the means available
to sense-conceptions for expressing what is experienced in a
super-sensible sphere. His experience is not to be conceived,
then, as if it were like his means of expression; but with the
realization that he uses this means only like the words of a
language which he requires. One must seek for the content of
his experience, *not in the means of expression*—that is, not in
the illustrative representations—but in the manner in which he
uses these instruments of expression. The difference between his
presentation and a fantastic combining of sensible representations
lies in the fact that fantastic combining arises out of a subjective
arbitrariness; whereas the presentation of the spiritual researcher
rests upon a conscious familiarity with the super-sensible

complex of laws, acquired through practice. Here, however, the reason is also to be found why the presentations of the spiritual researcher may so easily be misunderstood. That is, *the manner in which he speaks is more important than what he says.* In the *how* is reflected his super-sensible experience. If the objection is raised that, in this case, what the spiritual researcher says has no direct relationship with the ordinary world, it must be emphasized in reply that the manner of his presentation does, in fact, meet the practical requirements for an explanation of the sense world drawn from a super-sensible sphere, and that the understanding of the world process perceptible to the senses is aided by real attention to the findings of the spiritual researcher.

Another objection may be raised. It may be asked what the assertions of the spiritual researcher have to do with the content of ordinary consciousness, since this consciousness, it may be said, cannot subject them to testing. Precisely this latter statement is, in principle, untrue. For research in the super-sensible world, for discovering its facts, that condition of mind is necessary which can be acquired only by means of the exercises described. *But this does not apply to the testing.* For this purpose, when the spiritual researcher has communicated his findings, ordinary unprejudiced logic is sufficient. This will always be able to determine in principle that, if what the spiritual researcher says is true, the course of the world and of life as they proceed before the senses becomes understandable. The opinion which may be formed at first concerning the experiences of the spiritual researcher is not the important point. These may be viewed as hypotheses, regulative principles (in the sense of Kantian philosophy). But if they are simply applied to the sense world, it will be seen that the sense world confirms in the course of its events everything which is asserted by the spiritual researcher. (Naturally, this is valid only in principle; it is obvious that, in details, the assertions of so-called spiritual researchers may contain the gravest errors.)

Another experience of the spiritual researcher can come about only provided the exercises are carried still further. This continuation must consist in the fact that the spiritual researcher, after having attained to beholding the self, shall be able by energetic power of will to suppress this experience. He must be able to free the mind from everything that has been achieved through the continued after-effects of his exercises resting upon the outer sense world. The symbol-images are combined out of sense-images. The living and moving of the self within itself in connection with achieved inspired knowledge is, to be sure, free from the content of the symbols, yet it is a result of the exercises which have been carried out under their influence. Even though the inspired knowledge thus brings about a direct relationship of the self to the super-sensible world, the clear beholding of the relationship can be carried still further. This results from the energetic suppression of the self-view which has been attained. After this suppression, the self may, as one possibility, be confronted by a void. In this case the exercises must be continued. As a second possibility, the self may find that it is more immediately in the presence of the super-sensible world in its real being than it had been in connection with inspired knowledge. In the latter experience, there appears only the relationship of a super-sensible world to the self; in the case of the kind of knowledge we are now describing the self is completely eliminated. If one wishes an expression adapted to ordinary consciousness for this condition of mind, it may be said that consciousness now experiences itself as the stage upon which a super-sensible content, consisting of real being, is not merely perceived but perceives itself. (In the volume, *Knowledge*

of the Higher Worlds and Its Attainment, I have called this kind
of knowledge 'intuitive knowledge,' but in connection with this
expression the ordinary term intuition must be disregarded—
which is used to designate every direct experience of a content of
consciousness through feeling.)

Through intuitive knowledge, the whole relationship in
which the human being as 'soul' finds himself with respect to his
bodily organization is altered for the direct observation of the
inner being of the soul. Before the faculty of spiritual vision, the
etheric body appears, in a sense, as a super-sensible organism
differentiated within itself. And one recognizes its differentiated
members as adapted in a definite way to the members of the
physical bodily organization. The etheric body is experienced
as the primary entity and the physical body as its copy, as
something secondary. The horizon of consciousness appears to
be determined through the law-conforming activity of the etheric
body. The coordination of the phenomena within this horizon
results from the activity of the differentiated members of the
etheric body striving towards a unity. The etheric body rests upon
an all-embracing cosmic web of laws; basic in the unification of
its action is the tendency to relate itself to something as a center.
And the image of this uniting tendency is the physical body.
Thus the latter proves to be an expression of the World-Ego
['Welt-Ich'; 'World-I'], as the etheric body is an expression of the
macrocosmic web of laws.

What is here set forth becomes clearer if we refer to a special
fact of the inner-life of the soul. This shall be done with reference
to memory. As a result of the freeing of the self from the bodily
organization, the spiritual researcher experiences the act of
recollecting differently from one with ordinary consciousness.
For him, recollecting, which is otherwise a more-or-less

undifferentiated process, is separated into partial factors. At first, he senses the attraction toward an experience which is to be remembered, like a drawing of the attention in a certain direction. The experience is thus really analogous to the spatial directing of one's look toward a distant object, which one has first seen, then turns away from, and then turns toward again. The essential aspect of this is that the experience pressing toward remembrance is sensed as something which has stopped far away within the temporal horizon, and which does not merely have to be drawn up from the depths below in the soul's life. This turning in the direction of the experience pressing toward remembrance is at first a merely subjective process. When the remembrance now actually occurs, the spiritual researcher feels that it is the resistance of the physical body which works like a reflecting surface and raises the experience into the objective world of representations. Thus the spiritual researcher feels, in connection with the process of remembering, an occurrence which (subjectively perceptible) takes place within the etheric body and which becomes his remembrance through its reflection by the physical body. The first factor in recollecting would give merely disconnected experiences of the self. Through the fact that every remembrance is reflected by being impressed upon the life of the physical body, it becomes a part of the Ego-experiences.

From all that has been said it is clear that the spiritual researcher comes to the point in his inner experience where he recognizes that the human being perceptible to the senses is the manifestation of a human being who is super-sensible. He seeks for a consciousness of this super-sensible human being, not by way of inference and speculation based upon the world that is directly given, but, on the contrary, by so transforming his own condition of mind that this ascends from the perceiving of the sense-perceptible to real participation in the super-sensible. He arrives in this way at the recognition of a content of soul which proves to be richer, more filled with substance, than that of ordinary consciousness. What this road then leads to further can only be suggested here, of course, since a thorough exposition would require a comprehensive treatise. The inner being of the soul becomes for the spiritual researcher the producer, the builder, of that which constitutes the single human life in the physical world. And this producer manifests in itself that it has—interwoven into its life as realities—the forces, not only of the one life, but of many lives. That which may be considered as evidence of reincarnation, of repeated earthly lives, becomes a matter of actual observation. For what one learns of the inner core of the human life reveals, one might say, the telescoping together of interrelated human personalities. And these personalities can be sensed only in the relationship of the preceding and the succeeding. For one which follows is always manifested as the result of another. There is, moreover, in the relationship of one personality to another no element of continuity; rather, there is such a relationship as manifests itself in successive earthly lives separated by intervening periods of purely spiritual existence. To the observation of the soul's inner being, the periods during which the core of the human being was embodied in a physical corporeal organization are differentiated from those of the super-sensible existence through the fact that, in the former, the experience of the content of the mind appears as if projected against the background of the physical life; while, in the latter, it appears as merged in a super-sensible element which extends into the indefinite. It has not been the intention to present here anything more concerning so-called reincarnation than a sort of view of a perspective which is opened by the preceding reflections.

Anyone who admits the possibility that the human self may be able to become familiar with the core-of-being which is supersensibly visible will also no longer consider it unreasonable to suppose that, after further insight into this core-of-being, its content is revealed as differentiated, and that this differentiation provides the spiritual view of a succession of forms of existence extending back into the past. The fact that these forms of existence may bear their own time-indications may be seen to be intelligible through the analogy with ordinary memory. An experience appearing in memory bears in its content also its own time-indication. But the real 'resurvey in memory' of past forms of existence, supported by rigid self-supervision, is still very remote, of course, from the training of the spiritual researcher which has thus far been described, and great difficulties for the inner soul life tower up on the path before this can be attained in an incontestable form. Nevertheless, this lies on the direct continuation of the path to knowledge which has been described. It has been my desire at first to register here, so to speak, facts of experience in the inner soul-observation. It is for this reason that I have described reincarnation only as one such fact, but this fact can be established also on a theoretical basis. This I have done in the chapter entitled 'Karma and Reincarnation' in the book, *Theosophy*. I undertook there to show that certain findings of modern natural science, if thought out to their conclusion, lead to the assumption of the ideas of reincarnation of the human being.

Regarding the total nature of the human being, we must conclude from what has been said that his essential nature becomes understandable when viewed as the result of the interaction of the four members: 1) the physical bodily organization; 2) the etheric body; 3) the astral body; 4) the Ego (the 'I'), which develops in the last-named member and comes to

manifestation through the relationship between the central core
of man's being and the physical organization. It is not possible to
deal with the further articulation of these four life-manifestations
of the total human being within the limits of one lecture. Here
the intention has been to show only the basis of spiritual research.
Further details I have sought to provide: 1) as to the method, in
the volume, *Knowledge of the Higher Worlds and its Attainment;*
and, 2) as to the system, in *Theosophy* and *Occult Science, an
Outline.*

*The Experiences of the Spiritual Researcher
and the Theory of Knowledge*

The exposition which has been presented will render it clear that
anthroposophy, rightly understood, rests upon the foundation
of a way of developing the human soul which is to be rigidly
systematized in its character, and that it would be erroneous to
suppose that there exists in the condition of mind of the spiritual
researcher anything of the nature of what is ordinarily called
at present enthusiasm, ecstasy, rapture, vision, and the like.
Misunderstandings arise which may be presented in opposition
to anthroposophy precisely through the confusion between the
condition of mind here characterized and these other conditions.
First, the belief is created through this confusion that there exists
in the mind of the spiritual researcher a state of rapture, of being
transported beyond self-possession in one's consciousness, a sort
of striving after immediate instinctive vision. But the truth is just
the opposite. The condition of mind of the spiritual researcher
is even further removed than is ordinary consciousness from
what is ordinarily called ecstasy, vision, from every sort of
ordinary seership. Even such states-of-mind as those to which
Shaftesbury refers are nebulous inner worlds in comparison

with what is striven for by means of the exercises of the genuine spiritual researcher. Shaftesbury finds that by means of the 'cold intellect,' without the rapture of the feeling nature, no path can be discovered leading to deeper forms of knowledge. True spiritual research carries with it the whole inner mental apparatus of logic and self-conscious circumspection when it seeks to transfer consciousness from the sensible to the super-sensible sphere. It cannot be accused, therefore, of disregarding the rational element of knowledge. It can, however, elaborate its contents in concepts through thinking after perception, for the reason that, in passing out of the sense world, it always carries with it the rational element and always retains it, like a skeleton of the super-sensible experience, as an integrating factor of all super-sensible perception.

Naturally, it is impossible here to show the relationship of spiritual research to the various contemporary trends in theories of knowledge. The effort will be made by means of a few rather sketchy observations, therefore, to point out that particular conception of the theory of knowledge and its relationship to spiritual research which must experience the greatest difficulties in relation to spiritual research. It is, perhaps, not immodest to call attention to the fact that a complete basis for discrimination between philosophy and anthroposophy can be obtained from my two publications, *Truth and Science* and *The Philosophy of Freedom*.

To the epistemology of our time it has become increasingly axiomatic to maintain that there are given in the content of our consciousness only pictures, or even only 'tokens' (Helmholtz) of the transcendent-real. It will be needless to explain here how critical philosophy and physiology ('specific sense-energies,' views of Johannes Mueller and his adherents) have worked together to make of such a conception an apparently irrefutable idea. *Naïve Realism*, which views the phenomena within the horizon of consciousness as something more than subjective representations of something objective, was considered in the philosophical development of the nineteenth century to have been invalidated for all time. But from that which lies at the foundation of this conception, there follows almost as a matter of course the rejection of the anthroposophical point-of-view. From the critical point-of-view, the anthroposophical viewpoint can be considered only as an impossible leap over the limits of knowledge inherent in the nature of our consciousness. If we may reduce to a simple formula an immeasurably great and brilliant expression of the critical theory of knowledge, it may be said that the critical philosopher sees in the facts within the horizon of consciousness representations, pictures, or tokens, and holds that a possible relationship to a transcendental external can be found only within the thinking consciousness. He holds that consciousness, of course, cannot leap beyond itself, cannot get outside itself, in order to plunge into a transcendental entity. Such a conception, in fact, has within it something that seems self-evident, and yet it rests upon a presupposition which one need only see into in order to refute it. It seems almost paradoxical when one brings against the subjective idealism expressed in the conception just cited the charge of a veiled materialism. And yet one cannot do otherwise. Permit me to render clear by a comparison what can be said here. Let a name be impressed in wax with a seal. The name, with everything pertaining to it, has been transferred by the seal into the wax. What cannot pass across from the seal into the wax is the metal of the seal. For the wax, substitute the soul life of the human being and for the seal substitute the transcendental. It then becomes obvious at once that one cannot declare it impossible for the transcendental to pass over into the impression unless one conceives the objective content of the transcendental as not spiritual, since this passing over of a spiritual content could be conceived in analogy with the complete reception of the name into the wax. To serve the requirement of Critical Idealism, the assumption would have to be made that the content of the transcendental is to be conceived in analogy with the metal of the seal. But this cannot be done otherwise than by making the veiled materialistic assumption that the transcendental must be received into the impression in the form of a materially conceived flowing-across. In the event that the transcendental is spiritual, it is entirely possible that the impression could take this up.

A further displacement in the simple facts of consciousness is caused by Critical Idealism through the fact that it leaves out of account the question of the factual relationship existing between the cognitional content and the Ego. If one assumes *a priori* that the Ego, together with the content of laws of the world reduced to the form of ideas and concepts, is outside the transcendental, it will be simply self-evident that this Ego cannot leap beyond itself—that is, that it must always remain outside the transcendental. But this presupposition cannot be sustained in the face of an unbiased observation of the facts of consciousness. For the sake of simplicity, we shall here refer to the content of the cosmic web of law in so far as this can be expressed in mathematical concepts and formulae. The inner conformity to law in the relationships of mathematical forms is acquired within consciousness and is then applied to empirical factual situations. Now, no distinction can be discovered between what exists in consciousness as a mathematical concept when, on the one hand, this consciousness relates its own content to an empirical factual situation, and when, on the other, it visualizes this mathematical concept within itself in pure abstract mathematical thinking. But this signifies nothing else than that the Ego, with its mathematical representation, is not outside the transcendental mathematical law-conformity of things but inside this. Therefore, one will arrive at a better conception of the Ego from the viewpoint of the theory of knowledge, not by conceiving the Ego as inside the bodily organization and receiving impressions 'from without'; but by conceiving the Ego as being itself within the law-conformity of things, and viewing the bodily organization as only a sort of mirror which reflects back to the Ego through the organic bodily activity the living and moving of the Ego outside the body in the transcendental. If, as regards mathematical thinking, one has familiarized oneself with the thought that the Ego is not in the body but outside it, and that the bodily activity represents only the living mirror, from which the life of the Ego in the transcendental is reflected, one can then find this thought epistemologically comprehensible concerning everything which appears within the horizon of consciousness.

One could then no longer say that the Ego would have to leap beyond itself if it desired to enter the transcendental; but one would have to see that the ordinary empirical content of consciousness is related to that which is truly experienced in the inner-life of man's core-of-being as the mirrored image is related to the real being of the person who is viewing himself in the mirror.

Through such a manner of conceiving in relation to the theory of knowledge, conflict could be decisively eliminated between natural science, with its inclination toward materialism, and a spiritual research, which presupposes the spiritual. For a right of way should be established for natural scientific research, in that it could investigate the laws of the bodily organization uninfluenced

by interference from a spiritual manner of thinking. If one wishes
to know according to what laws the reflected image comes into
existence, one must give attention to the laws of the mirror. This
determines how the beholder is reflected; it occurs in different
ways depending on whether one has a plane, concave, or convex
mirror. But the being of the person who is reflected is outside
the mirror. One could thus see in the laws to be discovered
through natural scientific research the reasons for the form of the
empirical consciousness, and with these laws nothing should be
mixed of what spiritual science has to say about the inner-life of
man's core-of-being. Within natural scientific research one will
always rightly oppose the interference of purely spiritual points-
of-view. It is natural that, in the area of this research, there is more
sympathy with explanations which are given in a mechanistic
way than with spiritual laws. A conception such as the following
must be congenial to one who is at home in clear natural scientific
conceptions:—

'The fact of consciousness brought about by the stimulation
of brain cells does not belong in a class essentially different
from that of gravity connected with matter.'

Moriz Benedikt

"In any case, such an explanation gives with exact
methodology that which is conceivable for natural science. It is
scientifically tenable, whereas the hypotheses of a direct control
of the organic processes by psychic influences are scientifically
untenable. But the idea previously given, fundamental from
the point-of-view of the theory of knowledge, can see in the
whole range of what can be established by natural science only
arrangements which serve to reflect the real core of man's being.

This core-of-being, however, is not to be located in the interior of the physical organization, but in the transcendental. Spiritual research would then be conceived as the way by which one attains knowledge of the real nature of that which is reflected. Obviously, the common basis of the laws of the physical organism and those of the super-sensible would lie behind the antithesis, *being* and *mirror.* This, however, is certainly no disadvantage for the practice of the scientific method of approach from both directions. With the maintenance of the antithesis described, this method would, so to speak, flow in two currents, each reciprocally illuminating and clarifying the other. For it must be maintained that, in the physical organization, we are not dealing with a reflecting apparatus, in the absolute sense, independent of the super-sensible. The reflecting apparatus must, after all, be considered as the product of the super-sensible being who is mirrored in it. The relative reciprocal independence of the one and the other method of approach mentioned above must be supplemented by a third method coming to meet them, which enters into the depths of the problem and which is capable of beholding the synthesis of the sensible and the super-sensible. The confluence of the two currents may be conceived as given through a possible further development of the life of the mind up to the intuitive cognition already described. Only within this cognition is that confluence superseded.

It may thus be asserted that epistemologically unbiased considerations open the way for rightly understood anthroposophy. For these lead to the conclusion that it is a theoretically understandable possibility that the core of man's being may have an existence free of the physical organization, and that the opinion of the ordinary consciousness—that the Ego is to be considered a being absolutely within the body—is to be adjudged an inevitable illusion of the immediate life of the mind. The Ego—with the whole of man's core-of-being—can be viewed as an entity which experiences its relationship to the objective world within that world itself, and receives its experiences as reflections in the form of impressions from the bodily organization. The separation of man's core-of-being from the bodily organization must, naturally, not be conceived spatially; but must be viewed as a relatively dynamic state-of-release. An apparent contradiction is then also resolved which might be discovered between what is here said and what has previously been said regarding the nature of sleep. In the waking state the human core-of-being is so fitted into the physical organization that it is reflected in this through the dynamic relationship to it; in the state-of-sleep the reflecting ceases. Since the ordinary consciousness, in the sense of the epistemological considerations here presented, is rendered possible only through the reflection (through the reflected representations), it ceases, therefore, during the state-of-sleep. The condition of mind of the spiritual researcher can be understood as one in which the illusion of the ordinary consciousness is overcome, and which gains a starting point in the life of soul from which it actually experiences the human core-of-being in free release from the bodily organization. All else which is then achieved through exercises is only a deeper delving into the transcendental, in which the Ego of ordinary consciousness really exists although it is not aware of itself as within the transcendental.

Spiritual research is thus proved to be epistemologically conceivable. That it is conceivable will be admitted, naturally, only by one who can accept the view that the so-called critical theory of knowledge will be able to maintain its dogma of the impossibility of leaping over consciousness only so long as it fails to see through the illusion that the human core-of-being is enclosed within the bodily organization and receives impressions through the senses. I am aware that I have given only indications in outline in my epistemological exposition. Yet it may be possible to recognize from these indications that they are not isolated notions but grow out of a developed fundamental epistemological conception.

Δ

Cosmic Ego and Human-Ego, **Rudolf Steiner, January 9, 1912, Munich, GA 130**

"If we take a sort of prophetic glance into the future, at what is to come, if we say that man will develop the Spirit-Self, or Manas, in the next, the Sixth Post-Atlantean Period [Slavic Period, 3,574 A.D.-5,734 A.D.] then we recognize that Spirit-Self, or Manas, really lies above the sphere of the Ego ['I']. As matter of fact, man could not in this future develop the Spirit-Self out of his own forces; but if he is to develop his Spirit-Self, he must be helped in a certain way by that which flows to the Earth through the forces of higher Beings. Man has come to that stage in the evolution of his Ego where, out of his own forces, he really can develop only up to the Consciousness-Soul; but this development would not be complete if he should not anticipate in a certain sense that which will reach its true, complete, self-impelled human evolution only upon Jupiter, the next embodiment of our planet. Up to the end of the Earth evolution man should develop his Ego; and he will have had opportunity to accomplish this development within the Sentient-, Intellectual-, and Consciousness-Souls. But the actual Spirit-Self is to become the human possession only upon Jupiter

[Future 5th Planetary Condition]; only there will it become the fitting human endowment—for on Jupiter man will have about the same relation to the Spirit-Self that he has to the Ego ['I'] on Earth. If then the human being develops the Spirit-Self during the Earth-period, he cannot relate himself to it in the same way as the Ego. Of our Ego ['I'] we say:— *'We ourselves are that; it is our self in reality.'* When in the next Cultural Period, the Sixth Post-Atlantean, the Spirit-Self shall have come to expression, then we shall not be able to address this Spirit-Self as *our self*; but we shall say:— 'Our Ego has developed to a certain stage, so that our Spirit-Self can shine into it, as from higher worlds—*as a kind of Angel Being* (which we ourselves are not); but which shines into us and takes possession of us.'

"Thus, will our Spirit-Self appear to us; and only upon Jupiter will it appear as our own being, as our Ego now is. Human evolution moves forward in this way.

"Hence, in the next, the Sixth Post-Atlantean Period, we shall feel as if drawn upward to something which shines into us. We shall not say:— 'Thou Spirit-Self within me.' ...

"But rather we shall say: 'I, partaker in a Being who shines into me from upper worlds, who directs and leads me, who, through the grace of higher beings, has become my guide! ...

"That which will come to us only upon Jupiter as our very own, we shall feel in the sixth epoch as a kind of guide [Holy Guardian Angel] shining upon us from the higher worlds ... And thus it will be later with the Life-Spirit, or Budhi, with the Spirit-Man, and so on ... So, a time will come when man will speak of himself otherwise than he does now. How does one speak of himself now when he speaks in the sense of Spiritual Science? He says:— 'I have three sheaths, my physical body, my etheric body, and my astral body. Within these I have my Ego ['I'], *the essential*

Earth possession, which is evolving within these three sheaths. These sheaths are, as it were, my lower nature; I have grown beyond it, I look down to this, my lower nature; and I see in what my Ego has become a preparatory stage of my own being, which will grow and evolve further and further' ...

"In the future man will have to speak otherwise; then he will say:— 'I have not only my lower nature and my Ego; but I have a higher nature, to which I look up as to something which is a part of me in the same way as my sheaths, which I have from earlier stages.' ...

"So, in the future the human being will feel that he is placed midway, so to speak, between his lower and his higher nature. The lower nature he already knows now; the higher will in the future appear as if standing above him, just as now the lower is below him. So, we may say that man grows from his fourth to his fifth, sixth and seventh principles during the Earth evolution—*but his fifth, sixth and seventh principles will not be his direct possession during the actual Earth evolution—but rather, as something to which he will gradually attain.* The matter must actually be conceived in this way.

"We shall have to experience a time when we shall say:— 'Certainly, it was our Earth mission to develop our Ego ['I']. But with prophetic anticipation we see something which is to come to development in us on Jupiter.'

"What we are now experiencing during our Earth evolution: namely, that we permeate ourselves, so to speak, with a Human-Ego ['I'] nature; and that during the past Earth-time up to the present we have developed a finer fashioning of our lower principles; and that we shall perfect the higher principles in the future—all that we as human beings experience on Earth, more advanced beings whom we designate as Angels, or Angeloi,

experienced upon the earlier planetary embodiment [Old Moon].
But also the higher members of the Hierarchy, the Archangels,
or Archangeloi, and the Archai, have had this experience upon
even earlier embodiments of our Earth planet, upon Old Sun and
Old Saturn. For them also there was at that time a kind of fourth
member which they developed; and then in the second half of
the corresponding planetary embodiments, they anticipated
that which actually is to come to full development in them upon
the Earth, as with us the Spirit-Self will come to development
on Jupiter. They had not at that time fully embodied it within
themselves as their possession, but they looked up to it.

"If in the first place we look back to the Old Moon evolution,
we must speak of beings who during that time should have
reached their seventh principle, in exactly the same way that we
human beings during the Earth evolution come to the seventh
principle—*that is, not to embody it completely, but to look up to it.*
When we speak of Luciferic beings, we refer to those who during
the Old Moon evolution remained in the condition in which a
man would be who, during the Earth evolution, had not brought
to full development his fifth, sixth and seventh principles; but had
turned aside from such development—*who perhaps had stopped
with the fourth or with the fifth.* That is, those beings who were at
the very diverse stages of Luciferic beings *were not fully evolved.*
So, we can say that human beings came over from the Old Moon
evolution to Earth evolution. They came over in such a way that
those who completed the Old Moon evolution brought with them
a normal development: their physical body, etheric or life body,
and astral body; and on the Earth, quite properly, they should
develop the Ego ['I'], into which they should then take up the
other principles. Other beings who stand higher than man should
already have developed on Old Moon what for them corresponds

to the Human-Ego. But they could have brought this Old Moon Ego to full development only if they had anticipated what for them would be fifth, sixth and seventh principles, of which they should have then fully developed the fifth on Earth. They should have reached their seventh principle—*but these Luciferic beings did not do so.* They barely evolved the fifth or sixth; and thus, did not stop with the fourth; but they did not bring the fourth to full development, because they did not anticipate the fifth, sixth and seventh principles; but stopped with the fifth or sixth.

"We distinguish then two classes of these Old Moon beings: First, those who had developed only their fifth principle, so that they were as we human beings would be if we should develop the Spirit-Self in the Sixth Post-Atlantean Period, and then stop, and not develop the sixth and seventh principles. Let us keep in mind this one class, who as Luciferic beings had developed their fifth principle; and then note another class of Old Moon beings of the Luciferic sort who had developed their sixth principle but not their seventh. There were such at the beginning of the Earth evolution, when man began the development of his Ego. So, we can ask: What was the situation as regards these beings at the beginning of Earth evolution? There were beings there who eagerly expected to develop their sixth principle during the Earth evolution, beings of a Luciferic kind, who upon Old Moon had evolved only as far as their fifth principle and wished to develop their sixth upon the Earth. And there were beings of the second class, who had already developed their sixth principle on Old Moon, and who wished to develop their seventh on the Earth. They expected that of the Earth evolution. Then there was man, who came over with three principles, to develop his fourth ['I'].

"So, we can distinguish human beings waiting for the opportunity to develop their Ego, Luciferic beings expecting to evolve their sixth principle, and the Luciferic beings who would evolve their seventh. We shall disregard those who were ready to develop their fifth (but there were such).

"Now you see we have distinguished three classes, so to speak, of Microcosmic Earth beings, three classes of beings who arrived upon the scene of Earth evolution. Of the three classes, however, only one could win a physical body for itself on the Earth; for the conditions which the Earth presents for the development of a physical fleshly body can be furnished only in conformity with its entire earthly relationship to a fourth human principle ['I']. Only that being could acquire a physical body for himself who wished to develop his fourth principle as Ego. The other beings, who wished to develop a sixth and a seventh principle, could not get physical bodies for themselves. For there is no possibility on the Earth for the direct acquisition of physical human bodies for beings who come into this Earth evolution so unadapted to it. The possibility does not exist for the direct acquisition of such a physical body. What did these beings have to do? They had to say to themselves:— 'Of course, we cannot have direct access to a human physical body consisting of flesh and bones, for such bodies are for human beings who wish to develop their Ego. Hence, we must take refuge in a kind of substitute physical body; we must search for human beings who belong to the most highly developed, that is, those who have evolved, let us say, their fourth principle. We must creep into these human beings, and in them our nature must work in such a way that they will be enabled to form their sixth or seventh principle.' ...

"The consequence of this was that among the ordinary human beings of ancient times some appeared who could be possessed by higher Luciferic beings. These naturally stood higher than man, since they were to form their sixth or seventh principle, and man only his fourth ['I']. Such higher beings of a Luciferic kind went about on the Earth in earthly human bodies. They were the leaders of Earth humanity; they knew and understood much more and could do much more than other men. We are given accounts of these beings in ancient tales and legends, and it is told of them that here and there they were founders of great cities, were great leaders of peoples, and so on. They were not merely normal men upon Earth; but they were men who were possessed by such higher beings of a Luciferic sort—*possessed in the best sense of the word.* We can only understand human Earth evolution when we take account of such things.

"But especially the less highly evolved of these beings because they cannot get human bodies for themselves, are always trying to continue their evolution in the bodies of human beings. And that is just what we have been able to characterize. Luciferic beings always had the longing to continue their evolution in the way described—*by possessing human beings*; and they are still doing that today. Lucifer and his hosts work in the human soul; for we are the *stage* for the Luciferic evolution. While we human beings simply take the human earthly body in order to develop ourselves, these Luciferic beings take us and develop themselves within us. And that is the temptation of human beings—*that the Luciferic spirits work in them.*

"But meanwhile these Luciferic spirits have advanced, just as human beings have advanced; so that very many of them who, let us say, when man entered upon the Atlantean time, stood on the threshold ready to evolve their sixth principle, are now already forming their seventh; although, of course—*this evolution on the Earth is abnormal.* Such a spirit accomplishes this in the following way: He takes possession of a man, perhaps for only a few years, in order to make use of the experiences of this man, who on his part is thus furthering his own evolution. This is nothing evil in human nature; for since we can bring the Consciousness-Soul to expression in our time, we can be possessed by Luciferic spirits who are evolving their seventh principle. What does a person become when he is possessed by such a lofty Luciferic spirit? *A genius!* But because as man he is possessed, and the real human nature is irradiated by this higher being, he is impractical for ordinary accomplishments; but works in some one realm as a pioneer and a leader.

"One may not speak of the Luciferic spirit as if he were something altogether hateful; but because he develops himself as a parasite by entering into the human being, he causes the man possessed by him and under his influence to work as a man of genius, as if inspired. So, the Luciferic spirits are absolutely necessary, and the gifted men of Earth are they in whom a Luciferic spirit is working diligently—generally only for a couple of years. If that were not the case, Édouard Schuré would not have been able to describe Lucifer sympathetically (see Note 1); for Lucifer is actually assigned a share in the great cultural progress of the Earth, and it is narrow-mindedness in traditional Christianity to see in the Luciferic being only the wicked devil—this signifies nothing less than gross Philistinism ... "Nature is sin, Spirit is devil; they cherish between them Doubt, their deformed bastard child," we read in *Faust*. Certainly, it is fitting for the narrow, traditionally-formed Christianity to call Lucifer the devil, and to hate him; but he who has an understanding of human evolution knows that *the Luciferic principle works in the genius.* It is fitting for the Spiritual Scientist to look these things straight in the face. And we should have no inducement whatever to rise to our fifth and sixth principles, if these spirits did not push us forward. It is the Luciferic spirits to whom we really owe the forward thrust, given because they seek thereby their own evolution, and through which we ourselves are enabled to grow out beyond our Ego. For it is said trivially that poets and geniuses and artists grow above the narrowly confined Human-Ego.

"So, we look up to the Luciferic spirits in a certain way as to leaders of men. We must free ourselves from narrowness, from all orthodox Christianity which calls Lucifer only a devil worthy of hatred. We must recognize the liberating character of the Luciferic principle, which has also been ordained by the good gods; for it drives us out beyond ourselves during the Earth evolution, so that we prophetically anticipate what will come to us as our own possession only during Future Jupiter, and so on. Thus there actually exists upon Earth a reciprocal influence of Microcosmic beings, who were present at the beginning of the Earth evolution—such a reciprocal influence that human beings are led forward, while they are developing their own Ego—by beings related to them in such a way that it must be admitted that they are higher than man; for they have evolved their fifth principle and are developing their sixth, or are already evolving their seventh, while man is working only upon his fourth. So in these Luciferic beings we see superhuman beings—*Microcosmic superhuman beings.*

"And now we will turn aside from these spiritual beings whom we regard as Luciferic and consider the nature of Christ.

"The Christ is quite radically different from other beings who share in the Earth evolution. He is a Being of quite another order; He is a Being who remained behind, not only during the Old Moon evolution, as the Luciferic spirits did; but who, foreseeing the Old Moon evolution, actually remained behind still earlier, namely, during the Old Sun evolution; and it was from a certain assured wisdom far above the human that He remained behind during the Old Sun evolution. We cannot regard this Being as 'Microcosmic' in the sense which applies to the other beings we have been considering; for we have to regard as Microcosmic beings those who were connected with this Earth evolution from its beginning. The Christ was not directly connected with the Earth evolution—*but with the Old Sun evolution*. He was a *Macrocosmic being* from the beginning of the Earth evolution on, a Being who was exposed to entirely different conditions of evolution from those of the *Microcosmic* beings. And His evolutionary conditions were of a special sort; they were such that this Macrocosmic Christ Being evolved the Macrocosmic-I [Ego] outside earthly conditions. For this Christ evolution it was normal to bring to Ego-perfection, outside the Earth, an Ego of a Macrocosmic sort, and then to descend to Earth. And so, for the evolution of the Christ Being it was normal, when He descended from the Macrocosm to our Earth, to bring into it the great impulse of the Macrocosmic-I, in order that the Microcosmic-I, the Human-Ego, might take up this impulse, and be able to go forward in its evolution. It was normal for the Christ to have the Macrocosmic-I impulse—not the Microcosmic-I impulse— just as much evolved as man upon the Earth had developed the Microcosmic. Thus, the Christ Being is a Being Who in a certain sense is like the human being, only that man is *Microcosmic* and has brought his four principles to expression *microcosmically*, and hence has his Ego also microcosmically as *Earth-I*—but the Christ as *Cosmic-I*. His evolution was such that He was great and significant because of the perfect development of this I, which He brought down to Earth. And He did not have the fifth macrocosmic principle, and not the sixth—*for He will evolve these on Future Jupiter and on Future Venus, in order that He may give them to man.*

"The Christ, then, is a four-membered Being, including His Macrocosmic I, just as man himself is microcosmically a four-membered being. And as man during the Earth time has as his mission the development of his I, *in order to be able to receive,* so the Christ had to develop His I, *in order to be able to give.* When He descended to Earth His whole being was employed in bringing His fourth principle to expression in the most perfect possible form. Now each macrocosmic principle has an inner relationship to the corresponding microcosmic principle; the fourth macrocosmic principle in the Christ corresponds to the fourth microcosmic principle in man, and the fifth in the Christ will correspond to the Spirit-Self in man.

"Thus, the Christ entered upon His earthly course in that He brought down to man out of the Macrocosm what man was to evolve microcosmically—*only the Christ brought it as a macrocosmic principle.* He entered the Earth evolution in such a way that during its course He would not have a fifth, sixth and seventh principle as His personal possession, just as man in his way does not possess them.

"The Christ is a Being Who had evolved macrocosmically up to the fourth principle, and the evolution of His fourth principle during the Earth course consists in His bestowing upon man everything which will enable him to evolve his I.

"If we take a complete survey, we have at the beginning of Earth evolution three classes of beings: human beings who were to bring their fourth principle to full development on Earth; a class of Luciferic beings who were to evolve their sixth principle; and a class of Luciferic beings who were to develop their seventh principle—beings who, because they were ready to develop their sixth and seventh principles, stood higher than man,—in fact, ranged far above man in this respect. But they also ranged above Christ in this regard; for the Christ was to bring His fourth principle to expression on the Earth, in devotion to humanity. It will not be the Christ, let us say, that will quicken man in the future to bring to expression something other than the True-Ego, the innermost human being—to reach ever higher and higher stages. It will be the Luciferic spirits who will lead man out beyond himself in a certain sense.

"Anyone who looks at the matter superficially can say:— 'Of course then the Christ stands lower than, for example, the Luciferic spirits.' ...

"Because the Christ came to Earth with something which is fully related to man's fourth principle. For that reason, He is not at all fitted to lead man above himself; but only more deeply into his own soul being; He is fitted to lead the individual soul-being of man more and more to itself. The Luciferic beings have evolved the fourth, fifth and sixth principles, and hence in a certain way stand higher than the Christ. Practically, that will work out in the future so that through the admission of the Christ principle into human nature, this human nature will become more and more deepened, will take up more and more Light and Love into its own being; so that the human being will have to feel Light and Love as belonging to his very self. The immeasurable deepening of the human soul—that will be the gift of the Christ-Impulse, which will work on and on forever and ever. And when the Christ shall come, as that coming has been represented in many lectures, then He will work only upon the deepening of human souls. The other spirits who have higher principles than the Christ—*though only microcosmic principles*—will in a certain sense lead man out beyond himself. The Christ will deepen the inner-life of man— *but also make him humble.* On the other hand, the Luciferic spirits will lead man out beyond himself, and make him wise, clever, talented—*but also in a certain sense haughty*; will teach him that he might become something superhuman even during the Earth evolution. Everything, therefore, which in the future shall lead man to rise above himself, as it were, which will make him proud of his own human nature even here upon Earth—*that will be a Luciferic impulse*; but what makes a man more deeply sincere, what brings his inner-life to such depths as can come only through the complete development of the fourth principle—*that comes from the Christ.*

"People who look at the matter superficially will say that Christ really stands lower than the Luciferic beings; for He has developed only the fourth principle, and the others, higher principles. Only the difference is that these other beings bring the higher principles as something parasitic, grafted upon human nature; but the Christ brings the fourth principle ['I'] in such a way that it penetrates human nature, takes root within it, *and fills it with power.* As the fleshly body of Jesus of Nazareth was once permeated and empowered by the fourth Macrocosmic-Principle, so will the bodies of those who take the Christ into themselves be permeated by the fourth Macrocosmic-Principle. Just as the fourth Macrocosmic-Principle is the gift of Christ, so will the sixth and the seventh principles be the gifts of the Luciferic spirits. So that in the future—and such time is now being prepared for—we may experience that people lacking in understanding will say: If we examine the *Gospels*, or otherwise allow to work upon us what Christ gave to humanity, we see that in regard to His teaching He does not at all rank as high as perhaps do other spiritual beings who are connected with humanity ... For they are higher than man in a certain way.

They cannot penetrate the entire man; but they take root in his intellect, they make him a genius! And one who observes only outwardly says that these beings stand higher than the Christ ... And the time will come when the most powerful, the most significant of these Luciferic spirits, who will wish to lead the people out beyond themselves, so to speak, will be extolled, and looked upon as a great human leader; and it will be said that what the Christ was able to furnish was really only a bridge. Now already there are people who say:— 'What do the teachings of the *Gospels* amount to! We have outgrown them.'

"As has been said, men will point to a lofty, versatile spirit, a spirit of genius, who will take possession of a human fleshly nature, which he will permeate with his genius. It will be said that he surpasses even the Christ! For the Christ was one who gave opportunity to develop the fourth principle; but this one gives opportunity during the Earth evolution to attain to the seventh principle.

"Thus, will the Christ Spirit and the spirit of this being face one another—the Christ Spirit, from whom humanity may hope to receive the mighty Macrocosmic impulse of its fourth principle [I'], and the Luciferic Spirit, who will wish in a certain way to lead humanity beyond this.

"If people would agree that we must acquire from the Luciferic spirits only that to which we can look up in the same way that we look down to our lower nature ... then they would be doing right. But if people should come to say:— 'You see the Christ gives only the fourth principle; while these spirits give the sixth and seventh.' ...

People who think thus concerning Christ will worship and extol ... *the Antichrist*."

Esoteric Lessons for the First Class of the Free School for Spiritual Science at the Goetheanum, **Volume Two, by Rudolf Steiner, Lesson XIX, Dornach, August 2, 1924, Dornach, GA 270**

"…My dear sisters and brothers, if we wish to enter the esoteric realm, we should first feel that the ancient holy 'eyeh 'asher 'eyeh!—'I am I,' "I Am" is a holy word which resounds from that other worldly reality. What our fleeting thoughts understand as "I Am" is only a reflection of it.

"We must be aware that the true "I Am" does not come from us in the earthly realm, that if we wish to say "I Am" worthily, we must first enter the realm of the Seraphim, Cherubim and Thrones. Only there does "I Am" sound true. Here in the earthly realm it is illusion.

"In order to experience the true "I Am" within us, we must hear the Cosmic-Word. So, we must listen to the Guardian of the Threshold's question: Who speaks in the Cosmic-Word? Seraphim, who wend their way through the cosmic waves with spiritual flames of lightning, where we now stand. The Word is flame, a flaming voice. And in experiencing ourselves in this blazing cosmic fire, which speaks the fire-language in the flaming fire, we experience the true 'I am.'

"…The Cosmic-Spirit-Word must speak. Thoughts stream from it. But the thoughts are creative; the thoughts are permeated with forces; the thoughts stream; and cosmic beings and cosmic events, everything which is evolves from them. In it, in the thought bearing Cosmic-Word live the word-created cosmic thoughts. It is not mere thinking, it is not mere speaking, *it is force, forces streaming in the Words.* Forces inscribe the thoughts into the cosmic beings, into the cosmic events.

"…In a certain sense, my sisters and brothers, it is a kind of conclusion to the path that began in the realm of illusion, of maya, which led us to the Guardian of the Threshold, which led us to self-knowledge, and through self-knowledge over to the spiritual realm, and allowed us to hear the choirs of the hierarchies. In a certain sense it is a conclusion when we now stand at the place where we may experience in ourselves the true 'I am,' 'eyeh 'asher 'eyeh.

"In this dialog we can experience, when the threefold 'It is I' streams from the heart, where it may stream from the heart; when it streams from the heart in such a way that it is the echo of what resounds in these hearts from the Seraphim, Cherubim, Thrones..."

Sergei O. Prokofieff on the Three Human-Egos

Rudolf Steiner's Path of Initiation and the Mystery of the Ego, Sergei O. Prokofieff, Bologna, March 31, 2011, Temple Lodge Publishing: Forest Row, 2013

"On the basis of the exercises—where one works meditatively with different symbolic pictures—that Rudolf Steiner presented in the Bologna lecture[1] (and many more can be found in his other works), we can take the first steps in our consciousness which lead us to experience our own being outside the body. We are now achieving the first stage of supersensible consciousness. In anthroposophy it is called the imaginative stage, or that which pertains to *Imagination*. Here one is living and weaving in pictures...

"At the same time, one lives in the purified process of one's own thinking. When one has achieved this stage of higher knowledge, one can experience for oneself the awareness that the real being of man lives outside the body. Thus we learn that the

Ego consciousness otherwise experienced as the everyday Ego is only a mirror image of this higher Ego in the body.

"However, this path of seeking the transcendental Human-Ego goes further. We now no longer concentrate on the content of the symbolic pictures with which we have previously worked meditatively but must voluntarily extinguish them again and then concentrate on the pure power of consciousness necessary to engender these pictures within us. In other words: one directs one's attention to the inner-activity itself which unfolds behind the thought pictures. In this way we create a free space within the soul into which the spiritual world can flow. This is the next step on the path to a knowledge of higher worlds. In his writings and lectures, Rudolf Steiner calls this stage of knowledge *Inspiration*.

"...One perceives oneself in one's essential nature, thus yielding a definite experience of one's own consciousness outside one's body. By continuing the corresponding exercises on this path, one is able to grasp the nature of one's own Ego consciously. In other writings, Rudolf Steiner designates this second Ego as the higher Human-Ego.

"The path that has been begun now leads still further, and the next step is exceptionally difficult... Essentially, he says that the experience of the higher self must now be extinguished. A person is required to eliminate from his consciousness all the inner experience of living and weaving in his own self that he has achieved with so much effort. He must voluntarily eliminate the self that has been arrived at with such effort. This brings him to the next higher stage of supersensible consciousness. Rudolf Steiner calls it the stage of *Intuition*...

"At this stage we are drawing close to what in the Bologna lecture Rudolf Steiner calls the world Ego. It is what he describes as the third or true Human-Ego...

"…In accordance with the concept of three Egos, this means that a person must initially come to a conscious connection with the second, higher Ego. It is the intermediate station on the path leading from the earthly Ego via the higher Ego to the true Ego.

"…This [third Ego] embodies the mystery of the Human-Ego in connection with the whole world, with the cosmos…

"…This path covers three stages: from the earthly Ego to the higher Ego and then to the true Ego. This is at the same time the path to supersensible knowledge.

"What happens, however, when we proceed consistently along this path? We then come ever closer to the Christ Being… Christ represents the principle of the Ego as its highest example and also as its eternal archetype. Here they converge: the human soul developing upward from below and Christ, who mercifully inclines towards it from the heights.

"Naturally, in man we are only concerned with the microcosmic Human-Ego. With Christ we have to do with the world Ego, the comprehensive divine Ego. Nevertheless, there is a mysterious connection between the Human-Ego [Microcosmic-I] and Christ's world Ego [Macrocosmic-I]. In one place in his works, Rudolf Steiner asks: What is the esoteric name of Christ? He answers: His real name is 'I am.'

"When we come across the words "I Am" seven times in the Gospel of John (for example: I am the way, the truth and the life), then instead of representing a grammatical form these words "I Am" indicate the esoteric name of Christ Himself. His esoteric name is: I am. Rudolf Steiner summarizes this mystery by saying: 'The only true name of Christ is "I am": Whoever doesn't know and understand that and calls Him something else doesn't know anything at all about Him. "I am" is His only name.'

"This results in a quite new perspective of Christianity, which comes about from a new relationship of the human being to Christ. In other words, if we follow the path outlined by Rudolf Steiner in the Bologna lecture—which leads to the highest aspect of the Human-Ego—sufficiently far, that is, if we seek and find our deepest human nature, we also thereby encounter Christ. He is the greatest model of this development which is inherently possible—and will ever be possible—for man; the highest goal to which we as human beings are able to aspire.

"We want it not only because we are or want to be Christians, but because we are *human beings*; because every person possesses an Ego. Whether Christian, Muslim, or Buddhist, everyone is in the first instance a human being with an Individual-Ego that is reflected in the body and yet can only be found outside the body. Furthermore, there is also a third Ego that we cherish as the highest ideal of mankind's development, in which Christ is present in every person.

"Now we understand why Christ in his essential Being belongs not only to Christians, as is often thought, but to *all* people, because they are all Ego beings. Each person is following the path to Christ in so far as he has begun the journey to the source of his own being. It was this journey which, in his Bologna lecture, Rudolf Steiner described as the suitable path of schooling for the present-day. It is the modern path to Christ.

"When we reach the end of the path after many earthly incarnations, we will not only know but also really experience how the Human-Ego is related in its highest aspect to Christ.[3]

"Modern spiritual science makes us aware how Christ is connected with the true Human-Ego as its highest model and archetype. However, it is only since the Mystery of Golgotha, when Christ united Himself with the whole evolution of the Earth, that He can also be found in each true Human-Ego."

Notes:

1. Rudolf Steiner, Lecture held in Bologna, April 8, 1911 at the Fourth International Philosophy Conference.

2. From the esoteric lesson of May 27, 1909, in: Rudolf Steiner, *Esoteric Lessons*, Vol. I: 1904-1909 (GA 266/1)

3. About this, see further in Sergei O. Prokofieff, *Das Ratsel des menschlichen Ich Eine anthroposophische Betrachtung*, Dornach 2010. English edition: *Riddle of the Human "I": An Anthroposophical Study*, Temple Lodge Publishing: Forest Row, 2017

In light of this, further insights come to mind when we consider that the True-Ego is inseparably connected with the Christ Being; for Christ is the only one in the Spiritual World who possesses the Macrocosmic-Human-I with a consciousness that pervades everything in Heaven and on Earth. Therefore, the fulfillment of this spiritual destiny leads to the new Christ Consciousness within the free individual that will be the culmination of the 4th Planetary Condition, our present Earth Evolution, as a true Human Being—as a member of the '10th Hierarchy' referred to by Rudolf Steiner as 'the Spirits of Freedom and Love.' Beyond this, the complete union with Christ through His manifestation of the Macrocosmic Spirit-Human (Atman) will only possible in the 7th Planetary Condition or Future Vulcan Evolution as an Archai. but this will be preceded by His manifestation of the Macrocosmic Life-Spirit (Budhi) which will be possible in the 6th Planetary Condition / Future Venus Evolution as an Archangel; this, in turn, will be preceded by His manifestation of the Macrocosmic Spirit-Self (Manas) which will become possible in the 5th Planetary

Condition / Future Jupiter Evolution as an Angel. Nonetheless, these future exalted states of being are anticipated within a wholesome development, and stream into us from higher beings—as *Moral Imagination* (Angelic realm), *Moral Inspiration*, (Archangelic realm), and *Moral Intuition* (realm of the Archai).

And so, the Earthly-Ego examines the physical world of the senses while the Higher-Ego examines the supersensible world. Nonetheless, these two currents must be supplemented by a 'third' entelechy coming to meet them which is capable of beholding the *synthesis* of the sensible and the supersensible. The confluence of these two currents may be conceived of as arising through *intuitive cognition*, as it is only within this third current that the polarity of the sensible and the supersensible is superseded. For it is only at the stage of *Moral-Intuition* where the True-Human-Ego, which is so deeply connected with the Christ Being, can be grasped—*but will only find completion as a future state-of-being*—until then it is streaming to us from higher beings, out of the future as it were. For it is that which unites the polarity of the physical world of the senses and the supersensible world of soul and spirit through a higher synthesis that manifests a linking of Heaven and Earth and represents the conscious path leading from Earth to Heaven and back again.

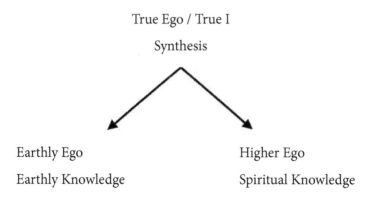

True Ego / True I

Synthesis

Earthly Ego
Earthly Knowledge

Higher Ego
Spiritual Knowledge

Unification Leading to the Holy Spirit and Group-Soul

The Festivals and their Meaning: Ascension and Pentecost, **Rudolf Steiner, Lecture V,** *Whitsun: The Festival of United Soul-Endeavour,* **Cologne, June 7, 1908**

"Now the kind of Ego ['I'] man has today is only to be found in man, in the human being living on the Earth; every man has his Ego enclosed within himself. It is different with the animals: they have a Group-Ego, a Group-Soul; that is to say, a group of animals with the same form have a common Group-Ego… We must not imagine the Animal-Ego to be like the human being of course, though if we consider man as he is as a spiritual being, we can then certainly compare the animal Group-Ego with him.

"In many animal species the Group-Ego is a wise being. If we think of how certain kinds of birds live in the north in the summer and in the south in the winter, how in spring they fly back to the north—in this migrating flight of the birds there are wise powers at work; they are in the Group-Egos of the birds. Anywhere you like in the animal kingdom you can find the wisdom of the Group-Egos. If we turn back to our schooldays, we can remember learning how modern times gradually arose out of the Middle Ages, of how America was discovered, and how gunpowder and printing were invented, and later still the art of making paper from rags. We have long been accustomed to such paper, but the wasp Group-Soul invented it thousands of years ago. The material of which the wasp's nest consists is exactly the same as is used in making paper out of rags. Only gradually will it become known how the one or the other achievement of the human spirit is connected with what the Group-Souls have introduced into the world."

"When the clairvoyant looks at an animal, he sees a glimmer of light along the whole length of its spine. The physical spine of the animal is enveloped in a glimmering light, in innumerable streams of force which everywhere travel across the Earth, as it were, like the trade winds. They work on the animal in that they stream along the spine. The Group-Ego of the animal travels in a continual circular movement around the Earth at all heights and in all directions. These Group-Egos are wise, but one thing they have not yet gotten—*they have no knowledge of love.* For only in man is wisdom found in his individuality together with love. In the Group-Ego of the animals no love is present; love is found only in the single animal. What underlies the whole Animal-Group as wise arrangements is quite devoid of love. In the physical world below the animal has love; above, on the astral plane, it has wisdom. When we realize this a vast number of things will become clear to us."

"Only gradually has man arrived at his present stage of development; in earlier times he also had a Group-Soul, out of which the Individual-Soul has gradually emerged. Let us follow the evolution of man back into ancient Atlantis. Mankind once lived in Atlantis, a continent now lying beneath the Atlantic Ocean. At that time the vast Siberian plains were covered with immense seas; the Mediterranean was differently distributed, and in Europe itself there were extensive seas. The farther we go back in the Old Atlantean Epoch, the more the conditions of life alter, the more the sleeping and the waking state of man changes. Since that time consciousness during the sleeping condition has darkened, as it were, so that today man has, so to say, no consciousness at all in this condition. In the earliest Atlantean times the difference between sleeping and waking was not yet so great. In his waking state at that time man still saw things with an aura around them; he did not attain to any greater clarity than this in his perception of the physical world. Everything physical was still filled out, so to say, with something unclear, as if with mist. As he progressed, the human being came to see the world in its clear-cut contours; but in return he lost his clairvoyance.

"It is in the times when men still saw clairvoyantly what was going on up above in the astral world that all the myths and sagas originate. When he was able to enter into the spiritual world, man learned to know the beings who had never descended into the physical world:— Wotan, Baldur, Thor, Loki. *These names are memories of living realities, and all mythologies are memories of this kind.* As spiritual realities, they have simply vanished from the sight of man. When in those earlier times man descended into his physical body, he got the feeling: 'Thou art a single being.' When he returned into the Spiritual World in the evening, however, the feeling came over him: 'Thou art in reality *not* a single being.' The members of the old tribal groups, the Herulians, the Cheruskans and the like, had still felt themselves far more as belonging to their group, than as single personalities. It was out of this condition of things that there arose such practices as the blood-feud, the vendetta. The whole people formed a body which belonged to the Group-Soul of the folk…

"Now we must put to ourselves the question: Can we compare the anthropoid apes with man himself? The vital difference is that the ape preserves the Group-Soul condition throughout, whereas man develops the Individual-Soul. But the ape Group-Soul is in a quite special position to other Group-Souls. We must think of a Group-Soul as living in the astral world and spreading itself out in the physical world, so that, for instance, the Group-Soul of the lion sends a part of its substance into each single lion. Let us suppose that one of these lions dies; the external physical part drops away from the Group-Soul, just as when we lose a nail. The Group-Soul sends out a new ray of being, as it were, into a new individual. The Group-Soul remains above and stretches out its tentacles in a continual process of renewal. The animal Group-Soul knows neither birth or death; the single individual falls away and a new one appears, just as the nails on our fingers come and go. *It is not at all so, however, with the apes.* When an ape dies, the essential part does return to the Group-Soul, but a part does not; a part is severed from the Group-Soul. The ape detaches substance too strongly from the Group-Soul. There are species where the single animal tears something away from the Group-Soul which cannot return to it. With all the apes, fragments are detached in each case from the Group-Soul. It is the same with certain kinds of amphibians and birds; in the kangaroo, for example, something is kept back from the Group-Soul. Now everything in the warm-blooded animals that remains behind in this way becomes an elemental being of the kind we call a *salamander* [fire elemental]."

"Under entirely different conditions from those on the earth today, the other types of elemental beings have detached themselves in the past. We have here a case where cast-off products of evolution, as it were, are made of service under the wise guidance of Higher Beings. Left to themselves, these would disturb the Cosmos; but under a higher guidance the sylphs, for example, can be used to lead the bees to the flowers. Such a service changes the harmful into something useful.

"Now it could happen that man himself might entirely detach himself from the Group-Soul in becoming an individual and find no means of developing further as an Individual-Soul. If he does not accept spiritual knowledge in the right way, he can run the risk of complete severance.

"What is it that protects man from an isolation which is, without the direction and purpose which, earlier on, the Group-Soul had given him? We must clearly recognize that man individualizes himself more and more, and today, he has to find a connection once again with other men out of his free will. All that connects men, through folk, race, and family, will be ever more completely severed; everything in man tends more and more to result in *individual* manhood."

"Imagine that a number of human beings on the earth have come to recognize that they are all becoming more and more individual. Is there not a real danger that they will split away from each other ever more completely? Already nowadays men are no longer held together by spiritual ties. Each one has his own opinion, his own religion; indeed, many see it as an ideal state of affairs that each should have his own opinion. *But that is all wrong.* If men make their opinions more inward, then they come to a common opinion. It is a matter of inner experience, for example, that 3 times 3 makes 9, or that the three angles of a triangle make up 180 degrees. That is inner-knowledge and matters of inner-knowledge need not be argued about. Of such a kind also are all spiritual truths. What is taught by Spiritual Science is discovered by man through his inner powers; along the inward path man will be led to absolute agreement and unity. The ideal lies in the greatest possible inwardness of knowledge; that leads to peace and to unity.

"In the past, mankind became free of the Group-Soul. Through spiritual-scientific knowledge mankind is now for the first time in the position to discover, with the utmost certainty of purpose, what will unite mankind again. When men unite together in a higher wisdom, then out of higher worlds there descends a Group-Soul once more. What is willed by the Leaders of the Spiritual-Scientific Movement is that in it we should have a society in which hearts stream towards wisdom as the plants stream towards the sunlight. In that together we turn our hearts towards a higher wisdom, we give a dwelling-place to the Group-Soul; we form the dwelling-place, the environment, in which the Group-Soul can incarnate. Mankind will enrich earthly life by developing what enables spiritual beings to come down out of higher worlds.

"This spirit-enlivened ideal was once placed before humanity in a most powerful way. It was when a number of men, all aglow with a common feeling of fervent love and devotion, were met together for a common deed: Then the sign was given, the sign that could show man with overwhelming power how in unity of soul he could provide a place for the incarnation of the common spirit. In this company of souls, the same thing was living: in the flowing together, in the harmony of feeling they provided what was needed for the incarnation of a common spirit. That is expressed when it is said that the Holy Spirit, the Group-Soul, sank down as it were into incarnation. It is a symbol of what mankind should strive towards, how it should seek to become the dwelling-place for the Being who descends out of higher worlds.

"The Easter event gave man the power to develop these experiences; the Whitsun event [Pentecost] is the fruit of this power's unfolding. Through the flowing of souls together towards the common wisdom there will always result that which gives a living connection with the forces and beings of higher worlds, and with something which, as yet, has little significance for humanity namely—*the Whitsun festival*. When men come to know what the down-coming of the Holy Spirit in the future can mean for mankind, the Whitsun festival will once more become alive for them. Then it will be not only a memory of the event in Jerusalem; but there will arise for mankind the everlasting Whitsun festival, the festival of united soul endeavor. It will depend on men themselves what value and what result such ideals can have for mankind. When in this right way they strive towards wisdom, then will higher spirits unite themselves with men."

Wisdom of Man, of the Soul, and of the Spirit, Rudolf Steiner, Lecture IV, _Supersensible Currents in the Human and Animal Organizations,_ Berlin, October 27, 1909, GA 115

"Here the error comes to light. In judging external things accessible to the senses we should never forget that they are built up from within, through the agency of spiritual currents. Suppose we are observing those parts of the human being that are accessible to perception proper, or we observe part of another person that the eye can see—his face, for example. In studying this face we must not imagine it as having been built up from without. On the contrary, we must realize the need to distinguish between two currents flowing into each other, the current of the Sentient-Body [Astral-Body] running backward from the front, and that of the Sentient-Soul running forward from the rear. In so far as we perceive the human countenance by means of the senses, the sense image is true. That is given us by sense perception and we will not go astray there. But now the human mind joins in, at first subconsciously, and is at once misled. It regards the human countenance as something merely fashioned from without, whereas in reality, this fashioning occurred from within, through the agency of the Sentient-Soul. What you see is not really outer body; it is the outer image of the Sentient-Soul.

"Disabuse your mind of the notion that the human face might be outer body, and you will see that in truth, it is the image of the soul. A fundamentally false interpretation results from reasoning in a way that ignores the true nature of the countenance as being the outer image of the Sentient-Soul acting outward. Every explanation of the human countenance based solely on physical forces is wrong. It must be explained through the soul itself, the visible through the invisible. The deeper we penetrate into theosophy the more we will see in it a great school for learning to think. The chaotic thinking that today dominates all circles, particularly science, finds no shelter in theosophy, which is therefore able to interpret life correctly...

"Returning once more to the sense of sound and the sense of visualization, let us ask ourselves: *Which of these came into being first in the course of human development?* Did man learn first to understand words or to perceive and understand the conceptions that came to him? This question can be answered by observing the child, who first learns to talk and only later to perceive thoughts. Speech is the premise of thought perception because the sense of sound is the premise of the sense of visualization. The child learns to talk because he can hear, can listen to something that the sense of sound perceives. Speech itself is at first mere imitation, and the child imitates long before he has any idea of visualization whatever. First the sense of sound develops, and then, by means of this, the sense of visualization. The sense of sound is the instrumentality for perceiving not only tones but also what we call sounds.

"The next question is how it came about that at one time in the course of his development man achieved the ability to perceive sounds and, as a result, to acquire speech? How was he endowed with speech? If he was to learn to speak, not just to hear, it was necessary not only that an outer perception should penetrate; but that a certain current within him should flow in the same direction as that taken by the currents of the Sentient-Soul when they press forward from the rear. It had to be something acting in the same direction. That was the way in which speech had to originate, and this faculty had to appear before the sense of visualization, before man was able to sense the conception contained in the words themselves. Men had first to learn to utter sounds and to live in the consciousness of them before they could combine conceptions with them. What at first permeated the sounds they uttered was *sentience*.

"This development had to take place at a time when the transposition of the circulatory system had already occurred; for animals cannot speak. The Ego ['I'] had to be acting downward from above with the blood system in a vertical position. As yet, however, man had no sense of visualization, consequently no visualizations. It follows that he could not have acquired speech through the agency of his own Ego, but rather, he received it from another Ego that we can compare with the Group-Ego of animals. In this sense speech is a gift of the gods. It was infused into the Ego before the latter itself was capable of developing it. The Human-Ego did not yet possess the organs needed to give the impulse for bringing about speech, but the Group-Ego worked from above into the physical, etheric, and astral bodies, and as it encountered an opposing current, a sort of vortex came into being at the point of contact. A straight line drawn through the center of the larynx would indicate the direction of the current employed by the speech-giving spirits, and the larynx itself represents the physical substance, the dam, that resulted from the encounter of the two currents. That accounts for the peculiar shape of the human larynx.

"It was under the influence, then, of a Group-Ego that man had to develop speech. In what manner do Group-Ego operate on Earth? In animals the current of the Group-Ego passes through the spinal cord horizontally, and these force currents are in continual motion. The force currents running downward from above move constantly around the Earth, as they did around the Old Moon [3rd Planetary Condition]. They don't remain in one spot but move around the Earth retaining their vertical direction of influence. If men were to learn to speak under the influence of a Group-Ego, they could not remain in one place, they had to migrate. They had to move toward the Group-Ego. Never could they have learned to speak if they had remained in one spot."

From Race and Tribe to Individuality

The Influence of Spiritual Beings Upon Man, **Rudolf Steiner, Lecture IX, Berlin, June 1, 1908, GA 102**

"We ventured on rather unusual ground in our last lecture when we turned our attention to certain beings who definitely exist amongst us. They are spiritual beings who in a certain way fall out of the regular course of evolution, and it is just this fact that gives them their significance. We were considering the elemental beings whose existence is naturally viewed by the enlightened mind of today as the utmost superstition; but who will play a significant role in a not very far-distant time of our spiritual evolution, precisely through the position they occupy in the Cosmos. We have seen how such elemental beings come into existence as a sort of irregularly severed parts of Group-Souls. We have said that these Group-Souls play the same role in the astral world as our Human-Soul in the physical world. The Human-Ego is really a Group-Ego which has descended from the astral plane to the physical plane, and thus becomes an Individual-Ego. The Animal-Egos are still normally on the astral plane, and what is here on the physical plane as the separate animal possesses only physical body, etheric body, and astral body. The Ego is in the astral world, similarly formed animals being members of their own Group-Ego. We can realize from this fact how birth and death in human life have not the same significance in the life of the animal. For when an individual animal dies, the Group-Soul or Group-Ego remains alive. The Group-Soul of the animals knows changes, metamorphoses; knows, so to speak, the severing of the members which then extend into the physical world, the loss of these members and their renewal.

"We have said, however, that there are certain animal forms which go too far in the process of severing, which are no longer in a position to send back to the astral plane what they bring down to the physical plane. When an animal dies, what falls away must be entirely exhausted in the surrounding world, while the soul and spirit nature of the animal must stream back into the Group-Soul, to be ex-tended afresh and grow to a new individual entity. There are in fact certain animal forms which cannot send everything back into the Group-Soul; and these parts which remain over, which are cut loose, torn loose from the Group-Soul, then lead an isolated life as elemental beings. Our evolution has gone through the most varied stages and at each stage such elemental beings have been separated off, so you can well imagine that we have a fairly large number of such elementals around us in what we call the supersensible world.

"...It will become increasingly indispensable to grasp the nature of Group-Souls, and such knowledge will play a great role even in the purely external evolution of humanity. If we go back thousands and thousands of years, we find man himself as a being still belonging to a Group-Soul. Human evolution on our Earth is from the Group-Soul nature to the Individual-Soul. Man advances through the gradual descent of his Ego-endowed soul into physical conditions, there having the opportunity of becoming individual. We can observe different stages in the evolution of mankind and see how the Group-Soul gradually becomes individual…

"So, we see a second stage of the evolution of mankind: the Group-Soul age which finds its external expression in the blood relationship of the generations. A people which has particularly developed this, lays very special value on continually emphasizing: As folk we have a folk Group-Soul in common. That was particularly the case for the people of the *Old Testament*, and the conservatives among them strongly opposed therefore the emphasis of the "I Am" of the Individual-Ego…

"…The human being has grown out of the Group-Soul condition and emancipates himself from it increasingly. If we look at groups instead of souls, we have family connections, connections of tribe and nation, and finally connected races. The race corresponds to a Group-Soul. All these group connections of early humanity are what man outgrows and the more we advance the more the race conception loses its meaning.

"We stand today at a transitional point; race will gradually disappear entirely and something else will take its place. Those who will again grasp spiritual truth as it has been described will be led together of their own free will. Those will be the connections of a later age. The human beings of earlier times were born into connections, born into the tribe, the race. Later we shall live in the connections and associations which men create for themselves, uniting in groups with those of similar ideas while retaining their complete freedom

and individuality. To realize this is necessary for a right
understanding of something like the Anthroposophical Society.
The Anthroposophical Society is intended to be a first example
of such a voluntary association—although we may be well aware
that it has not yet reached very far. The attempt had to be made
to create a group in which men find themselves together without
the differentiation of the ancient Group-Soul's nature and there
will be many such associations in the future. Then we shall no
longer have to speak of racial connections but of intellectual-
ethical-moral aspects with regard to the associations that are
formed. The individuals voluntarily allow their feelings to stream
together, and this again causes the forming of something which
goes beyond the merely emancipated man. An emancipated
human being possesses his Individual-Soul which is never lost
when it has once been attained. But when men find themselves
together in voluntary associations, they group themselves round
centers. The feelings streaming in this way to a center once more
give beings the opportunity of working as a kind of Group-Soul,
though in quite a different sense from the early Group-Souls.
All the earlier Group-Souls were beings who made man unfree.
These new beings, however, are compatible with man's complete
freedom and individuality. Indeed, in a certain respect we may
say that they support their existence on human harmony; it
will lie in the souls of men themselves whether or not they
give as many as possible of such higher souls the opportunity
of descending to man. The more that men are divided, the
fewer lofty souls will descend into the human sphere. The
more that associations are formed where feelings of fellowship
are developed with complete freedom, the more lofty beings
will descend and the more rapidly the earthly planet will be
spiritualized.

"So, we see that if man is to acquire any idea of future evolution, he must have a thorough understanding of the character of the Group-Soul element. For otherwise, if his Individual-Soul keeps itself aloof too long on the Earth, and does not find the link of companionship—*it could come about that it lets the chance of union go by.* It would then itself become a sort of elemental being, and the elemental beings originating from man would be of quite an evil nature. Whereas those which have arisen from the earlier kingdoms are very useful for our orderly course of nature, the human elemental beings will by no means possess this quality.

'We have seen that such severed beings arise in certain border regions, and they arise also on the boundary made by the transition from the Group-Soul nature to the independent group associations where the connections are of an aesthetic, moral, intellectual character. Wherever such connections arise, Group-Beings are there."

Egyptian Myths and Mysteries, Rudolf Steiner, Lecture XII, *The Christ-Impulse as Conqueror of Matter*, Leipzig, September 14, 1908, GA 106

"We have seen how, in the Egyptian myths and mysteries, all the mighty pictures of the Sphinx, of Isis, of Osiris, were memories of ancient human conditions. All this was like a reflection of ancient events on Earth. Man looked back into his primeval past and saw his origin. The initiate could experience again the spiritual existence of his forebears. We have seen how man grew out of an original Group-Soul condition. We could point out how these Group-Souls were preserved in the forms of the four apocalyptic beasts. Man grew out of this condition in such a way that he gradually refined his body and achieved the development of individuality. We can follow this historically. Let us read the *Germania* of Tacitus.[1] In the times described there, in the conditions of the Germanic regions in the first century after Christ as there portrayed, we see how the consciousness of the individual is still bound up with the community, how the clan spirit rules, how the Cherusker, for example, still feels himself as a member of his clan. This consciousness is still so strong that the individual seeks vengeance for another of the same group. It finds expression in the custom of the blood-feud. Thus, a sort of Group-Soul condition prevailed. This condition was preserved into late Post-Atlantean times; but only as a echo. In the last period of Atlantis, the Group-Consciousness generally died out. It is only stragglers whom we have just described. In reality, the men of that time no longer knew anything of the Group-Soul. In the Atlantean time, however, man did know of it. Then he did not yet say 'I' of himself. This Group-Soul feeling changed into something else in the following generations."

Note:

1. *Germania* of Tacitus: The passage referred to is probably the following (Loeb Classical Library Edition, pgs 293 and 295): "Sisters' children mean as much to their uncle as to their father; some tribes regard this blood-tie as even closer and more sacred than that between son and father… The more relations a man has and the larger the number of his connections by marriage, the more influence has he in his age; it does not pay to have no ties. It is incumbent to take up a father's feuds or a kinsman's not less than his friendship."

Passing through Four Animal Group-Souls

The Apocalypse of St. John, **Rudolf Steiner, Lecture X,
Nuremberg, June 27, 1908, GA 104**

"We have seen that we pass through 343 conditions of form.
Now, the subject grows more complicated when we learn that the
matter does not end here; but that man must also pass through
various conditions with each condition of form. In our mineral
condition of life during the Earth period three conditions of
form have preceded the present physical condition of form and
three others will follow it. But now the physical again passes
through seven conditions, and these are the seven of which we
have spoken in previous lectures; the first when the Sun is still
united with the Earth, the second when it separates, the third
when the Moon withdraws, the fourth that of the Atlantean
humanity. The Atlantean humanity lives in the Fourth Epoch
of the development of the physical condition of form. Thus
within each condition of form you have again seven Epochs or
so-called root-races, although the expression 'race' applies only
to the middle condition. We are now living in the Fifth Epoch,
the Post-Atlantean Epoch, [7,227 B.C.-7,894 A.D.] between the
great Atlantean flood and the great War of All against All. The
Sixth will follow this and then the Seventh. The Sixth Epoch is
indicated in the *Apocalypse of John* by the seven seals, and the
seventh by the seven trumpets. Then the Earth passes over into
the astral. That is a new condition of form which again will have
its Seven Epochs.

"And still our diagram is not at an end. Each Epoch as it runs
its course, between such events as the great Atlantean flood and
the great War of All against All, must again be divided into seven
ages. As regards the Fifth Epoch there are the Old Indian Period

of civilization [7,227 B.C.-5,067 B.C.], the Old Persian Period of civilization [5,067 B.C.-2,907 B.C.], the Assyrian-Babylonian-Chaldean-Egyptian-Jewish Period [2,907 B.C.-747 B.C.], the Graeco-Latin Period [747 B.C.-1,414 A.D.] our own Period [1,414 A.D.-3,574 A.D.], then the Sixth [3,574 A.D.-5,734 A.D.], which is indicated in the *Apocalypse* by the community of Philadelphia, and the Seventh Period of civilization which will follow that [5,734 A.D.-7,894 A.D.].

"Thus if we imagine the whole of evolution consisting of nothing but short ages such as these—which, however, are long enough—we have 7 x 7 x 7 x 7 x 7 stages of development such as the ancient Indian or the ancient Persian. The number of different conditions of this nature which man passes through between Saturn and Vulcan is 16,807:—

$$7 \times 7 \times 7 = 343$$
$$7 \times 343 = 2,401$$
$$7 \times 2,401 = 16,807$$

"Thus you see how the number 7 governs development in the successive Periods throughout the whole of evolution. Just as the tones in music progress from octave to octave, so does the whole of evolution take place in octaves of development.

"Let us now recall that we have seven of these conditions out of the 16,807 in our Epoch between the great Atlantean Flood and the great War of All against All, and that previously we had seven more in the Atlantean Epoch. But we also remember that man went through four of these seven ages of the Atlanteans Epoch under quite different conditions from the last three. You know the kind of conditions we have to enumerate. Four of the conditions, out of the total number, man went through

during the Atlantean Epoch in such a way that he felt himself as
a Group-Soul, as we have described—as *Eagle, Lion, Bull, and
Man.* He gradually developed these four Group-Souls during
these four root-races of the Atlantean Epoch. Now, because races
always continue, just as for instance, the Indian has continued,
although later ones have developed (they pass into one another);
for this reason the four heads indicating the Group-Souls also
remained at the beginning of the fifth Period of Atlantean
civilization and we have this four-headed beast. Now when man
began to harden himself from the etheric into the physical, he
developed four different parts of the body in accordance with
his fourfold Group-Soul. And through the former Group-Soul-
Consciousness changing into the Individual-Consciousness,
man had within him a conjunction of the earlier four-foldness
at the beginning of the Fifth Period of Atlantis. He bears within
him the four heads which are summed up in his head which
gradually arises. It is composed of the four Group-Heads as it
developed in the course of the Fifth Period."

"Man has four parts of the physical body corresponding to the
four heads. These are the four horns. So that you may imagine
that because man was etheric, he had four heads, four animal
heads, only the last is already human-animal; for that is what is
meant. He was four-headed, and each force-system corresponding
to one of these heads formed physical organs. We saw in our last
lecture that there was a force-system which formed the heart,
namely, that which is connected with the lion head. The various
organs of man are like condensations of the corresponding
parts of the etheric body. This is the view of the writer of the
Apocalypse. He says: That which is physical is a densification of
the etheric. Just as you would think: 'This skin thickens and forms

a callosity,' so the Apocalyptist thinks: 'man exists etherically and this condenses and becomes physical.' And because man is fourfold, consisting of four Group-Souls, four condensations are formed. These constitute his physical body. This is the reason why one described as 'horn' that which in the physical body corresponds to the etheric body. Horn is a callous thickening. Man is described, as far as he had developed in the fourth age of the Atlantean Epoch, as an animal with four heads and four horns. He then evolves further into an individual human being. This begins in the neighborhood of the present Ireland. Man passes through the last three ages in such a way that he possesses the germ of the Ego-Being ['I-Being']. He no longer develops an animal body outwardly—*but has risen to the human stage*. He matures his human nature more and more until he absorbs the Christ-Principle. If we regard present day man, we see that he was not always as he appears today. In order for him to become what he now is, he had to pass through four Animal-Group-Souls, he had to be incarnated in bodies corresponding to the present Lion form, the Bull form, the Eagle form, and the Human form. He then pressed forward and became more and more human, and the form of the earlier Group-Soul disappeared. It is no longer there and man has assumed human shape.

"We must now understand an important event which then took place when man assumed human form—for without this understanding one cannot comprehend the *Apocalypse of John*—it was an event of the greatest importance. Up to this event when man passed into the Human-Soul-Nature, something was totally hidden from his vision which later was revealed. Man had a kind of dim, hazy consciousness. When he awakened in the morning he saw everything surrounded by misty formations, so to speak; and when he went to sleep he was in the spiritual world. This appeared to him in pictures; *for such is the nature of the spiritual world*. I shall now describe something which took place before man passed over physically into the human condition, before he passed from the Group-Soul nature to full I-Consciousness.

"That which he lived through here upon the Earth consisted only of a number of experiences. He then went to sleep and during his sleep was in a dim consciousness in a spiritual world where he lived among gods and spirits, of which an echo remains in the myths and legends. He then experienced mighty pictures; for example, the picture in which he encountered two other beings who threw stones behind them, and out of these stones other beings like themselves grew out of the Earth. These were experiences which man had throughout the fourth age of the Atlantean Epoch. To express it plainly, we must say that reproduction took place in sleeping-consciousness, not in the waking-consciousness. When man was outside his physical body and in the spiritual world, he accomplished in this condition of picture-consciousness deeds which had to be brought about. The whole act of reproduction was veiled in a spiritual element and appeared to him in the picture of throwing stones behind him. The act of reproduction was enveloped in spiritual consciousness; it lay behind the day-consciousness. Man had no knowledge of sex. In the day-consciousness he did not see himself as existing in two sexes, his soul was untouched by any thought of sex. Not that it did not exist—*it did exist*—but it rested in the obscurity of a spiritual consciousness, and during the day-consciousness he knew nothing of it. With the acquisition of the first germ of the I-Consciousness man first became aware of sex. That is the moment presented to us in the *Bible* when Adam and Eve become aware that there is such a thing as sex. This important event took place at this stage in the Earth's evolution.

"If with spiritual vision you look back to the time which preceded that time, you see only that part of man which is the instrument of the spirit. The other part was invisible, only the upper part of man could be seen. From the point-of-time we have mentioned, the whole man began to be seen. It is now comprehensible why men began to cover themselves up. Previously they saw nothing which required covering. In this way man gradually emerged into the external world.

"If we consider the outer human form as the condensed part of the etheric, we have in the fourth Atlantean age the four horns in addition to the four Group-Soul heads. Now, however, in the last three ages of Atlantis something twofold begins to develop physically. At each stage where a Group-Soul head was to develop, a double physical, male and female, was formed. In the first four stages you find man formed with four heads, the condensed etheric with four horns. We now have three more heads which are invisible because the external human form absorbs then. These three are only perceptible to spiritual vision, three etheric heads, a principal human head between two others which are like shadows beside it—*like a double-shadow*. Thus when the Atlantean flood burst, we have seven Group-Soul heads, of which the last three always appear in such a way that they have their physical part in a double form, as male and female. From this you see that at the end of the Atlantean Epoch the entire Group-Soul nature of man—although the later portion remains invisible—has seven heads and ten horns. The horns of the first four heads are not separated into male and female—but only the last three. Man has the seven heads and ten horns within him. He must now work upon these through the reception of the Christ-Principle so that they shall be destroyed, so to speak. For each time a man dies the sevens-headed and ten-horned nature can clearly be seen in his astral body. This is merely held together like a piece of India-rubber which has been correspondingly formed. Now suppose a person hardened himself during our Epoch against the Christ-Principle and were to come to the time of the great War of All against All without having had the Christ-Experience, suppose he were to come to this time and had thrust the Christ away from him, then when the Earth passes over into the astral, that which was there and which he ought to have changed, would spring forth—*it would spring forth in its old form.* The beast with the seven heads and ten horns would appear; whereas in those who have received the Christ-Principle—*sex will again be overcome.* The hardened ones will keep the six-horned sexuality and will appear in their totality as the 'beast with the seven heads and ten horns' of which the rudiments were laid down in the Atlantean Epoch. They will be transformed through the reception of the Christ-Impulse; but if Christ is rejected they will remain and will reappear in the Epoch indicated by the falling of the vials of wrath and the Earth splitting, as it were, into two parts, one in which the Christ-Men appear with white garments as the elect, even in the Epoch of the Seals—and the other part in which men appear in the form of the beast with seven heads and ten horns. Then appears another beast with two horns, symbolized by the number 666."

Egyptian Myths and Mysteries, **Rudolf Steiner, Lecture VIII,** *The Stages of Evolution of the Human Form—The Expulsion of the Animal Beings—The Four Human Types,* **Leipzig, September 10, 1908, GA 106**

"We shall best understand evolution if we make it quite clear that, while man was becoming ever more human, animal beings remained stuck at certain stages. We have already said that man developed lungs, heart, and larynx through the influence of the moon forces. We have also shown to what extent Osiris and Isis participated in this. Now we must be quite clear that the higher organs, such as heart, lungs, larynx, and others, could develop only through the fact that the higher members of man—etheric body, astral body, and also the Ego ['I']—cooperated in a definite way as the really spiritual members of man. After the point that was reached under the Balance, these higher members cooperated much more than in the preceding Epochs. Thus the most manifold forms could appear. For example, the etheric body, or the astral, or the Ego, could work especially strongly. It could even happen that the physical body might predominate over the other three members. Through this, four human types developed. A number of men appeared who had worked out the physical body especially. Then there were men who had received their stamp from the etheric body, others whose astral nature predominated, and also Ego-men, strongly marked Ego-men. Each man showed what predominated in him. In the ancient times when these four forms originated, one could meet grotesque shapes, and the clairvoyant discovers what is present in the different types. There are representations, although these are not well known, in which the memory of this has been preserved. For example, those men in whom the physical nature became especially strong and worked on the upper parts, bore the mark of this in their upper part. Something was formed that was entirely suited to the baser form, and through what was thus active there appeared the shape that we see retained in the apocalyptic picture of the Bull, although not the bull of today, which is a decadent form.

"What was governed principally by the physical body at a certain time, remained stuck at the stage of the bull. This is represented by the bull and all that belongs to this genus, such as cows, oxen and so on. The human group in whom the etheric rather than the physical body was strongly marked, in whom the heart region was especially powerful, is also preserved in the animal kingdom. This stage, beyond which man has progressed, is preserved in the Lion. The lion preserves the type that was worked out in the group of men in whom the etheric body was intensely active. The human stage in which the astral body overpowered the physical and etheric is preserved for us, although degenerated, in the mobile bird-kingdom, and is portrayed in the *Apocalypse* in the picture of the Eagle. The predominating astrality is here repelled; it raised itself from the Earth as the race of birds. Where the Ego grew strong, a being evolved that should actually be called a union of the three other natures; for the Ego ['I'] harmonizes all three members. In this group the clairvoyant actually has before him what has been preserved in the Sphinx, for the Sphinx has the Lion-body, the Eagle-wings, something of the Bull-form—and in the oldest portrayals there was even a Reptilian-tail, pointing to the ancient reptile form—and then at the front there is the Human-face, which harmonizes the other parts.

"These are the four types. But in the Atlantean time the Man-form predominated, as the human shape gradually constructed itself out of the Eagle, Lion, and Bull natures. These transmuted themselves into the full Human-form, and this gradually transmuted itself into the shape that was present in the middle of Atlantis. Something else occurred through all these events. Four different elements, four forms, merged harmoniously in man. One is present in the physical body, in the Bull-nature; these are the predominating forces that evolved up to the evolutionary period of the Balance. Then we have the Lion-nature in the etheric body; in the astral body, in the predominating forces of the astral, the Eagle- or Vulture-nature; finally, the predominating forces of the Ego, the true Human-nature. In single beings, one or another of these members had the upper hand. Through this the four types arose. But one could meet still other combinations. For example, the physical, astral, and Ego might be equal, while the etheric predominated; that is a particular type of mankind. Then there were beings in whom the etheric, astral, and Ego had the upper hand, while the physical was less developed, so that we have men in whom the higher members prevail over the physical body. Those human beings in whom the physical, astral, and Ego predominated—*are the physical ancestors of the males of today*; while those in whom the etheric, astral, and Ego predominated—*are the physical ancestors of the females of today*. The other types disappeared more and more—*only these two remained and evolved into the male and female forms.*"

Theosophy of the Rosicrucian, Rudolf Steiner, Lecture XII, *Evolution of Mankind on the Earth* Pt. II, Munich, June 4, 1907, GA 99

"Thus, we have reached the period in which we have seen the earlier dual-sexed organism, representing a kind of Group-Soul, divide into a male and a female, so that the similar is reproduced through the female, what is varied and dissimilar through the male. We see in our humanity the feminine to be the principle which still preserves the old conditions of folk and race, and the masculine that which continually breaks through these conditions, splits them up and so individualizes mankind. There is actually active in the human being an ancient feminine principle as Group-Soul and a new masculine principle as Individualizing-Element. It will come about that all connections of race and family stock will cease to exist, men will become more and more different from one another, interconnection will no longer depend on the common blood, but on what binds soul-to-soul. That is the course of human evolution.

"In the first Atlantean races there still existed a strong bond of union and the first sub-races grouped themselves according to their coloring. This Group-Soul element we have still in the races of different color. These differences will increasingly disappear as the Individualizing-Element gains the upper hand. A time will come when there will no longer be races of different color; the difference between the races will have disappeared—*but on the other hand there will be the greatest differences between individuals.* The further we go back into ancient times the more we meet with the encroachment of the racial element—*the true Individualizing-Principle begins as a whole only in later Atlantean times.*"

The Four Human Group-Souls—Lion, Bull, Eagle, Man, Rudolf Steiner, Berlin, October 29, 1908, GA 107

"…Where was the Human-Ego then, in reality? Where was the present Ego? It was not really within man at that time but still in his environment. We can say: *the upper members of man harden through the entry of the Egos.* Because the Ego was outside man, it was still endowed with a quality which later became different. Through entering the physical body, the Ego was enabled to become an Individual-I; whereas before it was still a kind of Group-Soul.

"I will here give a picture of the facts of the case. Imagine a circle of twelve men are sitting somewhere. These twelve men are sitting in a circle. Through evolution as it is today, each of these men has his Ego within himself. Thus twelve Egos are sitting in this circle. Let us consider such a circle of men in the Atlantean

Epoch; then the physical bodies sat thus around, but the Ego is only in the etheric body which is still outside. The Ego is thus to be found in front of each one. This Ego, however, has another characteristic. It is not so centralized. It develops, as it were, its forces and unites with the Egos of the other men so that they form a ring which again sends its forces towards its center. Thus we have here an etheric circular body which forms a unity in itself, and within it, the Egos. Thus there is a circle of physical bodies, and within an etheric circular surface, which forms a unity because the Egos are caught up in it, and the single Ego is enclosed. Through this image we come to a pictorial idea of the Group-Souls.

"If we go further back, then we can keep this image; but we must not imagine such a regular circle of men. For these human beings can be scattered in the world in the most manifold way. Let us imagine one in West France, another in the East of America, etc.—that is to say, not sitting together. Where the laws of the spiritual world are in question the Egos can still be connected, although the human beings are scattered over the world. These human beings form, then, this 'round.' That which is formed through the flowing together of their Egos is not indeed such a beautifully formed etheric body, but still it is a Unity. Thus, a group of people existed at that time, who were united because their Egos formed a unity—and indeed, there were actually four such Group-Egos. You must imagine these human beings in accordance with the laws of the Spiritual World. The Group-Souls of the four groups passed into each other. They were not inwardly united but passed into each other. One calls these four Group-Souls by the names of the apocalyptic beasts: Bull, Eagle, Lion, Man. The Man, however, was at another stage of evolution than the man of today. The names are taken from the organization of the Group-Souls. Why could one call them thus? I should like to make that clear today from another aspect.

"Let us place ourselves as vividly as possible in the early ages of Lemurian life. The souls which today are incarnated in human bodies had not yet descended as far as the physical bodies. They had not yet the tendency to unite themselves with physical matter. Even the bodies which later were to become human bodies were very, very animal-like. The most grotesque physical beings were on Earth, which would even seem grotesque compared with what we should call today the most grotesque creatures. Everything was still in a soft, slippery form—seething, watery, or fiery—human beings, as well as the environment. Among these grotesque forms were already, of course, the ancestors of the human physical bodies; but these were not yet taken possession of by the Egos. The four Group-Souls, whom we have already characterized as four Group-Souls before the entry of the spirit into the physical organization, actually represented four Egos who waited to incarnate—for such Egos as were adapted to quite special forms, which were down there below. One category was adapted to enter the organizations already existing physically, in quite definite shapes, another category to enter another. The forms which were below must correspond in their formation, in a certain way, to the kinds of Egos which waited. There were forms existing which were especially adapted to receive the Lion-Egos, others the Bull-Egos, etc. That was in a very early age of Earth evolution. Now consider that the Group-Soul we have called the Bull-Soul enters quite definite forms which are there below. These have a quite definite appearance. Similarly, the Lion-Soul was drawn to other special forms.

"Thus, what is physical on Earth shows us a fourfold picture. The one group especially develops the organs whose functions

coincide more with those of the heart. They were organized one-
sidedly in the heart nature; an especially aggressive, courageous,
attacking element was in them. They were courageous, self-
assertive, sought to overcome the others—were, as it were, already
conquerors, born as conquering natures even in their form. They
were those in whom the heart, the seat of the Ego, had been made
strong. In others, the organs of digestion, of nourishment, of
procreation, were especially developed. In the third group, it was
especially the organs of movement. In the fourth group, these
tendencies were equally shared—both the courageous, aggressive,
and the tranquil—which comes through the development of the
digestive organs. Both were developed. The group in which the
aggressive quality belonging to the organization of the heart was
specially developed, formed the human beings whose Group-Soul
belonged to the Lion. The second group was that of the Bull. The
third group, with the mobile element that does not wish to know
much of the Earth, belongs to the Group-Soul of the Eagle. They
are the ones who can raise themselves above what is earthly. And
those in whom these things were held in equilibrium belonged to
the Group-Soul *Man*. Thus, we have, in due form, the projection
of the four Group-Souls into the physical. At that time, a quite
peculiar sight would have offered itself to the observer. One
would have found one kind of race, of which someone with a
prophetic gift could have said: Those are physical beings who
remind one somewhat of the lion, who reproduce the character of
the lion, even though they looked different from the lion of today.
They were lion-hearted people, aggressive human germs. Then
again there was a group of bull-like people, everything adapted
to the physical plane. You can easily complete for yourselves
the third and fourth races. The third race was already strongly
visionary. While the first were combative, while the second

cultivated everything connected with the physical plane and working it over, you would have found the third class of people, who were very visionary. As a rule, they had something which, in relation to the other bodies, was misshaped. They would have reminded you of people who have much psychism and believe in visions, and because they do not bother much about the physical, have something dried-up, something stunted compared with the abundant force of the other two groups. They would have reminded you of the bird nature. 'I will hold back my Spirit,' that was the tendency of the Eagle-men. The others had something which, as it were, was mixed out of all the parts. Something else must be added to this.

"If we go so far back as to meet with these conditions on the Earth, then we must also bear in mind that everything that happened in the course of Earth evolution, occurred in such a way that the affairs of the Earth were regulated from out of the spiritual world. Everything was a detour in order to arrive at the man of today. One who could have seen more deeply into these things, could have made the experience that these lion natures (who reminded one of what we see today in quite another way in the lion body) developed a special attractive force for the male forms of the etheric bodies. These felt themselves especially drawn to the Lion-men, so that these were beings who had outwardly a lion body—inwardly, however, a male etheric body. There was a powerful etheric being with a male character, and a small part of this etheric being densified itself to the physical lion body. The Bull-race, however, had a special attractive force for the female etheric body. Thus the bull body had the special force to attract the female etheric body and unite with it. And now think further—the etheric bodies go on continually working, penetrating and transforming. The relation of the lion-like men to the bull-like was especially important in older times. The others come less into consideration. The male etheric bodies which crystallized a physical lion body out of themselves, had the power of fructifying the physical lion body itself, so that the procreation of humanity was especially cared for by the lion-like race. It was a kind of fructification from out of the spiritual, a non-sexual procreation. The bull-race, however, could also bring about the same thing. That which had become physical worked back here on the female etheric body. In the course of evolution, the process fashioned itself differently. Whereas the lion nature retained this mode of procreation, since the fructifying force came from above, out of the spiritual, whereas here this process intensified, the other process was driven more and more back. The bull humanity became more and more unfruitful. The result was that on the one side there was a humanity which was maintained by fructification, on the other side, another half which became more and more unfruitful. The one side became the female sex, the other the male. The modern female physical nature has in fact a male etheric body, whereas the etheric body of the man is female. The physical body of the woman has proceeded from the lion nature; whereas the physical Bull-body is the ancestor of the male body.

"The spiritual in man has a common origin, is neutral, and first entered the physical body when the sexes had already differentiated. Only then was the spirit taken hold of, and only then the head hardened. The etheric body of the head united for the first time with the physical body; it was all the same to it whether it joined on to a male or female body, since both sexes were the same for it.

"We must say that woman, so long as we look away from what in general transcends this differentiation, has, through her evolution, something Lion-like in her nature. The male physical body has that which in the true sense we can call the Bull-nature. You thus see how these Group-Souls have worked together. They so work that the Lion and Bull Group-Souls cooperate in their work. These Divine Beings cooperate and, in the man of today, the labors of the different Divine Group-Souls are concealed.

"These pictures which I have here put before you, in outline, will certainly have their effect. If you follow humanity ever further back, to the time when no procreation was yet possible, then we must say: The external physical female body changes into something which was Lion-like, whereas the male body was Bull-like. Such things, however, must be taken in a holy, earnest sense, if we will understand them aright. It would be easy for those who have studied human anatomy, to deduce the anatomical differences between the physical bodies of man and woman from these Lion- and Bull-natures. Physical science will be utterly fruitless and only describe external facts as long as it does not penetrate into the spirit of these facts. Now it will no longer appear so strange to you that once a race of people existed who had a Lion-like body. These took up the Ego nature, and through this the Lion-nature was changed more and more into the female body. Those who received nothing of this spiritual element changed in quite another way; i.e., into the modern lion, and what is related with it. We will deal another time with the reason why these animals too are bisexual. Those who shared nothing of spirituality formed the modern lion, whereas those who did so developed the modern female body. In the course of time many, many other aspects of these things can be shown. Theosophical learning is not like the mathematical. First it was shown, for instance, that there exist four Group-Souls of which only the names are at first given. Then some or other aspect is chosen, and the matter is illuminated from outside. And so we approach continually from another side. We go around what is first presented, and illuminate it from the most diverse aspects. Whoever grasps this will never be able to say that theosophical matters contradict each other. This is also the case, even in the greatest things we consider. The differences come from the various standpoints from which one observes the matter. Let us take with us from this gathering what one might call inner tolerance. May we succeed in our special theosophical stream in bringing this inner-spirit of tolerance into the theosophical movement. Let us take that with us as a content of feeling and try and work externally in such a way that this spirit of the most inner understanding may become effective."

The Vision of Ezekiel

The *Bible* story of Ezekiel's wheel features a vision of four wheels and four living creatures. This story is predominately found in the first chapter of the *Book of Ezekiel*. God approaches Ezekiel as the divine warrior, riding in his battle chariot. The chariot is drawn by four living creatures, each having four faces (those of a Man, a Lion, an Ox, and an Eagle) and four wings. Beside each 'living creature' is a 'wheel within a wheel,' with 'tall and awesome' rims full of eyes all around. Ezekiel's vision dramatically illustrates the power of God. The wheels were associated with the 'four living creatures' (*Ezekiel* 1:4), who were later described (*Ezekiel* 10:5-20) as cherubim, angelic beings appointed as guardians of the holiness of God.

> "Wherever the spirit would go, they would go, and the wheels would rise along with them, because the spirit of the living creatures was in the wheels. When the creatures moved, they also moved; when the creatures stood still, they also stood still; and when the creatures rose from the ground, the wheels rose along with them, because the spirit of the living creatures was in the wheels." *Ezekiel* 1:20-21

Studying the Biblical description of the Group-Souls of early humans is quite instructive. Ezekiel's vision of the archetypical Group-Souls of humanity is one of the best places to start.

Ezekiel

1 Now it came to pass in the thirtieth year, in the fourth month, in the fifth day of the month, as I was among the captives by the river of Chebar, that the Heavens were opened, and I saw visions of God.

2 In the fifth day of the month, which was the fifth year of king Jehoiachin's captivity,

3 The word of the Lord came expressly unto Ezekiel the priest, the son of Buzi, in the land of the Chaldeans by the river Chebar; and the hand of the Lord was there upon him.

4 And I looked, and, behold, a whirlwind came out of the north, a great cloud, and a fire enfolding itself, and a brightness was about it, and out of the midst thereof as the color of amber, out of the midst of the fire.

5 Also out of the midst thereof came the likeness of four living creatures. And this was their appearance; they had the likeness of a man.

6 And every one had four faces, and every one had four wings.

7 And their feet were straight feet; and the sole of their feet was like the sole of a calf's foot: and they sparkled like the color of burnished brass.

8 And they had the hands of a man under their wings on their four sides; and they four had their faces and their wings.

9 Their wings were joined one to another; they turned not when they went; they went every one straight forward.

10 As for the likeness of their faces, they four had the face of a man, and the face of a lion, on the right side: and they four had the face of an ox on the left side; they four also had the face of an eagle.

11 Thus were their faces: and their wings were stretched upward; two wings of every one were joined one to another, and two covered their bodies.

12 And they went every one straight forward: whither the spirit was to go, they went; and they turned not when they went.

13 As for the likeness of the living creatures, their appearance was like burning coals of fire, and like the appearance of lamps: it went up and down among the living creatures; and the fire was bright, and out of the fire went forth lightning.

14 And the living creatures ran and returned as the appearance of a flash of lightning.

15 Now as I beheld the living creatures, behold one wheel upon the Earth by the living creatures, with his four faces.

16 The appearance of the wheels and their work was like unto the color of a beryl: and they four had one likeness: and their appearance and their work was, as it were, a wheel in the middle of a wheel.

17 When they went, they went upon their four sides: and they turned not when they went.

18 As for their rings, they were so high that they were dreadful; and their rings were full of eyes round about them four.

19 And when the living creatures went, the wheels went by them: and when the living creatures were lifted up from the Earth, the wheels were lifted up.

20 Whithersoever the spirit was to go, they went, thither was their spirit to go; and the wheels were lifted up over against them: for the spirit of the living creature was in the wheels.

21 When those went, these went; and when those stood, these stood; and when those were lifted up from the Earth, the wheels were lifted up over against them: for the spirit of the living creature was in the wheels.

22 And the likeness of the firmament upon the heads of the living creature was as the color of the terrible crystal, stretched forth over their heads above.

23 And under the firmament were their wings straight, the one toward the other: every one had two, which covered on this side, and every one had two, which covered on that side, their bodies.

24 And when they went, I heard the noise of their wings, like the noise of great waters, as the voice of the Almighty, the voice of speech, as the noise of a host: when they stood, they let down their wings.

25 And there was a voice from the firmament that was over their heads, when they stood, and had let down their wings.

26 And above the firmament that was over their heads was the likeness of a throne, as the appearance of a sapphire stone: and upon the likeness of the throne was the likeness as the appearance of a man above upon it.

27 And I saw as the color of amber, as the appearance of fire round about within it, from the appearance of his loins even upward, and from the appearance of his loins even downward, I saw as it were the appearance of fire, and it had brightness round about.

28 As the appearance of the bow that is in the cloud in the day of rain, so was the appearance of the brightness round about. This was the appearance of the likeness of the glory of the Lord. And when I saw it, I fell upon my face, and I heard a voice of one that spake.

The Festivals and Their Meaning, **Rudolf Steiner, Part II,** *Pentecost and the Ascension,* **Lecture I,** *The Whitsun Mystery and its Connection with the Ascension,* **Dornach, May 7, 1923, GA 224**

"In the course of the evolution of mankind, the different world-religions have placed mighty pictures before humanity. If these pictures are to be fully understood a certain esoteric knowledge is required. In the course of years, such a knowledge, based on Anthroposophy, has been applied to the interpretation of all the four *Gospels*, in order that their deeper content and meaning may be brought to light. This content is for the most part in the form of pictures, because pictures refuse to communicate themselves in the narrow, rationalistic way that is possible with concepts and ideas. People think that once a concept has been grasped they have got to the root of everything to which it is relevant. No such opinion is possible in the case of a picture, an imagination. A picture or an imagination works in a living way, like a living being itself. We may have come to know one aspect or another of a living person; but ever and again he will present new aspects to us. We shall not be satisfied, therefore, with definitions purporting to be comprehensive; but we shall endeavor to look for characteristics which contribute to the picture from different angles, giving us increasing knowledge of the person in question."

Imagination, Inspiration, Intuition and the Three Egos

The question of the source and nature of the Human-Ego(s) is one that plagued my years as a Waldorf teacher trainer. Explaining where the Ego ['I'] arises and how it develops requires a cosmology to ground the seemingly timeless and divine nature of the Human-Ego(s) and its future. After teaching Rudolf Steiner's book *Theosophy* to first- and second-year Waldorf student teachers for years, *I finally got brave enough to try and teach the past and future natures of the Three-Egos.* Rudolf Steiner's basic book of spiritual definitions, *Theosophy*, is often overlooked as one of the greatest books in his collected works. *Theosophy* is difficult to understand because translations mix old theosophical terms with Steiner's new anthroposophical terms. It takes a theosophical background to fully appreciate the profound insight Rudolf Steiner presents in this book. Anthroposophy is a marvelous cosmology from which we can shed some light on the question of the Human-Ego(s).

First, we should define what is meant by an Ego, as it seems somewhat undefinable but is the source and goal of all spiritual evolution. According to Steiner, "The Ego is a name for the mysterious force of consciousness that finds itself everywhere that consciousness goes but finds no one place to rest. The Ego ("I Am") is always developing towards the example of the Cosmic-Ego, Christ."

Some other definitions are helpful in this discussion so that we share a common terminology and meaning. In this book, the

'I' is the "I Am" awareness of the wakeful self-consciousness of the human being. We can be awake, dreaming, or in a dreamless sleep condition of consciousness. In this discussion, we focus on the awake person's experience of their "I am." In short, we will use the terms 'I,' 'I-Consciousness,' 'Ego,' and 'Ego-Awareness' as synonymous.

If we paraphrase some of the salient points of Rudolf Steiner's *Theosophy* that address the nature of the Ego, we will be on firm ground to begin to build the temple in which the Ego resides. Normally, what we experience of our I, or Ego, is the total experience of body and soul wherein awakened Ego-Consciousness has its source in the soul. This Ego remains invisible, and we perceive it as our true being while our body and soul seem to be garments. The Ego is difficult to find or define and is held in the deepest part of the individual. Sense perception reveals one world to us, while the Ego can also perceive another world of spirit. The body and soul give themselves over to the Ego to serve its needs on one hand, while the Ego gives itself over to the spirit to serve its needs on the other.

The Ego lives within the body and soul; but the spirit lives within the Ego. What there is of spirit in the Ego is eternal; for the Ego receives its nature and significance from that which it is united.

The Ego dwells in the Consciousness-Soul and radiates outward from there, filling the entire soul and exerting its influence on the body through the soul. Within the Ego, the spirit is alive and actively streaming into the Ego, taking it as its 'garment.' The spirit shapes the Ego from the inside-out and the mineral world shapes it from the outside-in. We call that part of our spirit, the Spirit-Self that shapes the Ego.

The Consciousness-Soul touches the autonomous truth that is independent of all sympathy and antipathy, but the Spirit-Self carries this truth inside itself by taking it up, enclosing it and individualizing it by means of the Ego, thereby incorporating itself into the individual's independent being. Through becoming independent and uniting with the truth, the Ego itself achieves immortality.

The Spirit-Self is a revelation of the Spiritual World within the Ego, just as a sense perception, coming from the other side, is a revelation of the physical world within the Ego. We call the revelation of physical things 'Sensation,' and we call the revelation of spiritual things 'Intuition.' Even a very simple thought already contains intuition because we cannot touch it with our hands or see it with our eyes; we must receive its revelation from the spirit by means of the Ego. As we grow on the path of spiritual self-development, we learn to create 'Intuition-filled thinking.' This Intuition announces itself in its lowest manifestation to the Spirit-Self; what can be called Manas, or Manasic thinking. This is sense-free thinking or supersensible-thinking.

Through Intuitions, the Ego awakening in our soul receives messages from the Spiritual World, just as it receives messages from the physical world through sensations. We take in spiritual substance from our spiritual surroundings and make it our own. This spiritual substance is eternal nourishment for human beings.

The Spiritual World has built the organ of Intuition into the higher parts of the Consciousness-Soul called the Spiritual-Soul. This Spiritual-Soul merges with the Spirit-Self. The Spiritual-Body is capable of unlimited expansion. Through the Spirit-Body, "wings" are grown that give the 'I' mobility in the Spiritual World.

Over the course of spiritual self-development, the Spirit-Self (Manas) transforms the astral body, the Life-Spirit (Budhi) transforms the etheric body, and the Spirit-Human (Atman) transforms the physical body. The Ego can then begin to recognize that its own Ego arises out of what happens to the individual through its biography, what comes from the outside. The body is subject to the laws of heredity; the soul is subject to self-created destiny or karma; and the spirit is subject to the laws of reincarnation or repeated Earth lives.

It must be emphasized above all that this Spiritual World is woven out of the substance that constitutes human thought. When our spiritual senses are awakened, we actually perceive the *thought being* itself, just as our physical eyes perceive a table or chair. We are surrounded and accompanied by thought beings. *Those who have learned to use their spiritual eyes perceive their surroundings as filled with a whole new world of living thoughts or spiritual beings.*

Sense-perceptible things are nothing other than condensed Spirit-Beings. Those who can lift their thoughts to the level of these spirit beings may understand them. Sense-perceptible things originate in the spirit world and are another manifestation of Spirit-Beings. When we formulate thoughts about things, we are inwardly directed away from their sense-perceptible forms and toward their spiritual archetypes. We must imagine this sense-perceptible thing as a condensed Thought-Being.

If we want to set out on the path to higher knowledge, we must practice until we are able to obliterate ourselves and all our prejudices at any moment so that something else can flow into us. Only high levels of selfless devotion enable us to perceive the higher spiritual phenomena all around us.

Truth itself must become sovereign over us, filling our whole being and transforming us into a replica of Spirit-Land's eternal laws. We must imbue ourselves with these eternal laws in order to let them flow out into life. We cannot achieve living in the spirit merely by being beholders of it—*it has to be experienced.*

Initiation is bestowed upon aspirants who become disciples of wisdom through the great spiritual powers guiding humanity. The less we see this initiation as consisting of any outward human relationship, the more accurate the idea we have of it. The disciples of wisdom are able to converse with the spirit itself.

Through these sweeping images of the nature of the Threefold-Ego, we can see outlined a dynamic where the 'Earthly-Ego' comes to birth in the soul realm and merges with the Spirit-Self, creating the Higher-Ego, the reincarnating soul/spirit of the individual. On the other hand, the Christened-Ego that is a replica of Christ and is intimately connected to the Life-Spirit part of the threefold spiritual constitution of the human being (Spirit-Self, Life-Spirit, Spirit-Human) may be found in the realm of the Life-Spirit that is the home of the Christened-Group-Soul of Humanity. This realm is also called Budhi in theosophical terms. It is out of this realm that Christ pours forth the Waters of Life to renew the etheric realms of the Earth and the human etheric body. When the soul is purified and the astral body is tamed, the eternal thoughts gleaned from life by the Consciousness-Soul/Spiritual-Soul are offered as the 'Virgin Sophia' to the Spirit-Self as a Bride of Wisdom, ready for the spiritual wedding of the Higher-Ego/Spirit-Self to the Christened-Self/Life-Spirit.

This merging, or wedding of Higher-Ego to Christened-Ego is depicted in many spiritual traditions with images of weddings, alchemical marriages, sacred unions, and such. The wedding at Cana also had to 'transform' water into wine, an alchemical transubstantiation of earthly substance into spiritual nourishment. The Virgin Soul (Sophia) unites with the Spirit-Self which then can wed the Life-Spirit of Christ, the Christened-Ego. This stage is described clearly in the images from *Theosophy* above.

Most traditions are clear about this aspect of the Higher-Ego uniting with its Spiritual Betrothed/Christened-Ego/World-Ego. But what isn't clear from these remarks is where the Third-Ego, the True-Ego/Zodiacal-Ego, the substance of the Spirit-Human (Atman) can be found or what the process is that brings this about.

Rudolf Steiner indicates in *The Foundations of Anthroposophical Methodology*, Bologna, April, 1911, that: "The epitome of supersensible observation consists of the fact that in the Spiritual World Christ is recognized as the guiding force. The more the soul develops supersensible cognitive powers, the nearer it comes to the Christ Being."

Part of the problem with describing the Third-Ego is the confusion between the First-Ego called the reincarnating Ego (Spirit-Self), the Second-Ego called the Christened-Group-Soul of Humanity (Life-Spirit), and the Third-Ego, the Ego of the Zodiac (Spirit-Human). This third realm of the Spirit-Human, or Atman, is little understood because the conditions of consciousness to perceive this realm lie in future supersensible organs that have yet to be developed. To live in this realm, the initiate would know Sophia (Anthroposophia) as an ever-present companion on the spiritual path leading directly to union with the Holy Spirit, Christ, and the Father-Ground-of-Being; the ultimate completion of the trinity of human Spiritual-Egos. Each individual takes on a part of the Etheric Christ to exist in these higher spiritual realms. Initiates may use all Three-Egos at this time in history if they are in constant resonance with the Spirit-Self, Life-Spirit, and Spirit-Human realms of humanity's future spiritual development; the realms of Angels, Archangels, and Archai. Moral Imaginations, Moral Inspirations, and Moral Intuitions live in these realms where divine mercy and grace is bestowed on the initiate who can visit these angelic kingdoms of consciousness and return with spiritual nourishment.

We illuminate the stages of the Three-Egos as we describe the three stages of initiation that must be traversed to ascend through the realms of Spirit-Self, Life-Spirit, and Spirit-Human. The stages of Imagination, Inspiration, and Intuition are transformed from the higher thinking, feeling, and willing of the initiate. Each realm transforms and redeems a complementary realm of the astral (thinking), etheric (feeling), and physical (willing). The human body is a Temple of Wisdom wherein the spiritual nature of the Ego comes to birth. Using these bodies (astral, etheric, physical) as tools of initiation can free and release spiritual beings who have been 'enchanted' into material substances that create the world we encounter through sense perception. As we evolve into these higher worlds using our various bodies as spiritual tools for supersensible perception, we are participating in a process of transubstantiation that returns matter to its source of existence within the world of spirit.

To spiritually develop through the stages of initiation, the aspirant must first understand that earth-bound intellectual thinking is limited to the physical body's sense-bound perception and cannot produce the living thoughts necessary to reach the etheric realm. Living thinking can lead to 'thinking about thinking'; wherein the very process of thinking itself becomes the focus of perception. This can lead to metamorphic and morphological thinking that examines, through direct perception of a phenomena, the processes of growth and decay in the outside world's stream-of-time that lead to the 'invisible' worlds of forces and 'beings.' Observing how one seed can grow to leaf, stem, blossom and then eventually to many seeds and subsequently begin the cycle again—*leads to a living thinking that is mobile and not subject to decay and entropy*. Morphological thinking 'witnesses' the invisible levity and life that causes 'form' to metamorphose into the next stage of life—*within higher 'forms'*—as a conscious living process raying into matter from the worlds of spirit that are the source of life. Image becomes sound as we grow from Imagination to Inspiration, from 'thinking about thinking' to feeling and knowing the wisdom of the cyclic processes of life manifesting from the invisible worlds of spirit. Sound becomes the 'Word' (the Language of Spirit) in the next stage of initiation and those 'Words' become Moral Intuitions given by the Archai from the realm of Spirit-Human (Atman). Thus, the Third-Ego manifests the will of the divine through Moral Intuition and the human being evolving through the realms of Angels and Archangels, and into the realm of the Archai (Spirits of Time).

Beyond normal thinking is an exceptional state of thinking, a spiritual thinking that is an experiential contemplation of thinking. When this is achieved, thinking births an inner-life that is real and connected to the Spiritual World. Once a regulated and harmonious thought organism is developed in the soul, the deeper powers of thinking can be consciously directed, observed, and understood. Sense perception and 'true thinking' become one as the subject and object coincide in the experience of perception. Deep powers of thinking arise that must be examined and studied when 'thinking about thinking' starts to produce results. Finally, the ability arises that the initiate can control thinking and perception to the point that it can go outside of the human body in full consciousness and grasp the

'Real-Ego' that lives and weaves outside of the human body. It is this independent thinking that can then go into the Spiritual World and use supersensible organs to commune with the divine.

Let's take a look at what these three realms of the Spiritual World, or the three steps of initiation, might look like to the developing aspirant.

Stage One: Imagination

The first stage of initiation is called Imagination, and it involves the Consciousness-Soul merging with the Spirit-Self to embody the reincarnating Human-Ego. During this stage we feel our Ego outside of our physical body in the world, as if it is coming at us. The Ego that we generally experience, we will call the everyday Ego, or Earthly-Ego, in contradistinction to the Higher-Ego and the World-Ego/Christened-Ego. The Earthly-Ego is a mirror image of the Higher-Ego. This Higher-Ego was donated to us before 'creation' began. The creation of new Egos throughout the evolution of a solar system is the original intent of creation, a certain type of 'creation out of nothingness.' Christ has donated all Three-Egos and is intimately connected to the progress and evolution of them.

During the Old Moon incarnation of the Earth, objective perception of thought as a living being appeared in the astral body through pictures, signs, and symbols. Human beings were not confused into believing that their thoughts were their own property or that they had created the thoughts out of their own capacities of thinking. Only in our times are thoughts considered to 'belong' to the thinker. This illusion of thinking as 'personal' and the 'product of human effort' has led to the development of a false Egohood filled with pride and evil in the realm of thinking.

Sense perception is observation of things that are essentially made from thoughts. Things are thoughts slowed down as an illusion of solid matter so that humans could have a realm of isolation in which to be born as 'new thinkers.' Transforming sense perception into food for the gods is the intent of the Spiritual World being acted out through human evolution. Through enlivened thinking called Moral Imagination. Higher thinking can be born by finding eternal truths that are objective, even in the outside-world of seeming illusion. These thoughts can rise into the realm of Moral Imagination, called the Manasic realm or the realm of Spirit-Self. These eternal truths are objective and have a basis of reality in both the physical and Spiritual Worlds.

The personal, everyday Ego can be found in the interaction between the seeming center of consciousness inside the human being and the picture of that human being coming to him from the outside-world. For example, it takes another to reflect to us who we are. Our actions in the world and the response of the world to those actions tell us much about our Ego. We see ourselves through others and find our Ego coming to us as our destiny and karma. This 'self-knowing' is the first step in understanding the Higher-Ego.

Imagination is the first step of initiation that begins with transforming 'thinking about thinking' into a force of self-knowing. Studying the same processes of thinking that have produced the outer-world's laws of nature tunes us into the true nature of the Ego inside of us and outside of us.

For readers who require a foundation of these concepts from Rudolf Steiner's own words, please review the selections below.

The Festivals and Their Meaning, Rudolf Steiner, Part II, *Ascension and Pentecost,* Lecture IV, *The Whitsun: A Symbol of the Immortality of the Ego,* Berlin, June 6, 1916, GA 169

"It would then be realized that the purpose of instituting the Christmas and Easter festivals was to provide man with tokens of remembrance that he is connected with spiritual nature, with that nature that brings death to the physical, and to provide him with tokens reminding him that in his etheric body and astral body he is himself a bearer of the spiritual.—In our days these things have been forgotten. They will come to light again when humanity has the will to acquire understanding of spiritual truths such as these.

"But now, besides the etheric body and the astral body, we bear within us as that which is supremely spiritual, our Ego ['I']. We know something of the complex nature of the Ego. We know especially that it is the Ego which passes from incarnation to incarnation, that the inner forces of the Ego build themselves up and shape themselves to that form which we carry forward into our being in each new incarnation. In the Ego we rise again from death to prepare for a new incarnation. It is by virtue of the Ego that we are individuals. If we can say that the etheric body represents in a certain sense that which is akin to birth and is connected with the elemental forces of nature, that the astral body symbolizes the death-bringing principle that is connected with the higher spirituality, so we can say that the Ego represents our continual rising again in the spirit, our resurrection into the spiritual realm which is neither nature nor the world of stars; but pervades them all. And just as the Christmas festival can be connected with the etheric body and the Easter festival with the astral body, so the Whitsun festival can be connected with the Ego. This is the festival which, representing the immortality of the Ego, is a token of the fact that we, as men, do not share only in the universal life of nature, do not merely undergo death—*but that we are individual immortal beings, rising ever and again from death*."

The Christmas Thought and the Secret of the Ego, Rudolf Steiner, Dornach, December 19, 1915, GA 165

"...If the Mystery of Golgotha continues to live on in the human soul through earthly existence—amid what is connected with this

Mystery of Golgotha in the Christmas mystery—it can serve as an impulse resounding in the soul. Fichte is a perfect example of how, when this is the case, a path is opened on which we can find the consciousness in which our own 'I' flows together with the Earth 'I'—for this Earth 'I' is the Christ. Through this, we develop something in the human being that must become greater and greater if the Earth is to move toward the development for which it was destined from the beginning."

The Being of Man and His Future Evolution, **Rudolf Steiner, Lecture XVIII,** *The Manifestation of the Ego in the Different Races of Men*, **Berlin, May 3, 1909, GA 107**

"What we need is an Ego that keeps itself mobile, neither losing itself in external physical observation or in external physical experience, nor remaining stationary at one point, but really advancing in spiritual development. That is why the great masters of wisdom and of harmony of the perceptions have not been telling us all the time in the theosophical movement that we should let the divine man within us speak; on the contrary they have given us quite specific impulses for finding the wisdom of the world in all its different aspects. And we are not pupils of the great masters by only wanting to let the God within us speak, or by imagining that each individual carries his own master within himself, but by wanting to get to know the structure of the world in all its aspects. Anthroposophical development is a striving to know all the subtle aspects of cosmic happenings. We attain our Higher-Ego by evolving upwards from stage-to-stage. Our Ego is there outside, manifest in the wonders of the world. For we are born out of the world and want to live our way back into it."

The Contents of Esoteric Classes Esoteric Lessons, **Part III,**
Rudolf Steiner, Stuttgart, May 18, 1913, GA 266/3

"If an esoteric wants to make progress he should make certain
things increasingly clear to himself meditatively. For example,
just as the lungs breathe in air, so the physical and etheric
bodies inhale the spirit on awaking in the morning. Our
materialistic age only wants to accept what's perceived through
the senses; but just as it denies the spirit someone could deny
the existence of air, because it's perceived by a finer sensibility.
An esoteric should become accustomed to look upon outer
happenings as only letters or signs of a world word. For instance
an esoteric wouldn't ask whether the 'b' in 'about' is the effect of
the 'a'; for he knows that this sequence of letters is necessary to
form the word. So an esoteric should ask less about cause and
effect; but should say that things and events are necessary to
form world words.

"An exoteric is all too inclined to look at things only from
the viewpoint of sympathy and antipathy. He readily accepts and
notices what pleases him, and he ignores other things if possible.
A form of mental disease that's sometimes observed is that an
otherwise normal person suddenly travels from one place to
another and finally seems to wake up; but he can't remember what
happened while he was travelling. If one investigates the past of
such a sick person occultly one can find that he passed by many
things in the world with great indifference and thereby weakened
his Ego a great deal. It's a weakening, almost like an occasional
loss of the Ego.

"Theosophists also often tend to turn away from the outer-
world. But a loving interest in our surroundings is absolutely

necessary if one wants to make progress. One doesn't have to neglect what one is striving for theosophically thereby.

"So the Ego grasps itself in memory, and high beings gave us the Ego and memory. The Ego that grasps itself in memory is like a letter that an esoteric must learn and that the Gods have written into world space. The high beings who gave the Ego have their seat on the Sun; they give us what goes from incarnation to incarnation. We got our physical body from forces that work down through the incarnations, and these forces work on us from the circle that's described by the Moon's orbit. What goes from one generation to the next like this is like a second letter. We can draw this schematically. We draw the Ego that becomes conscious through memory as the Earth or a point, and around it the Moon's orbit as a circle. If the Moon would be moved to another place by some force, what would result for the Earth thereby? The reproductive forces working through the generations would dry up. Men would no longer reproduce and would die out. So a real esoteric must look up to the beings who work on him through Moon forces from outside full of reverential thanks and must tell himself that he owes his development through the generations to them. Mankind will have reached the end of its physical evolution when the Moon is attracted by the Earth's forces so much that it goes into it, as is supposed to happen later. We receive the forces that strengthen our Ego from the Sun, and we shouldn't just stare at the Sun but should let these ideas arise in us: You marvelous world body, it was through you, through your Sun-grace forces that I received my Ego and all the forces that are connected with it. I thank you in shy reverence.—We can draw the Sun forces as another circle.

Man, Offspring of the World of Stars, **Rudolf Steiner, Stuttgart, May 5, 1921, GA 204**

"We take earthly life today as the basis of our ideas and concepts and build up a conception of the Universe in line with the conditions of this earthly life. But the picture of the Universe thus arising has been evolved by simply transferring earthly conditions to the world beyond the Earth. By means of spectro-analysis and other methods—admirable as they are in their way—a conception of the Sun has grown up which is really modelled wholly upon earthly conditions. Everyone is familiar with the appearance of luminous, incandescent gas, and this picture is then transferred to the Sun in the heavens. But we must learn to think of the Sun in the light of Spiritual Science. The Sun which the physicist believes to be a luminous body of gas out in cosmic space is spiritual through and through. The Sun receives the cosmic light and radiates it to the Earth—*but the Sun is not physical at all*. It is spiritual in its whole nature and being. The Greek was right when he felt that the Sun was connected with the development of his Ego, for the development of the Ego is associated with the intelligence and the faculty of forming ideas. The Greek conceived the rays of the Sun to be the power which kindled and quickened his Ego. His was still aware of the spirituality of the Cosmos, and to him the Sun was a living being, related to the Human-Ego in an absolutely concrete way. When a man says 'I' to himself, he experiences a force that is working within him, and the Greek, as he felt the working of this inner force, related it to the Sun. The Greek said to himself: Sun and Ego are the outer and inner aspects of one and the same being. The Sun out there in space is the *Cosmic* Ego. What lives within me is the *Human-Ego*.

"As a matter of fact, this experience still comes to those who have a deeper feeling for Nature. The experience is not nearly

as vivid as it was in the days of Greece; but for all that it is still
possible to become aware of the spiritual forces indwelling
the rays of the Sun in springtime. There are people here and
there who feel that the Ego is imbued with a new vigor when
the rays of the Sun begin to shine down upon the Earth with
greater strength. But this is a last faint echo, an outward shell
of an experience that is dying out altogether in the abstract,
shadowy intellectualism prevalent in every branch of civilized
life today. The task before us is to begin once again to realize
and understand the connection of the being of man with super-
earthly existence.

"If we study and compare many things that are to be found
in anthroposophical literature, we shall be able to understand
the way in which the Sun is related to the Ego, and we shall also
realize that the forces which stream down to the Earth from
the Sun and from the Moon are entirely different in character
and function. In a certain respect, Sun and Moon stand in polar
antithesis. The forces streaming from the Sun enable the human
being to become the bearer of an Ego. We owe to the rays of the
Sun the power which molds the human form into an image of the
Ego. The forces which determine the human form from outside,
even during the period of embryonic life, are the active forces of
the Sun. While the embryo is developing in the mother's body,
a great deal more is happening than modern science dreams of.
Modern science is of the opinion that the forces all originate
from the fertilized germ, but the truth is that the human embryo
merely rests there in the body of the mother and is given form by
the Sun forces. These Sun forces are, of course, associated with the
Moon forces which are also working but in a different way. The
Moon forces work above all in the inner, metabolic processes. We
may therefore say: the Sun forces give form to the human being

from outside. The Moon forces radiate outwards from within the metabolic process; they are centrifugal forces. This does not contradict the fact that these Moon forces are working, for instance, in the shaping and molding of the human countenance. The Moon forces stream out from a center in the metabolic system and work as it were by attraction upon the forming of the human face, differentiating the features; but there is an interplay between these Moon forces and the Sun forces. The organism that is connected with procreation is subject to the Sun forces. The whole being of man is involved in this way in the interplay between the forces of the Sun and the forces of the Moon."

The Gospel of St. John, **Rudolf Steiner, Lecture V, Basel, November 20th, 1907**

"Through the work of the Ego upon the astral body the latter is transformed into Spirit-Self. But this takes place step by step, through the Sentient-Soul being developed first, then the Intellectual-Soul, and finally the Spiritual-Soul; then the Spirit-Self pours into the purified and mature Spiritual-Soul [Consciousness-Soul]. In the same way the Ego works upon the etheric body, and the impulses which are most effective in this case are the influences of art, religion and occult training."

Stage Two: Inspiration

The second stage of initiation is called Inspiration. This stage happens when the Spirit-Self (Manas) merges with the Life-Spirit (Budhi). The realm of Life-Spirit is the Archangelic realm where Christ reigns supreme through creating an atmosphere of redeemed etheric life-force that nourishes the Life-Spirit and helps the Higher-Ego/Spirit-Self wed the Christened-Ego (World-Ego/Life-Spirit). This is often depicted as the Virgin Sophia being a bride who is wedding the Lamb of God, Christ the bridegroom. This Heavenly marriage is found in many religions and spiritual practices. It is accomplished by emptying our being so that spirit can flow into the prepared sacred space made for the 'Christ in me.'

On the path to the Second-Ego, we develop the Christened-Ego through the etheric body transforming the experience of Moral Inspiration, hearing the Music of the Spheres, into the substance of Life-Spirit. To reach this level of initiation, the initiate must extinguish the pictures that were so abundant in the first stage of Moral Imagination/Spirit-Self. One must push past the images to the experience of the inner-activity behind thought processes, the Beings who create thought. No sense perception is allowed into this realm, only sense-free, higher-order feeling and spiritual harmonies. New supersensible organs of perception must be developed to perceive and understand these realms. It is there that the Higher-Ego/Spirit-Self can unite with the Christened-Ego/Life-Spirit and join the Christened-Group-Soul of Humanity. This creates the spiritual anointing of the Christened-Ego/World-Ego/Life-Spirit that unites with the Higher-Ego/Spirit-Self. The etheric blood donated by Christ to create the Earthly-Ego can create the ascending energy to the pineal gland through the earthly and cosmic nutrition stream, which at this stage can witness New Jerusalem descending as the Temple of Wisdom or the Grail Castle.

In the second stage of initiation, Moral Inspiration/Life-Spirit, the initiate's Higher-Ego/Spirit-Self becomes the 'Not I but Christ in me' and takes on the Life-Spirit/Christened-Ego in the realm of the Archangels as the human etheric body is spiritualized. In the first stage of initiation, the Moral Imagination/Spirit-Self develops the Higher-Ego through a process called the 'etherization of the blood' and is a type of spiritual communion which nourishes the Spiritual World and the initiate. The etherization of the blood creates direct contact with the Higher-Ego, or Higher-Self, as it is commonly referred to.

The experience of the Higher-Ego comes from the outside world and is experienced in the inner-soul-world; in a sense, raying in from the outside towards the inside. Your Higher-Ego is developed by your spiritual practice, but the substance of the Christened-Ego/Life-Spirit is taken from the common substance provided by Christ to all Higher-Egos ready to participate in the Resurrection-Body of Christ. This is why the Christened-Ego/World-Ego is called the Christened-Group-Soul of Humanity. The individual's second Spiritual-Ego becomes one with the World-Ego of Christ, through the agency of Higher-Beings raying into man in service to Christ.

The Earthly-Ego is realized through the outside world coming at you; whereas your Higher-Ego is witnessed from the outside world looking towards you. The perspective changes from a dynamic of outward raying in, to one of outward witnessing. One is a type of 'being beheld,' whereas the other is one of 'beholding.' There is a distinct sense of 'selflessness' that comes with the Higher-Ego that is quite different from the Earthly-Ego and the perspective changes radically.

The Threshold of the Spiritual World, Rudolf Steiner, XIV, Concerning Man's Real-Ego, GA 17

"When the soul experiences itself in its astral body and has living thought-beings as its environment, it knows itself to be outside both the physical and etheric bodies. But it also feels that its thinking, feeling, and willing belong but to a limited sphere of the universe; whereas in virtue of its own original nature it should embrace much more than is allotted to it in that sphere. The soul that has become clairvoyant may say to itself within the spiritual world:—

'In the physical world I am confined to what my physical body allows me to observe; in the elemental world I am limited by my etheric body; in the spiritual world I am restricted by finding myself, as it were, upon an island in the Universe and by feeling my spiritual existence bounded by the shores of that island. Beyond them is a world which I should be able to perceive if I were to work my way through the veil which is woven before the eyes of my spirit by the actions of living thought-beings.'

"Now the soul is indeed able to work its way through this veil, if it continues to develop further and further the faculty of self-surrender which is already necessary for its life in the elemental world. It is under the necessity of still further strengthening the forces which accrue to it from experience in the physical world, in order to be guarded in supersensible worlds from having its consciousness deadened, clouded, or even annihilated. In the physical world the soul, in order to experience thoughts within itself, has need only of the strength naturally allotted to it apart from its own inner-work. In the elemental world, thoughts which immediately on arising fall into oblivion, are softened down to dreamlike experience; i.e., *do not come into the consciousness at all, unless the soul, before entering this world, has worked on the strengthening of its inner-life.* For this purpose it must specially strengthen the will-power; for in the elemental world a thought is no longer merely a thought—*it has an inner-activity, or life of its own.* It has to be held fast by the will if it is not to leave the circle of the consciousness. *For in the spiritual world thoughts are completely independent living beings.* If they are to remain in the consciousness, the soul must be so strengthened that it develops within itself and of itself the force which the physical body develops for it in the physical world, and which in the elemental world is developed by the sympathies and antipathies of the etheric body. *It must forgo all this assistance in the spiritual world.*

For there the experiences of the physical world and the elemental world are only present to the soul as memories—*and the soul itself is beyond those two worlds.* Around it is the spiritual world. This world at first makes no impression upon the astral body. The soul has to learn to live by itself on its own memories. The content of its consciousness is at first merely this:— 'I have existed, and now I am confronting nothingness.'

"But when the memories come from such soul-experiences as are not merely reproductions of physical or elemental occurrences; but represent free thought-experiences induced by those occurrences, there begins in the soul an exchange of thought between the memories and the supposed nothingness of the spiritual environment. And that which arises as the result of that intercourse becomes a world of conceptions in the consciousness of the astral body. The strength which is needful for the soul at this point of its development is such as will make it capable of standing on the shore of the only world hitherto known to it— *and of enduring the facing of supposed nothingness.* This supposed nothingness is at first an absolutely real nothingness to the soul. Yet the soul still has, so to speak, behind it the world of its memories. It can, as it were, take a firm grip of them. *It can live in them.* And the more it lives in them, the more it strengthens the forces of the astral body. With this strengthening begins the intercourse between its past existence and the beings of the spiritual world. During this intercourse the soul learns to feel itself as an astral being. To use an expression in keeping with ancient traditions, we may say:— 'The human soul experiences itself as an astral being within the Cosmic-Word.'

"By the Cosmic-Word are here meant the thought-deeds of living thought-beings, which are enacted in the spiritual world like a living discourse of spirits; but in such a way that the discourse exactly corresponds in the spiritual world to deeds in the physical world.

"If the soul now wishes to step over into the super-spiritual world, it must efface, by its own will, its memories of the physical and elemental worlds. It can only do this when it has gained the certainty, from the spirit discourse, that it will not wholly lose its existence if it effaces everything in itself which so far the consciousness of that existence has given it. The soul must actually place itself at the edge of a Spiritual Abyss—*and there make an act of will to forget its willing, feeling, and thinking.* It must consciously renounce its past. The resolution that has to be taken at this point may be called a bringing about of complete sleep of the consciousness by one's own will, not by conditions of the physical or etheric body. Only this resolution must not be thought of as having for its object a return, after an interval of unconsciousness, to the same consciousness that was previously there; but as if that consciousness, by means of the resolution, really plunges into forgetfulness by its own act of will. It must be borne in mind that this process is not possible in either the physical or the elemental world—*but only in the spiritual world.* In the physical world the annihilation which appears as death is possible—*in the elemental world there is no death.* Man, insofar as he belongs to the elemental world—*cannot die; he can only be transformed into another being.* In the spiritual world, however, no positive transformation, in the strict sense of the word, is possible; for into whatever a human being may change, his past experience is revealed in the spiritual world as his own conscious existence. If this memory existence is to disappear within the spiritual world, it must be because the soul itself—*by an act of will*—has caused it to sink into oblivion. Clairvoyant consciousness is able to perform such an act of will when it has won the necessary inner-

strength. If it arrives at this, there emerges from the forgetfulness
it has itself brought about—*the real nature of the Ego.* The super-
spiritual environment gives the human soul the knowledge of
that Real-Ego [True-I]. Just as clairvoyant consciousness can
experience itself in the etheric and astral bodies, so too can it
experience itself in the Real-Ego.

"This Real-Ego is not created by clairvoyance—*it exists in the
depths of every human soul.* Clairvoyant consciousness simply
experiences consciously a fact appertaining to the nature of every
human soul, of which it is not conscious.

"After physical death man gradually lives himself into his
spiritual environment. At first his being emerges into it with
memories of the physical world. Then, although he has not
the assistance of his physical body, he can nevertheless live
consciously in those memories, because the living thought-
beings corresponding to them incorporate themselves into the
memories, so that the latter no longer have the merely shadowy
existence peculiar to them in the physical world. And at a definite
point-of-time between death and rebirth, the living thought-
beings of the spiritual environment exert such a strong influence
that—*without any act of will*—the oblivion which has been
described is brought about. *And at that moment life emerges in
the Real-Ego.* Clairvoyant consciousness, by strengthening the life
of the soul, brings about as a free action of the spirit that which
is, so to speak, a natural occurrence between death and rebirth.
Nevertheless, memory of previous Earth-lives can never arise
within physical experience—*unless the thoughts have, during
those Earth-lives, been directed to the spiritual world.* It is always
necessary first to have known of a thing in order that a clearly
recognizable remembrance of it may arise later. Therefore we
must, during one Earth-life, gain knowledge of ourselves as

spiritual beings if we are to be justified in expecting that in our next earthly existence we shall be able to remember a former one.

"Yet this knowledge need not necessarily be gained through clairvoyance. When a person acquires a direct knowledge of the spiritual world through clairvoyance, there may arise in his soul, during the Earth-lives following the one in which he gained that knowledge, a memory of the former one, in the same way in which the memory of a personal experience presents itself in physical existence. In the case, however, of one who penetrates into Spiritual Science with true comprehension—*although without clairvoyance*—the memory will occur in such a form that it may be compared with the remembrance in physical existence of an event of which he has only heard a description."

The Threshold of the Spiritual World, **Rudolf Steiner, XV,** *Summary of Part of the Foregoing,* **GA 17**

"Man bears within him a Real-Ego [True-I], which belongs to a super-Spiritual World. In the physical world this Real-Ego is, as it were, concealed by the experiences of thinking, feeling, and willing. Even in the Spiritual World man only becomes aware of his Real-Ego when he effaces in himself the memories of everything which he is able to experience through his thinking, feeling, and willing. The knowledge of the Real-Ego emerges out of forgetfulness of what is experienced in the physical world, the elemental world, and the Spiritual World."

Cosmic Ego and Human-Ego, **Rudolf Steiner, January 9, 1912, Munich, GA 130**

"For this Christ evolution it was normal to bring to Ego-perfection, outside the Earth, an Ego of a Macrocosmic sort, and then to descend to Earth. And so, for the evolution of the Christ Being it was normal, when He descended from the Macrocosm to our Earth, to bring into it the great impulse of the Macrocosmic-Ego, in order that the Microcosmic-Ego, the Human-Ego, might take up this impulse, and be able to go forward in its evolution. It was normal for the Christ to have the Macrocosmic-Ego-impulse—*not the Microcosmic Ego-impulse*—just as much evolved as man upon the Earth had developed the Microcosmic. Thus, the Christ Being is a Being Who in a certain sense is like the human being, only that man is *Microcosmic* and has brought his four principles to expression Microcosmically, and hence has his Ego also Microcosmically as Earth-Ego—but the Christ as Cosmic-Ego [Macrocosmic-I]. His evolution was such that He was great and significant because of the perfect development of this Ego [I], which He brought down to Earth. And He had not the fifth Macrocosmic principle [Spirit-Self; Manas], and not the sixth [Life-Spirit; Budhi]; for He will evolve these on Jupiter and on Venus, in order that He may give them to man."

Stage Three: Intuition

The third stage of initiation is called Moral Intuition wherein the Christened-Ego/World-Ego streams in from the Archangelic realm of the Life-Spirit (which Christ will fully manifest in the Future Venus Planetary Condition) and becomes one with all other Christened beings in the Cosmic-Ego/Zodiacal-Ego [Macrocosmic-I] of Christ which will fully manifest in the Archai realm of the Spirit-Human (Atman) in the Future Vulcan Planetary Condition. This Cosmic-Ego/Zodiacal-Ego of Christ is the Third-Ego, the True-Ego. Again, this True-Ego is found outside of the human body (on the Sun during the Future Vulcan Planetary Incarnation) and is found only when, through personal effort, the Earthly-Ego, Higher-Ego, and World-Ego are extinguished. All of the effort to develop the different Egos and become selfless and Christ-like must then be voluntarily surrendered and annihilated until nothing of the self remains. This embodiment of the True-Ego (Macrocosmic-I of Christ) fills the hollow sacred space surrendered for the reception of this Being within the human heart. The awareness of this 'presence' fills the prepared space with a spherical temple called a 'Zodiac.'

When we can empty ourselves and go beyond sense perception, beyond perception of thoughts as beings, beyond the extinguishing of our Egos, we are then ready to be filled by the Zodiacal-Ego of Christ [Macrocosmic-I] and become a sphere of stars (Zodiac) that can become co-creative through Christ with the Holy Trinity to give birth to a new Zodiac of beings who will, in time, come to their birth out of nothingness and ultimately develop as new Ego-beings on the path to ascension.

The stage of Moral Intuition/Spirit-Human is one wherein the will of the initiate becomes united with the will of Christ. There is nothing of the physical world in this realm and human cognition cannot comprehend it. It was from this realm of Spirit-Human (Atman) that the Earthly-Ego was designed. It is to this realm that the Ego ['I'] eventually returns; but now as a creator similar to his own maker—'in the image and likeness of god.' The mirroring of the True-Ego (Macrocosmic-I of Christ) within the human Earthly-Ego is the basis of Ego consciousness in the physical realm which can become self-consciousness and develop higher consciousness that can align with the Macrocosmic-I of Christ.

There is no time or space as we know it in the Spiritual World; so therefore, the Earthly-Ego and the True-Ego are one and the same, simply divided by time, space, and consciousness. This type of hyper-connectivity through time and space constitutes the ultimate path of human self-development from birth (creation) through ascension back into Heaven. Christ is the perfect example, model, and archetype of what the 'I' must go through in its entire evolution from the descent from Heaven to Earth to the ascent from Earth to Heaven—the story of the 'prodigal son.'

There is much confusion in spiritual circles about the Higher-Ego, Christened-Ego, and the True-Ego; the comprehensive Threefold-Ego. The True-Ego is the Cosmic-Ego which we are all on a path to gain or recover through grace, love, and mercy. The path to supersensible knowledge proceeds from Earthly-Ego to Higher-Ego to Christened-Ego to True-Ego. Christ is the living, eternal archetype of the Human-Ego whose only 'true' name is 'I Am.' The human being is developing upward from below while Christ is descending from above offering the true "I Am" to His children on Earth. Christ is the model and the goal as we make the journey to our own three spiritual Egos that is filled with challenges. We need unlimited trust in Christ and the Spiritual World to bridge the chasm over the abyss between the physical and Spiritual Worlds. We need the loving arms of Christ to catch us if we fall into the abyss. Only complete trust in Christ can see us beyond the abyss. Or, as Rudolf Steiner says in *Theosophy*: "In order to approach the abyss as nothing, it is necessary that one trusts that the True-Ego will be brought to one out of the Spiritual World."

To know that the True-Ego will be brought to us from beyond the abyss is the greatest of comforts and only arises through our faith in the grace and mercy of the Spiritual World. Then, once one meets Christ, the Cosmic Ego, man ascends to his True-Ego and no longer experiences Christ outside of oneself but within. This is the culmination of the stage of Moral Intuition. 'Not I, but the Christ in me.'

The True-Ego remains in the Spiritual World and can only be found there and cannot fully come into the physical world except through the spiritual impulses that are received as *Moral Intuitions*. The Earthly-Ego works through sense perception to find itself in the outer-world. The Higher-Ego is the gift of Christ from the outer-world alighting in us. The Christened-Ego joins us with all other Christened humans and with Christ personally. The True-Ego is a merciful gift of Christ from Heaven at the edge of the Abyss that was donated through the agency of Christ's Resurrection-Body; and thereby, along with Christ's Ascension will carry all true believers upwards into Heaven. The True-Ego can develop supersensible perception of the Spiritual Worlds through Moral Intuitions and the supersensible gift of Moral Technique that unites with the efforts of Christ and the Holy Trinity.

It is often the case that Western esotericists' tend towards a greater focus on the development of the Higher-Ego/Spirit-Self; whereas Eastern esotericists' often focus on the True-Ego/Spirit-Human, the heavenly Ego that is not tied in any way to material things. A balanced path of the development of the Three-Spiritual-Egos would include the use of a synthesis of both the sensible and supersensible to develop all Three-Egos based upon the living example of Christ's deeds.

The Threshold of the Spiritual World, **Rudolf Steiner, IX,** *Concerning the Ego-Feeling and the Human Soul's Capacity for Love; and the Relation of these to the Elemental World,* **GA 17**

"The experiences of consciousness that is becoming clairvoyant, manifest special peculiarities with regard to what has just been stated. Whereas the Ego-feeling—necessary as it is for experience in supersensible worlds—is easily deadened, and often behaves like a weak, fading thought in the memory—feelings of hatred and lovelessness, and immoral impulses become intense experiences immediately after entering the supersensible world. They appear before the soul like reproaches come to life, and become terribly real pictures. In order not to be tormented by them, clairvoyant consciousness often has recourse to the expedient of looking about for spiritual forces which weaken the impressions of these pictures. But by doing so the soul steeps itself in these forces, which have an injurious effect on the newly-won clairvoyance. *They drive it out of the good regions of the spiritual world—and towards the bad ones.*

"On the other hand—*true love and real kindness of heart are experiences of the soul which strengthen the forces of consciousness in the way necessary for acquiring clairvoyance.* When it is said that the soul needs preparation before it is able to have experiences in the supersensible world, it should be added that one of the many means of preparation is the capacity for true love, and the disposition towards genuine human kindness and fellow-feeling.

"An over-developed Ego-feeling in the physical world works against morality. An ego-feeling too feebly developed causes the soul, around which the storms of elemental sympathies and antipathies are actually playing, to be lacking in inner firmness and stability. These qualities can only exist when a sufficiently strong Ego-feeling is working out of the experiences of the physical world upon the etheric body; which of course remains unknown in ordinary life. But in order to develop a really moral temper of mind it is necessary that the Ego-feeling, though it must exist, should be moderated by feelings of good-fellowship, sympathy, and love."

The Gospel of St. John, Rudolf Steiner, Lecture V, Basel, November 20, 1907, GA 100

"*The Gospel of St. John* is a book of life. No one who has merely enquired into it with his intellect has understood this book; he alone who has experienced it really knows it. If a man meditates upon the first fourteen verses day-after-day for some time, he will discover the purpose of these words. They are really words which, when one meditates upon them, awaken in the Human-Soul the capacity to see the various parts of the *Gospel*, such as the marriage at Cana in chapter two, the conversation with Nicodemus in chapter three, as one's own experiences in the great astral tableau. Through these exercises clairvoyance develops in the human being and he can then experience for himself the truth of what is written in *St. John's Gospel*. Hundreds have experienced this. The writer of *St. John's Gospel* was a great Seer who was initiated by Christ Himself.

"The disciple 'John' is never mentioned by name in this *Gospel*. We read of him as 'the disciple whom the Lord loved,' for example in Chapter 19:26. This is a technical expression and signifies the one who was initiated by the Master Himself. 'John' describes his own initiation in the story of the 'raising of Lazarus.' (Chapter 11). It was only through the writer of *St. John's Gospel* being initiated by the Lord Himself that the most secret connections between Christ and the evolution of the world could be revealed. As we have already said, the old initiations lasted for three and a half days; hence the raising of Lazarus on the fourth day. It is also said of Lazarus that the Lord loved him (*John* 3:35-36.)

"While the body of Lazarus lay as if dead in the grave, his etheric body was lifted out in order to undergo the initiation, and to receive the same force that is in Christ. Thus the one whom the Lord loved, the one to whom we owe *St. John's Gospel*, was raised, he was awakened. Not a line in *St. John's Gospel*, contradicts this fact; the process of initiation is represented in a veiled way.

"Let us now consider another scene in this *Gospel*. In (*John* 19:25), we read:—

'Now there stood by the cross of Jesus, His mother, and His mother's sister, Mary the wife of Cleophas, and Mary Magdalene.'

"If we wish to understand this *Gospel* it is necessary to know who these three women are. We do not usually give two sisters the same name; neither was it the custom in former times. The passage we have quoted proves that, according to *St. John's Gospel*, the mother of Jesus was not called Mary. If we search through the whole of this *Gospel* we nowhere find it said that the mother of Jesus was called Mary. In the scene of the Marriage of Cana, for example, Chapter 2, we only read, 'the mother of Jesus was there.' In these words something important is indicated, something we only understand when we know how the writer of this *Gospel* uses his words. What does the expression 'the mother of Jesus' mean? We have seen that man consists of physical, etheric and astral bodies. We must not consider the transition of the astral body to the Spirit-Self so simply. The Ego transforms the astral body very slowly and gradually into Sentient-Soul, Intellectual-Soul and Spiritual-Soul [purified Consciousness-Soul]. The Ego goes on working and only when it has developed the Spiritual-Soul is it able so to purify it that Spirit Self can arise in it. The following diagram represents the constitution of man:—

Father	**7. Spirit-Human**	
Son	**6. Life-Spirit**	
Holy Spirit	**5. Spirit-Self**	**Virgin Sophia (purified Spiritual-Soul)**
	4. Intellectual Soul	**Mary the wife of Cleophas**
	3. Astral Body	**Sentient-Soul—Mary Magdalene**
	2. Etheric Body	
	1. Physical Body	

"The Spirit-Human will only be developed in the distant future, and Life-Spirit is also only germinal in most people of the present day. The development of the Spirit-Self has only just begun; it is closely united with the Spiritual-Soul (somewhat like a sword in its sheath). The Sentient-Soul is similarly united with the astral body. The human being thus consists of nine parts or principles; but as the Spirit-Self and the Spiritual-Soul, and the Sentient-Soul and the astral body are so closely united, we often speak of seven parts. Spirit-Self is the same as the 'Holy Spirit,' who according to Esoteric Christianity, is the guiding Being in the astral world. According to the same teaching, Life-Spirit is called the 'Word' or the 'Son'; and Spirit-Man is the 'Father Spirit' or the 'Father.'

"Those human beings who had brought the Spirit-Self to birth within them, were called 'Children of God'; in such men 'the light shone into the Darkness and they received the light.' Outwardly they were, men of flesh and blood; but they bore a Higher-Man within them; the Spirit-Self had been born within them out of the Spiritual-Soul. The 'mother' of such a spiritualized man is not a bodily mother, she lies within him; she is the purified and spiritualized Spiritual-Soul; she is the principle who gives birth to the Higher-Man. This spiritual birth, a birth in the highest sense, is described in *St. John's Gospel*. The Spirit-Self or the Holy Spirit pours into the most highly purified Spiritual-Soul. This is referred to in the words:—

'I saw the Spirit descending from heaven like a dove, and it abode upon him.'

(*John* 1:32)

"As the Spiritual-Soul [the refined Consciousness-Soul] is the principle in which the Spirit-Self develops, this principle is called the 'mother of Christ,' or, in the occult schools, the 'Virgin Sophia.' Through the fertilization of the Virgin Sophia the Christ could be born in Jesus of Nazareth. In the occult school of Dionysius, the Intellectual-Soul was called 'Mary,' and the Sentient-Soul 'Mary Magdalene.'

"The Physical man is born of the union of two human beings; but the higher man can only be born of a Spiritual-Soul which embraces a whole people. Among all the peoples of olden times the method of initiation was essentially the same. Each initiation had seven stages or degrees. Among the Persians, for example, they were called as follows:—

1. *The Raven.* One at this stage had to bring information from the outer world into the temple. The Raven has always been called the spiritual messenger; for instance in the legend of the Ravens of Barbarossa, and also in the German legends of Odin and his two ravens.
2. *The Occult.*
3. *The Warrior. In the occult school the warrior was allowed to go forth and announce the* teachings.
4. *The Lion. The Lion was one who was firmly grounded in himself; he not only had the Word, but he possessed also the magical forces; he had stood the test which guaranteed that he would not misuse the powers entrusted to him.*
5. *The Persian.*
6. *The Sun Hero.*
7. *The Father.*

"Let us consider the title of the fifth degree, the 'Persian,' a little more closely. In all the occult schools an initiate of the fifth degree was called by the name of the people to whom he belonged; for his consciousness had widened where it included the whole people. He felt all the sorrow of the people as his own; his consciousness had been purified and expanded to the consciousness of the whole people. Among the Jews the initiate at this stage was called an 'Israelite.' Only when we grasp this fact do we understand the conversation between Christ and Nathanael (*John* 1:46-49). Nathanael was an initiate of the fifth degree. The words of Christ Jesus to Nathanael, that he had seen him under the fig tree, refer to a special process in initiation, namely, the reception of the Spiritual-Soul.

"The following considerations will help towards the understanding of the inner-process of initiation. The individual 'I-consciousness' of man is in the physical world; men walk the Earth with their Ego. But the Egos of the animals are on the astral plane; each group of animals there possesses an Ego-consciousness in common. There is, however, in the astral world, not only the Ego of the animal; but also the Ego of the body which man has in common with the animals, the Ego of the human astral body. In the Lower Spirit World [Lower Devachan], we find the Ego of the plants, and also the Ego of the body man possesses in common with the plants, the Ego of the etheric body. If we rise still higher, into the Higher Spirit World [Higher Devachan], we there find the Ego of the minerals and the Ego of that part which man has in common with the minerals—the Ego of the physical body. Thus, through our physical body we are connected with the Higher Spiritual World. We are here in the physical world with our Individual-Ego only. When, in the case of an initiate, the Ego of the astral body is permeated by his Individual-Ego, the consequence is that he becomes conscious in the astral world; he can then perceive the beings around him there and become active in that world. He then meets Beings who are incarnated in astral bodies; he also meets the Group-Souls of the animals, and the Higher Beings who in Christianity are called Angels. On being initiated still more deeply, the Ego of the etheric body is also permeated by the Individual-Ego. The consciousness of the human being then extends into the Lower Spiritual World. There he encounters the Egos of the plants and the Spirit of the Planet. A still deeper initiation takes place when the Individual-Ego permeates the Ego of the physical body, man then rises to personal consciousness in the Higher Spiritual World. There he meets the Egos of the minerals and still higher Spirits. Thus, continued initiation raises a man to higher and higher worlds, in which he meets with higher and higher Beings."

"When the Individual-Ego has gained full control over the three bodies, it has brought about inner-harmony. Christ possessed this harmony to the fullest extent; he appeared on the Earth in order that men might develop this power of inner-harmony. In this Son of Man, we see represented the full development of humanity, up to the highest spiritual stage. Formerly this inner-harmony did not exist, outer laws worked in its place; this inner-harmony is the new impulse which humanity received through Christ. Man is to acquire the 'Christ capacity,' that is to say, he is to develop the Inner-Christ. Goethe said: 'The eye is built by light to receive light'; in the same way this inner-harmony, this Inner-Christ is only kindled through the presence of the outer, historical Christ; before His appearance it was not possible for man to reach this stage of spiritual development. Those human beings who lived before the appearance of Christ on Earth are not excluded from the blessings He brought to humanity; for it should not be forgotten that, according to the law of reincarnation, they will come again to the Earth—and will, therefore, have the opportunity to develop the Inner-Christ. It is only when people forget the law of reincarnation that they can speak of injustice. St. John's *Gospel* shows the way to the historical Christ, to that Sun which enkindles the inner-light in man, just as the physical Sun has enkindled the light of the eyes. The Ego of the etheric body may be compared to the engineer who builds a motorcar; the Ego of the astral body may be compared to the one who drives it; and the Ego of the individual to the one who owns it."

The Nature of the "I Am"

Secrets of the Threshold, Rudolf Steiner, Lecture VIII, Munich, August 31, 1913, GA 147

"A person can actually ascend into the spiritual worlds—this has often been said—and have quite a few experiences there without having a meeting with the Guardian, something that is partly terrifying but on the other hand highly significant, indeed of infinite importance for the sake of a clear, objective perception of those worlds. I have pointed to this and everything connected with it in my book, *The Threshold of the Spiritual World*, at least as far as I could while treating the material in an aphoristic way. I have gone further in the course of these lectures, and now I should like to add only a few details to characterize the Guardian of the Threshold. Should I try to describe everything about the meeting with the Guardian, I would indeed have to hold another long cycle of lectures.

"May I point out again that when a human being leaves his physical body in which he lives with the physical world around him, he enters the elemental world and lives in his etheric body, just as in the physical world he lives in the physical body. Then when he leaves the etheric body clairvoyantly, he lives in the astral body surrounded by the spiritual world. We have pointed out that on leaving the astral body the human being can then be within his True-Ego. Around him will be the supra-spiritual world. When he enters this world, he has finally attained what he has always possessed in the depths of his soul, his True-Ego. He reaches now the spiritual world in such a way that his True-Ego, his other-self, is revealed, actually enveloped in the element of living thought-being. All of us walking about on the physical plane have this other-self within us; but our ordinary consciousness not only is not aware of it—*but cannot know that we will not perceive it until we ascend into the spiritual and supra-spiritual worlds.* Our True-Ego is actually our constant companion within us; but when we meet it on the threshold of the Spiritual World, it is there in a remarkable way, in fact one can say—*decked out quite peculiarly.* There on the threshold our True-Ego is able to clothe itself in all our weaknesses, all our failings, everything that induces us to cling with our whole being either to the physical sense-world or at least to the elemental-world. Thus, we confront our own True-Ego on the threshold."

Background to the Gospel of St. Mark, **Rudolf Steiner, Lecture XI,** *Kyrios, the Lord of the Soul,* **Berlin, December 12, 1910, GA 124**

"In ancient days man was endowed with a kind of clairvoyance and through the forces of his soul was able to rise into the Divine-Spiritual World. When this happened, he was not using his Ego, his 'I' at the stage of development it had then reached; he was using his astral body which contained the powers of seership—whereas the forces rooted in the Ego were only gradually being awakened by perception of the physical world. The 'I' uses physical instruments—but in earlier times, if a man were seeking revelation, he used his astral body, seeing and perceiving through it. The process of evolution itself consisted in the transition from use of the astral body to use of the 'I'. The Christ-Impulse was to be the most powerful factor in the development of the 'I.' If the words of St. Paul: 'Not I but Christ in me' are fulfilled in the 'I,' then the 'I' is able to grow into the Spiritual World through its own forces, whereas formerly this was possible only for the astral body.

"This, then, is how evolution proceeded: Man once used his astral body as an organ of perception; but the astral body became less-and-less able to serve that purpose. When the time of Christ's coming was drawing near, it was losing its power to see into the Spiritual World. Man could no longer be united with that world through his astral body and the 'I' was not yet strong enough to reveal it. That was the state of things when the time of Christ's coming was approaching.

"In the course of human evolution the important steps which are eventually to take place have always to be prepared in advance. This was so in the case of the Christ Impulse too; but there was necessarily a period of transition. There could be no sudden change from the time when man felt his astral body becoming unreceptive to the Spiritual World, becoming barren and desolate, to a time when the 'I' was kindled into activity through the Christ-Impulse. What happened was that as the result of a certain influence from the Spiritual World, a few human beings were able to experience in the astral body something of what was later to be seen and known by the 'I.' Egohood was prepared for, anticipated as it were in the astral body. It was through the 'I' and its development that man became Earth-man in the real sense. The astral body properly belonged to the evolutionary period of the Old Moon, when the *Angels* were at the human stage. Man is at the human stage on the Earth. On the Old Moon it was appropriate for man to use his astral body. Everything else was merely preparation for the development of the 'I.' The earliest stages of Earth-evolution proper were a recapitulation of the Old Moon-evolution. For man could never become fully man in the astral body; on the Old Moon it was only the Angels who could reach the human stage in the astral body. And just as the Christ lived in earthly man in order to inspire his 'I,' so there were Angels who, having reached the human stage on the Old Moon, prophetically inspired man's astral body as a preparation for Egohood. A time was to come in human evolution on the Earth when man would be ready for the development of the 'I.' On the Old Moon the Angels had developed to the highest stage; but as we have heard, only in the astral body. Now, in order that man might be prepared for Egohood, it was necessary that in exceptional conditions, and through grace, certain individuals should be inspired to work on the Earth as Angels; although they were men, the reality was that Angels were working in and through them.

"This is a concept of great importance, without which there can be no understanding of human evolution in line with that of occultism. It is easy enough to say simply that everything is 'maya'—*but that is a mere abstraction.* We must be able to say: Yes, a man is standing in front of me, but he is *maya*—indeed who knows if he is really a man? Perhaps what seems to be a human figure is only the outer sheath; perhaps some quite other being is using this sheath in order to accomplish a task that is beyond man's capacity.—I have given an indication of this in *The Portal of Initiation.*

"Such an event in the history of humanity actually took place when the Individuality who had lived in Elijah was reborn as John the Baptist. An Angel entered into the soul of John the Baptist in that incarnation, using his bodily nature and also his soul to accomplish what no human being could have accomplished. In

John the Baptist there lived an Angel whose mission was to herald in advance the Egohood that was to be present in its fullness in Jesus of Nazareth."

***Background to the Gospel of St. Mark,* Rudolf Steiner, Lecture XII, *Mystery Teachings in St. Mark's Gospel,* Munich, December 18, 1910, GA 124**

"When we read the lines at the very beginning of St. Mark's *Gospel* we can feel how necessary it is to think in this way about language and its secrets… The passage from Isaiah reads: 'Behold I send my Angel before thee who shall prepare thy way before thee.' It is the voice of the preacher in the wilderness: "Prepare the way of the Lord, make straight his path."

"…In the words just quoted, Isaiah is giving voice to something he knew through Initiation, namely that an impulse of supreme importance is to be given to the evolution of humanity. Why did he, and all other Initiates, regard this event to which he was pointing as being of such significance? His picture of the evolution of humanity was true and he knew that in earlier times men possessed a natural clairvoyance, moreover that through the astral body they were able to see into the spiritual worlds. In earlier times men possessed a natural clairvoyance, moreover that through the astral body they were able to see into the Spiritual Worlds. The astral body gradually lost the power of vision and became inwardly dark, but man's progress lay in this very loss of astral clairvoyance. It was now to be made possible for the 'I' to function. Out of his Initiation-knowledge Isaiah might also have said:—

'In those days men will speak only of their Ego and as long as that Ego is not filled with Christ it will be restricted to perception of the physical plane furnished by the senses and intellect. Men will be forsaken by the world of the spirit.' But then Christ will come, bringing consolation, and human souls will be permeated more and more with the Christ-Impulse so that they can again look upwards into the Spiritual World. Before this is possible, however, they will experience the darkening of the astral body.'

"The very first beginnings of man's physical body came into being on Old Saturn, of his etheric body on Old Sun, of his astral body on Old Moon; and the Ego ['I'] evolves on the Earth. Until the astral body lost its clairvoyant powers and became dark, the Ego had at first to work in the darkness. Before Earth-evolution began in the real sense a kind of recapitulation of the Old Moon-evolution took place. During that period man's astral body had developed to a stage where the activity of the whole Universe was mirrored within it. When the recapitulation of the Moon-evolution was completed, the Ego began to enter into the process of evolution and Isaiah could say that Egohood would become more and more dominant on the Earth."

The Solar Elohim and
Lunar Pitris

According to the *The Secret Doctrine*, of H. P. Blavatsky (the references
can be found online at: *Theosophy World*) the Solar and Lunar Pitris
are two of the seven classes of Dhyan-Chohan or Dhyāni-Chohan;
which is a generic term for all celestial beings who besides Pitris are
also called Dhyani-Buddhas, Angels, Archangels, Devas (Sanskrit:
a "shining one"), Barhishads (in Hindhism one of two classes of
Pitris, the other one being the Agnishvatta), Manasaputras, Elohim,
Prajapatis, Kumaras, etc. The nature and powers of the Dhyan-
Chohans far exceed those of human beings. These 'ancestors' are only
limited by the boundaries that separate the various solar systems in
the Cosmos.

Early in his theosophical lectures and writings Rudolf Steiner
frequently used some these terms in reference to the Angelical
Hierarchies when lecturing to theosophists, as they were the used
within the Theosophical Society.

"The Dhyan Chohans are the agents of the Karmic and Cosmic
Laws."
H.P. Blavatsky, *The Secret Doctrine: the Synthesis of Science,
Religion and Philosophy*, Vol. I, Theosophical Publishing Co., Ltd.:
London:, 1888 (pg. 274)

The theosophical term Lunar Pitris literally means 'lunar fathers.'
(Sanskrit: Pitṛs = fathers) According to *The Secret Doctrine*, these are
advanced beings from the Moon Chain [Old Moon] who gave the form

of the physical body of human beings. They are called in *The Secret Doctrine* by many other names: Barhishads, Agnishvattas, Lords of the Moon, Sons of Soma, Sons of the Moon, Celestial Ancestors, Lunar Sons, Lunar Gods, Lunar Progenitors, Sons of Twilight, Moon-Gods, Lunar Monads, Lunar Fathers, Lunar Ancestors, Will-born Lords, and Sons of the Lord of the Lotus.

The Lunar Pitris completed the human stage of evolution during the Old Moon Chain. This was how the astral form of humanity was formed prior to the solid physical body.

The Solar Pitris, often called 'Lords of the Flame,' or 'Lords of Spiritual Life' are said to be superior to the Lunar Pitris. They provided the intelligence for human beings and quickened the mind principle of human beings. They are also called the 'Sons of Mahat' who work with the fifth principal of Manas [Rudolf Steiner's Spirit-Self] to awaken the mind of humanity.

Helena Petrovna Blavatsky used the term 'Pitris' in her writings to refer to the divine fashioners of humanity (Progenitors, Forefathers, Ancestors) in: *The Secret Doctrine,* Vol. II:

> "The ancestors, or creators of mankind are of seven classes, three of which are incorporeal, arupa, and four corporeal, rupa. Occultism defines and limits the number of primordial races to seven, because of the 'seven progenitors,' or prajapatis, the evolvers of beings. These are neither gods, nor supernatural Beings, but advanced Spirits from another and lower planet, reborn on this one, and giving birth in their turn in the present Round to present humanity."

> "Exoteric Hindu books mention seven classes of Pitris, and among them two distinct kinds of Progenitors or Ancestors: the Barhishad and the Agnishvatta; or those possessed of the 'sacred fire' and those devoid of it. The Agnishwatta Pitris are devoid of fire, because too divine and pure; whereas the Barhishad, being the lunar spirits more closely connected with

Earth, became the creative Elohim of form, or the Adam of dust."

"The Progenitors of Man, called in India 'Fathers,' or Pitris, are the creators of our bodies and lower principles. They are ourselves, as the first personalities, and we are they. As stated, they were 'lunar Beings.' The Endowers of man with his conscious, immortal Ego, are the 'Solar Angels.' The esoteric name of these 'Solar Angels' is, literally, the 'Lords' (Nath) of 'persevering ceaseless devotion.'"

In the following is notes from an early lecture cycle given to members of the Theosophical Society in Berlin by Rudolf Steiner. It is amongst the most useful of Rudolf Steiner's works for bridging the esoteric teachings of East and West.

Foundations of Esotericism, Rudolf Steiner, Lecture XXIII, Berlin, October 25, 1905, GA 93a

"The last human beings during the Old Moon existence are our physical forefathers. On the Earth they now developed somewhat further. The Earth-men of the pre-Lemurian Epoch are the actual descendants of the inhabitants of the Moon. This is why we call the inhabitants of the Moon the Fathers or Pitris of Earth-men. They were irradiated and an inner fire shone through them. When human beings were going through an earlier stage of evolution, they were still more beautiful and nobler in their form.

"During the Age which preceded the Lemurian Epoch, we have the Hyperborean Epoch on the Earth, that of the Sun-men, of the Apollo-men. They were formed out of a still nobler and even more delicate substance. Then we go still further back to the very first Race, to the Polarian-men. At that time, they lived in the tropical polar climate, a Race which was able to attain to special heights through the fact that a remarkable and great help had been granted them. The most beautiful of the Moon Pitris descended to the Earth. The Polarian human beings were very similar to four-footed animals, but they were formed out of a soft, pliant substance similar to a jellyfish, but much warmer. The human beings with the best forms, consisting of the noblest components, received at that time help of a special nature, for beings were still connected with the Earth who had earlier reached a higher stage.

"All esotericism recognizes that the Sun was at first a planet; it only later became a fixed star. The sequence of stages that the Earth has passed through is: Old Saturn, Old Sun, Old Moon, Earth. When the Sun was itself a planet, then everything which is now on the Moon and Earth was still in the Sun. Later Sun and Moon separated themselves from the Earth.

"Let us think back to the time of the Old Sun. Then everything which now lives on the Earth, dwelt on the Sun. The beings were then quite differently formed, having only a physical body, much less dense than it is now, and an etheric body. Man's whole way of life was plant-like. The beings lived in the light of the Sun. Light came to them from the center of their own planet. They were totally different from present-day man. In comparison with present-day man the Sun-man stood upside down and the Sun shone upon his head. Everything connected with reproduction developed freely on the other side. Man at that time stretched his legs, so to say, into the air. The plant has remained at this stage, its roots are in the earth and it stretches its organs of reproduction, stamens and pistil, into the air (plant). This Sun-man developed in seven different stages. His direction on the planet is the same as the growth of the plant on the Earth. Then, with the third incarnation of the Earth he became a Moon-man. He bent over, the vertical becoming the horizontal (animal). The tendency towards a spine developed. The symbol for this is the Tau = T. On the Earth he turns completely round. For this the symbol is the Cross. The symbolism of the Cross depicts the development from the Sun, through the Moon to the Earth. On the Earth the symbol of the Cross was attained by the addition of the upper vertical member above the 'T.' This developed further in the bearing of the Cross on the shoulders.

"The Sun-men too had attained a certain high development. There were also Sun Adepts, who had progressed further than the other Sun-men. They passed over to the Moon. There also they had the possibility of being on a higher level than the Moon-men, and they developed to quite special heights. They were the forefathers of the Earth-men; but had hastened much further ahead. When now in the second Epoch of the Fourth Round the Hyperboreans lived in their soft forms, these 'Sons of the Sun' were in position to incarnate, and they formed a particularly beautiful Race. They were the Solar Pitris. Already in the Hyperborean Epoch they created for themselves an upright form, completely transforming the Hyperborean bodies. This the other human beings were unable to do. In the Hyperborean Epoch the Solar Pitris became the beautiful Apollo-men, who in the Second Race had already attained the upright posture.

"In the Old Sun everything was contained which was later extrapolated as Moon and Earth. All life and all warmth streamed up from the center of the Sun. Then, in the next Manvantara (the Old Moon) the following took place: Out of the darkness of Pralaya the Sun emerged. A part of the Sun substance had the urge to detach itself. At first a kind of biscuit formation developed.

Then, the one part severed itself completely and the two bodies continued side-by-side as Sun and Old Moon. The Sun

retained the possibility of emitting light and warmth. The Old
Moon retained the power of reproduction. It was able to bring
forth again the beings who had been on the Sun; but they had
to be dependent on the Sun for light and warmth. Because the
Old Moon itself possessed no light, the beings had to orientate
themselves towards the Sun. All plants therefore completely
reversed their position on the Old Moon. The animals turned
half round and human beings also only turned halfway; but to
compensate for this they received on the Moon the astral body,
Kama, and thereby, developed warmth from within outwards.

"The Kama was at that time still an essentially warming
force. This is why the human beings did not already then turn
themselves completely towards the Sun. Life was in the darkness.
The Old Moon also circled round the Sun; but not as our Earth
does today. The Moon rotated around the Sun, in such a way that
only one side was turned towards it. A Moon-day therefore lasted
as long as a half year does today. Thus, on the one side there was
an intense heat and on the other side an intense cold.

"On the Old Moon the predecessors of man again went
through a certain normal development. But there were also Moon
Adepts who hastened on in advance of the rest of mankind. At
the end of the Old Moon evolution these Pitri beings were much
more advanced than the rest of humanity, just as the Adepts are
today.

"Now for the first time we reach the actual Earth evolution. In
the next Pralaya which followed the Moon evolution, the Moon
fell back into the Sun. As one body they went through Pralaya.
When the Earth eventually emerged out of the darkness the whole
Sun-mass was united with it. In that Epoch the first Polarian
Race began. Then the previous Sun-men, in accordance with
conditions at that time, were able to form this specially favored

species, the 'Sons of the Sun,' because the Sun was still united with the Earth.

"During the Hyperborean Epoch the whole again divided. One part severed itself and the Earth emerged out of the Sun … Now the second, or Hyperborean Race, evolved. Gradually the seeds of the Moon-Men appeared on the Earth, the Pitris in various degrees of perfection. They all still had the possibility of reproducing themselves through self-fertilization.

"A second severance followed. With the Moon everything connected with self-reproduction departed from the Earth, so that there were now three bodies: Sun, Earth, Moon. Then the possibility of self-fertilization ceased; the Moon had drawn out what made this possible. Then the Moon was outside and there were beings who were no longer able to reproduce themselves; thus in the Lemurian Epoch the two sexes originated.

"Such forms of evolution take their course only under the special guidance of higher beings, the Devas, in order to further evolution in a certain way. The leader of this whole progression is the God who in the Hebraic tradition is called Jahve; Jehovah. He was a Moon-God. He possessed in the highest sense of the word, the power that had developed on the Moon and accordingly he endeavored to develop mankind further in this direction. In the earthly world Jahve represents that God who endows beings with the possibility of physical reproduction. Everything else (intellect) did not lie in the Jahve-Intention. If Jahve's intention alone had continued to develop, the human being would eventually have ceased to be able to reproduce himself; for the power of reproduction would have become exhausted. He would then only have been concerned with the creation of beautiful forms; for he was indifferent to what is inward, intellectual. Jehovah wished to produce beautifully-formed human beings, like beautiful statues.

His intention was that the power of reproduction should be continued until it had expended itself. He wanted to have a planet that only bore upon it beautiful but completely motionless forms. If the Earth had continued its evolution with the Moon within it, it would have developed into a completely rigid, frozen form. Jehovah would have immortalized his planet as a monument to his intention. This would doubtless have come about had not those Adepts, who had hastened beyond the Moon evolution now come forward. It was just at this time that they made their appearance. They had already developed on the Moon intelligence and the Spirit which we first developed on the Earth. They now took the rest of humanity into their charge and rescued them from the fate which otherwise would have befallen them. A new spark was kindled in the human astral body. Just at that time they gave to the human astral body the impetus to develop beyond this critical point. Jahve could now save the situation only by altering his manner of working. He created man and woman. What could no longer be contained in one sex was divided between the two sexes.

"Two streams now existed, that of Jahve and that of the Moon Adepts. The interest of the Moon Adepts lay in spiritualizing mankind. Jahve, however, wished to make of them beautiful statues. At that time these two powers contested with one another.

"Thus on the Earth we have to do with a force having the power of self-reproduction; Kriyashakti. This power is only present on the Earth today in the very highest Mysteries. At that time everyone possessed it. Through this power man could reproduce himself; he then became divided into two halves with the result that two sexes came into being on the Earth.

"Jehovah withdrew the entire power of self-reproduction from the Earth and placed it in the Moon side-by-side with the

Earth. Through this arose the connection between the power of reproduction and the Moon beings. Now we have human beings with a weakened power of reproduction; but not yet having the possibility of spiritualizing themselves. These were the predecessors of present-day man. The Moon Adepts came to them and said: *You must not follow Jehovah. He will not allow you to attain to knowledge—but you should.* That is the Snake. The Snake approached the woman, because she had the power to produce offspring out of herself. Now Jehovah said: Man has become like unto ourselves, and brings death into the world and everything connected with it.

"Luciferic is the name given to the Moon Adepts; they are the bestowers of human intellectuality. This they gave to the astral and physical bodies; had it been otherwise the Monads would not have been able to enter into them and the Earth would have become a planetary monument to Jehovah's greatness. By the intervention of the luciferic principle human independence and spirituality were saved. Then Jehovah, so that man should not be completely spiritualized, divided the self-reproduction process into two parts [Male and Female]. What would have been lost however if Jehovah had continued his work alone will reappear in the Sixth Root-Race, when man will have become so spiritualized that he will regain Kriyashakti, the creative power of reproduction. He will be in the position to bring forth his own kind. In this way mankind was rescued from downfall.

"Through Jehovah's power man carries within himself the possibility of rigidifying. When one observes the three lower bodies we find that these bear within them the possibility of returning to the physical condition of the Earth. The upper parts: Atman, Budhi, Manas, were only able to enter into human beings because the influence of the Snake was added. This gave man new life and the power to remain with the earthly planet. Reproduction however became bisexual and thereby birth and death entered into the world. Previously this had not happened...

"Thus we have the human being as he evolved from the unisexual into the bisexual state, and together with him bisexual animals, male and female. It was only through the Lunar Pitris that man became mature enough to have a body capable of receiving the Monads. It was only then that the body formed itself in accordance with the Monad. The other forms which were less advanced failed to satisfy the descending Monad; hence they poured only a part of their spiritual force into the imperfect human bodies and the third stream utterly refused to incarnate. Because of this there existed very poorly endowed human bodies and also others quite devoid of spirit.

"In the middle of the Lemurian Epoch we find the first Sons of the Fire Mist; these incarnate in the fiery element, which at that time surrounded the Earth. The Sons of the Fire Mist were the first Arhats. In the first Lemurian human race those who had received only a small spark were little adapted to forming a civilization and soon went under. On the other hand those who had received absolutely nothing found full expression for their lower nature. They mingled with the animals. From them proceeded the last Lemurian races. The wild, animal instincts lived in wild animal-like human forms. This brought about a degeneration of the entire human substance.

"Had all human beings been fructified with Monads, the whole human race would have greatly improved. The first evil arose through the fact that certain Monads refused to incarnate. From this, through intermingling, deterioration set in. In this way the human being suffered an essentially physical degradation. Only in the Atlantean Epoch did the Monads regret their previous refusal; they came down and populated all mankind. In this way arose the various Atlantean races.

"We have now reached a time when something happened to bring about the deterioration of the Earth. The wholesale deterioration of the races brought this about. It was then that the seed of Karma was planted. Everything that came later is the result of this original Karma; for had the Monads all entered into human forms at the right time, human beings would have possessed the certainty of animals, they could not have been subject to error, but they would not have been able to develop freedom. The original Arhats could not go astray; they are angels in human form. The Moon Adepts however had so brought things about that certain Monads waited before incarnating. Through this the principle of asceticism entered into the world—reluctance to inhabit the Earth. This discrepancy between higher and lower Nature arose at this time. Because of it man became uncertain; he must now try things out, oscillating from one experience to another, in an attempt to find his way in the world. Because he had original Karma, his own further Karma came about. Now he could fall into error.

"The intention was that man should attain knowledge. This could only be brought about through the original Karma. The Luciferic Principle, the Moon Adepts, wanted to develop freedom and independence to an ever-greater degree…

"We have thus learned to know a two-fold order of human beings: those who succumbed to the Jehovah Principle, the bringing of perfection to the physical Earth, and also spiritual human beings who were becoming more highly developed. Jehovah and Lucifer are engaged in an unceasing battle. It is the intention of Lucifer to develop everything upwards, towards knowledge, towards the light. In Devachan the human being can bring a certain degree of advancement to the Luciferic Principle. The longer he remains in Devachan the more of this can he develop. He must pass through as many incarnations as are necessary in order to bring this Principle fully to perfection.

"Thus, there exists in the world a Jehovah Principle and a Lucifer Principle. If the Jehovah Principle alone were to be taught, man would succumb to the Earth. If the teaching of reincarnation and karma were allowed to disappear entirely from the Earth, we should win back for Jehovah all the Monads and physical man would be given over to the Earth, to a petrified planet. If, however, one teaches reincarnation and karma, man is led upwards to spiritualization. Christianity therefore made the absolutely right compromise, and for a period of time did not teach reincarnation and karma, but the importance of the single human existence, in order that man should learn to love the Earth, waiting until he is mature enough for a new Christianity, with the teaching of reincarnation and karma, which is the saving of the Earth and brings the whole of what has been sown into Devachan. As a result, in Christianity itself there is conflict between the two Principles: the one without reincarnation and karma, the other with this teaching. In the former case, everything which Lucifer could bring about would be taken from human beings. They would actually drop out of reincarnation and turn their backs on the Earth, becoming degenerate angels. In that case the Earth would be going towards its downfall. Were the hosts of Jehovah to be victorious on the Earth, the Earth would remain behind as a kind of Moon, as a rigidified body. The possibility of spiritualization would then be a missed opportunity. The battle in the *Bhagavad Gita* describes the conflict between Jehovah and Lucifer and their hosts.

"It might still be possible today for the teaching of Christianity without reincarnation and karma to prevail. Then the Earth would be lost for the Principle of Lucifer. The whole Earth is still a battlefield of these two principles. The principle that leads the Earth towards spirituality is Lucifer. Lucifer is the prince who reigns in the kingdom of science and art; but he cannot descend altogether on to the Earth: for this, his power does not suffice. Quite alone, it would be impossible for Lucifer to lead upwards what is on the Earth. For this, not only is the power of a Moon Adept necessary, but of a Sun Adept, who embraces the universality of human life, not manifesting only in science and art. Lucifer is represented as the Winged Form of the Dragon; Ezekiel describes him as the Winged Bull.

"Now there came a Sun Hero, similar to those who appeared in the Hyperborean Epoch, represented by Ezekiel as the Winged Lion. This Hero, who gave the second impulse, is the Christ, the Lion out of the tribe of Judah. The representative of the Eagle will come only later; he represents the Father Principle. Christ is a Solar Hero, a Lion-Nature, a Sun Pitri.

"The third impulse will be represented by an Adept who was already an Adept on [Old] Saturn. Such a one cannot, as yet incarnate on the Earth. When man is not only able to develop his higher nature upwards, but working creatively is able to renounce completely his lower nature, then will this highest Adept, the [Old] Saturn Adept, the Father Principle, the Hidden God, be able to incarnate."

Superhuman Beings of Venus, Mercury, and Vulcan

The question of 'Superhuman Beings of Venus, Mercury, and Vulcan' and their relationship with humanity is written about by numerous authors and yet little is understood concerning what Rudolf Steiner has said about this topic. It is often debated whether these beings are Angels, Archangels, and Archai who are intimately connected to human development through thinking, feeling, and willing; or are these beings aspects of our own threefold spirit that manifest through the forces of Moral Imagination, Moral Inspiration, and Moral Intuition? Some authors have even argued that these beings are, in fact, the higher nature of humanity from the future coming to us to bring the three spiritual principles of the Spirit-Self, Life-Spirit, and Spirit-Human into the souls of humans.

Much could be said about these different opinions and thus, the debate continues. Personally, I take up the side of the debate that these 'superhumans' are higher spiritual hierarchies, since in one place Steiner refers to 'other beings—not of the human order'; and in another place, calls them 'Heavenly Beings.' Unfortunately, these indications are not definitive and leave plenty of wiggle-room for further debate. These quotes are also confounded by the fact that Rudolf Steiner has also referred to our 'older brothers and sisters from the Pleiades' who are working together with human beings for the advancement of Spiritual Science and human spiritual development. Exactly what these few indications mean, is up for future conversations and speculation.

References to 'supermen from Vulcan' and 'older brothers and sisters from the Pleiades' stir the imagination and bring many unanswered questions to mind. But the bottom line seems clear in that the 'ever present help of the Spiritual World' is always there to support humans in taking the next step in uniting their soul to their spirit. The Being Anthroposophia is called the 'mid-wife of the soul helping birth the spirit' who 'passes through' the human being whenever another step is taken towards the spirit. So, whether it is Anthroposophia, the Archangel Michael, our Guardian Angel, one or another of the nine hierarchical ranks of spiritual beings, the Holy Trinity, supermen from Venus/Mercury/Vulcan, our Higher-Self, or siblings from the Pleiades doesn't seem to matter so much as long as we know that our efforts toward the spirit will be aided by spiritual beings anxious for our higher evolution.

We present below a few selections of Rudolf Steiner's indications concerning the future Incarnations of the Earth called Future Jupiter, Future Venus, and Future Vulcan and the beings associated with those future stages of human spiritual development. These stages align with human evolution becoming in-turn Angels, Archangels, and Archai. But since time and space will transform radically as these stages of development unfold, we could rightly ask the question: Are these spiritual beings who are here to help us actually our three higher spiritual Egos coming to unite our soul to the spirit? This question, and many others concerning these indications are yet to be fully answered and understood. Only time will tell if our spirit is working with hierarchical beings to aid in our personal spiritual development, or that our own three higher selves are helping our personal evolution from the future, or if our world is populated by other spiritual beings who wish to help us evolve. We hope that the selections below will help you formulate your own opinions concerning these transcendent questions and aid in developing Spiritual Science within your soul and spirit.

Materialism and the Task of Anthroposophy, **Rudolf Steiner,**
Lecture XIV, Dornach May 13, 1921, GA 204

"Thus, since the eighties of the nineteenth century, Heavenly
beings are seeking to enter this Earth existence. Just as the
Vulcan men were the last to come down to Earth [during the
Atlantean Epoch], so Vulcan beings are now actually entering
this Earth existence. Heavenly beings are already here in our
Earth existence. And it is thanks to the fact that beings from
beyond the Earth are bringing messages down into this earthly
existence that it is possible at all to have a comprehensive
Spiritual Science today.

"Taken as a whole, however, how does the human race
behave? If I may say so, the human race behaves in a cosmically
rude way toward the beings who are appearing from the Cosmos
on Earth, albeit, to begin with, only slowly. Humanity takes no
notice of them, ignores them. It is this that will lead the Earth
into increasingly tragic conditions. For, in the course of the next
few centuries, more and more spirit beings will move among us
whose language we ought to understand. We shall understand it
only if we seek to comprehend what comes from them, namely,
the contents of Spiritual Science. This is what they wish to bestow
on us. They want us to act according to Spiritual Science; they
want this Spiritual Science to be translated into social action and
the conduct of earthly life.

"Since the last third of the nineteenth century, we are actually
dealing with the influx of spirit beings from the Universe. Initially,
these were beings dwelling in the sphere between Moon and
Mercury; but they are closing in upon Earth, so to say, seeking
to gain a foothold in earthly life through human beings imbuing
themselves with thoughts of spiritual beings in the Cosmos. This
is another way of describing what I outlined earlier when I said

that we must call our shadowy intellect to life with the pictures of Spiritual Science. That is the abstract way of describing it. The description is concrete when we say: Spirit-Beings are seeking to come down into Earth existence and must be received. Upheaval upon upheaval will ensue, and Earth existence will at length arrive at social chaos if these beings descended and human existence were to consist only of opposition against them. For these beings wish to be nothing less than the advance guard of what will happen to Earth existence when the Moon reunites once again with Earth.

"Nowadays it may appear comparatively harmless to people when they think only those automatic, lifeless thoughts that arise through comprehension of the mineral world itself and the mineral element's effects in plant, animal, and man. Yes, indeed, people revel in these thoughts; as materialists, they feel good about them—*for only such thoughts are conceived today*. But imagine that people were to continue thinking in this way, unfolding nothing but such thoughts until the eighth millennium when Moon existence will once more unite with the life of the Earth. What would come about then? The beings I have spoken about will descend gradually to the Earth. Vulcan beings, Vulcan supermen, Venus supermen, Mercury supermen, Sun supermen, and so on will unite themselves with Earth existence. Yet, if human beings persist in their opposition to them, this Earth existence will pass over into chaos in the course of the next few thousand years. People will indeed be capable of developing their intellect in an automatic way; it can develop even in the midst of barbaric conditions. The fullness of human potential, however, will not be included in this intellect and people will have no relationship to the beings who wish graciously to come down to them into earthly life.

"All the beings presently conceived so incorrectly in people's thoughts—incorrectly because the mere shadowy intellect can only conceive of the mineral, the crudely material element, be it in the mineral, plant, animal or even human kingdom—these thoughts of human beings that have no reality all of a sudden will become realities when the Moon and the Earth will unite again. From the Earth, there will spring forth a horrible brood of beings. In character they will be in-between the mineral and plant kingdoms. They will be beings resembling automatons, with an over-abundant intellect of great intensity. Along with this development, which will spread over the Earth—*the latter will be covered as if by a network or web of ghastly spiders possessing tremendous wisdom*. Yet their organization will not even reach up to the level of the plants. They will be horrible spiders who will be entangled with one another. In their outward movements they will imitate everything human beings have thought up with their shadowy intellect, which did not allow itself to be stimulated by what is to come through new Imagination and through Spiritual Science in general.

"All these unreal thoughts people are thinking will be endowed with being. As it is covered with layers of air today, or occasionally with swarms of locusts, the Earth will be covered with hideous mineral-plant-like spiders that intertwine with one another most cleverly but in a frighteningly evil manner. To the extent that human beings have not enlivened their shadowy, intellectual concepts, they will have to unite their being, not with the entities who are seeking to descend since the last third of the nineteenth century, but instead with these ghastly mineral-plant-like spidery creatures. They will have to dwell together with these spiders; they will have to seek their further progress in cosmic evolution in the evolutionary stream that this spider brood will then assume.

"You see, this is something that is very much a reality of Earth humanity's evolution. It is known today by a large number of those human beings who hold mankind back from receiving spiritual scientific knowledge. For there are those who are actually conscious allies of this spidery entangling of human Earth existence. Today, we must no longer recoil from descriptions such as these. For descriptions of this kind are behind what is said to this day by many people who, based on ancient traditions, still have some awareness of things like these, and who would like to surround these ancient traditions with a certain veil of secrecy. The evolution of earthly humanity is not such that it can be veiled in secrecy any longer. However great the resistance in hostile quarters, these things must be said; for, as I have stated again and again, the acceptance or rejection of spiritual scientific knowledge is a serious matter facing mankind. It is not something that can be decided on the basis of more or less indifferent sympathies or antipathies; we are dealing with something that definitely affects the whole configuration of the Cosmos.

"We are dealing with the question of whether humanity at the present time will resolve to grow gradually into what benevolent spirits, wishing to ally themselves with human beings, bring down from the Universe, or whether mankind will seek its continued cosmic existence in the gradual entanglement, in the spider-brood of its own, merely shadowy thoughts. It does not suffice today to set down in abstract formulas the need for spiritual scientific knowledge. It is necessary to show how thoughts become realities. This is what is so dreadful about all abstract theosophists who appear on the scene and place abstractions before people, for example: *Thoughts will become realities in the future.* But it does not occur to them to present the full and actual implications of these matters. For the concrete implication is that the intellectual, shadow-like thoughts, spun inwardly by human beings today, will one day cover the earth like a spider's web. Human beings will become entangled in it if they are not willing to rise above these shadowy thoughts.

"The path of the ascent, my dear friends, is indeed outlined. We must take profoundly serious thoughts such as the one with which I concluded my lectures on color last Sunday where I said:— The point is to lift the comprehension of color out of the abstractions of physics into a region where the creative fancy, the feeling of the artist who understands the being of color, will harmonize effectively with a spiritual scientific insight into the world.

"We have seen how the beings and nature of color can be taken hold of, how the artistic element, which physics with its dreadful diagrams lets slide down into the ahrimanic sphere, can be lifted up. Thus, a theory of color can be founded; it would be remote from the established thought habits of modern science, yet can provide a basis for artistic creativity, if we will only imbue ourselves with its insight. *Such thoughts must certainly be taken seriously.*

"Another thought must be earnestly considered. What do we witness today throughout the civilized world? Our young people are sent into the hospitals and to the scientific faculties of the universities; there the human being is explained to them. They become acquainted with the human skeleton and with the human organism by studying the corpse. They learn to put together the human being logically in abstract thoughts.

"Yet, my dear friends, this is no way to comprehend the human being; in this way, one only gets to know the mineral aspect of man. What we learn about the human being through such a science is something that simply and solely has significance

from the moon's separation until its return, something that out of
the spider thoughts of today will then turn into spider beings. A
knowledge must be prepared that takes hold of the human being
quite differently, and this can be done only if science is lifted
into artistic vision. We must admit that science in the present-
day sense of the word can reach only to a certain level. It reaches
only as far as the mineral element in the mineral, plant, and
human kingdoms. Already in the plant kingdom science must
change into art; still more so in the animal. It is sheer nonsense
to try to understand the animal form in the way the anatomists
and physiologists do. And as long as we do not admit that it is
nonsense, the shadowy intellect cannot really be transformed into
a living, spiritual grasp of the world.

"What our young people are taught in so wretchedly abstract
a form in the universities must everywhere turn into an artistic
comprehension of the world. For nature around us creates
artistically. Unless it is understood that nature around us is an
artistic creation and can be grasped only with artistic concepts,
no good will come of our world conceptions. The idea should take
hold that the torture chambers in medieval castles, where people
were locked into the 'Iron Maiden,' for instance, and them pierced
through with spears, remind us of a procedure that, though more
physical and concrete, is the same as the one that occurs when
young people today are introduced to anatomy and physiology
and told that this will make them understand something of
human nature. No, they comprehend nothing but what has been
produced by a soul-spiritual element of torture: The human being
torn limb from limb, the mineralized human being—that part of
man that one day will be woven into the spider-cover of the Earth.

"Is it not sad that the power of civilization belongs now to
those who consider the thoughts of truth itself, which most

inwardly and intimately relate to the salvation and whole mission of mankind's development in the world, nonsense! It is tragic and we must be mindful of this tragedy. For only if we place this clearly and objectively before our soul's eye, shall we perhaps bestir ourselves to resolve to do what we can so that the intellect, *shadowy as it has become,* may find the way to admit the spiritual world that is approaching from the heavenly realms. Then, this shadowy intellect will be made fit for the potential it is to achieve. After all, this shadowy intellect should not be cast back into the realm beneath the plant kingdom, into a spider brood that will spread over the Earth. *No, it is intended that the human being shall be lifted up, in that time when women will no longer be fertile, when the eighth millennium will have arrived and the Moon will unite again with the Earth.* The earthly shall then remain behind, and the human being only direct it from outside—like a foot stool. It will be something he is not supposed to take along with him into his cosmic existence. Human beings should prepare themselves so that they need not become one with what will someday have to develop on the surface of this Earth in the manner described above.

"Mankind entered from a pre-earthly existence into this physical existence. At the time of the departure of the Moon, physical birth commenced. The human being began to be born of woman. Just as this came to pass, so in the future the human being will no longer be born of woman. For that is only a passing episode in the whole of cosmic evolution. It is the episode that is to bring to man the feeling of freedom, the consciousness of freedom, the integrated wholeness of individuality and personality. It is an episode that must not be disdained, an episode that was necessary in the whole cosmic process; but it must not be retained. Human beings must not give themselves up to the indolence of merely looking up to an abstract divine principle; they must concretely behold everything connected with their evolution. For they can attain a true inner revitalization of the whole soul-spirit being only if they comprehend that great period of time—but in its concrete evolutionary configuration—through which they will live in successive earth incarnations."

A Picture of Earth-Evolution in the Future, Rudolf Steiner, Dornach, May 13, 1921, GA 204

"This quickening to life of the shadow-pictures of the intellect is not only a human but a cosmic event. You will remember the passage in the book *Occult Science* dealing with the time when the human souls ascended to the planets and afterwards descended once more to Earth-existence. I spoke of how the Mars-men, the Jupiter-men and the others descended again to Earth. Now an event of great significance came to pass at the end of the seventies of last century. It is an event that can be described only in the light of facts which are revealed to us in the Spiritual World. Whereas in the days of old Atlantis human beings came down to the Earth from Saturn, Jupiter, Mars, and so on—that is to say, beings of soul were drawn into the realm of Earth-existence— since the end of the seventies of last century, other Beings—*not of the human order*—have been descending to the Earth for the purposes of their further development. From cosmic realms beyond the Earth, they come down to the Earth and enter into a definite relationship with human beings. Since the eighties of the nineteenth century, super-earthly Beings have been seeking to enter the sphere of Earth existence. Just as the Vulcan-men were the last to come down to the Earth—*so now Vulcan Beings are actually coming into the realm of earthly existence*. Super-earthly Beings are already here, and the fact that we are able to have a connected body of Spiritual Science at all today is due to the circumstance that Beings from beyond the Earth are bringing the messages from the Spiritual World down into Earth existence.

"But, speaking generally, what is the attitude adopted by the human race? The human race is behaving, if I may put it so very shabbily to these Beings who are appearing from the Cosmos and coming down—slowly and by degrees, it is true—to the Earth. The human race does not concern itself with them; it ignores their existence. And it is this which will plunge the Earth into tragic conditions; for in the course of the next centuries more and more Spiritual Beings will be among us—*Beings whose language we ought to understand.* And this is possible only if we try to grasp what comes from them: namely, the substance and content of Spiritual Science. They want to give it to us, and they want us to act in the sense of Spiritual Science. Their desire is that Spiritual Science shall be translated into social behavior and action on the Earth.

"I repeat, then, that since the last third of the nineteenth century Spiritual Beings from the Cosmos have been coming into our own sphere of existence. Their home is the sphere lying between the Moon and Mercury; but they are already pressing forward into the realm of Earth existence and seeking to gain a foothold there. And they will be able to find it if human beings are imbued with the thought of their existence. This can also be expressed as I expressed it just now, by saying that our shadowy intellect must be quickened to life by the pictures of Spiritual Science. We are speaking of concrete fact when we say: Spiritual Beings are seeking to come down into Earth-existence and ought to be willingly received. Catastrophe after catastrophe must ensue, and earthly life will fall at length into social chaos, if opposition is maintained in human existence to the advent of these Beings.

They desire nothing else than to be the advance-guards of what will happen to Earth existence when the Moon is once again united with the Earth.

"Today people may consider it comparatively harmless to elaborate only those automatic, lifeless thoughts which arise in connection with the mineral world and the mineral nature of plant, animal, and man. Materialists revel in such thoughts which are—well—thoughts and nothing more. But try to imagine what will happen if men go on unfolding no other kinds of thoughts until the time is reached in the eighth millennium for the Moon existence to unite again with the Earth. These Beings of whom I have spoken will gradually come down to the Earth. Vulcan Beings, 'Supermen' of Vulcan, 'Supermen' of Venus, of Mercury, of the Sun, will unite with this Earth existence. But if human beings persist in nothing but opposition to them—*Earth existence will pass over into chaos in the course of the next few thousand years.*

"It will be quite possible for the men of Earth, if they so wish, to develop a more and more automatic form of intellect—but that can also happen amid conditions of barbarism. Full and complete manhood, however, cannot come to expression in such a form of intellect, and men will have no relationship to the Beings who would fain come towards them in Earth existence. And all those Beings of whom men have such an erroneous conception because the shadowy intellect can only grasp the mineral nature, the crudely material nature in the minerals, plants, and animals, nay even in the human kingdom itself—all these thoughts which have no reality will in a trice become substantial realities when the Moon unites again with the Earth. And from the Earth there will spring forth a terrible brood of beings, a brood of automata of an order of existence lying between the mineral and the plant kingdoms and possessed of an overwhelming power of intellect.

"This swarm will seize upon the Earth, will spread over the Earth like a network of ghastly, spider-like creatures, of an order lower than that of plant-existence, but possessed of overpowering intelligence. These spidery creatures will be all interlocked with one another, and in their outward movements they will imitate the thoughts that men have spun out of the shadowy intellect that has not allowed itself to be quickened by the new form of Imaginative Knowledge by Spiritual Science. *All the thoughts that lack substance and reality will then be endowed with being.*

"The Earth will be surrounded—as it is now with air and as it sometimes is with swarms of locusts—with a brood of terrible spider-like creatures, half-mineral, half-plant, interweaving with masterly intelligence, it is true—*but with intensely evil intent.* And in so far as man has not allowed his shadowy intellectual concepts to be quickened to life, his existence will be united not with the Beings who have been trying to descend since the last third of the nineteenth century—*but with this ghastly brood of half-mineral, half-plantlike creatures.* He will have to live together with these spider-like creatures and to continue his cosmic existence within the order of evolution into which this brood will then enter.

"This is a destiny that is very emphatically part of human evolution upon the Earth, and it is quite well known today by many of those who try to hold humanity back from the knowledge of Spiritual Science. For there are men who are actually conscious allies of this process of the entanglement of Earth-existence. *We must no longer allow ourselves to be shocked by descriptions of this kind.* Such facts are the background of what is often said today by people who out of old traditions still have some consciousness of these things and who then see fit to surround them with a veil of mystery. But it is not right any longer for the process of the earthly evolution of humanity to be veiled in mystery. However great the resistance, these things must be said; for, as I constantly repeat, the acceptance or rejection of spiritual-scientific knowledge is a grave matter for all mankind.

"I have been speaking today of a matter upon which we cannot form a lukewarm judgment; for it is part and parcel of the very texture of cosmic existence. The issue at stake is whether human beings will resolve in the present Epoch to make themselves worthy to receive what the Good-Spirits who want to unite with men are bringing down from the Cosmos, or whether men intend to seek their future cosmic existence within the tangled, spider-brood of their own shadowy thoughts."

Cosmic Memory, **Rudolf Steiner, Chapter XIII,** *The Earth and Its Future,* **GA 11**

"A fact which will play a certain role in the following essays will be briefly indicated here. This concerns the speed with which the development on the different planets takes place. For this is not the same on all the planets. Life proceeds with the greatest speed on Old Saturn, the rapidity then decreases on the Old Sun, becomes still less on the Old Moon and reaches its slowest phase on the Earth. On the latter it becomes slower and slower, to the point at which self-consciousness develops. Then the speed increases again. Therefore, today man has already passed the time of the greatest slowness of his development. Life has begun to accelerate again. On Future Jupiter the speed of the Old Moon, on Future Venus that of the Old Sun will again be attained. The last planet which can still be counted among the series of earthly transformations, and hence follows Future Venus, is called Future Vulcan by mystery science. On this planet the provisional goal of the development of mankind is attained. The condition

of consciousness into which man enters there is called piety or
spiritual consciousness. Man will attain it in the seventh cycle
of Future Vulcan after a repetition of the six preceding stages.
Not much can be publicly communicated about the life on this
planet. In mystery science one speaks of it in such a way that it
is said, 'No soul which, with its thinking is still tied to a physical
body, should reflect about [Future] Vulcan and its life.' That is,
only the mystery students of the higher order, who may leave
their physical body and can acquire supersensible knowledge
outside of it, can learn something about [Future] Vulcan."

Mystery Centers, **Rudolf Steiner, Lecture IX,** *The Great Mysteries of Hibernia*, **Dornach, December 9, 1923, GA 232**

"I have related to you different things concerning the nature of
the Hibernian Mysteries, and you saw in the last lecture that
the peculiar path of evolution which men pursued on the island
of Ireland led them to gain an insight, first of all, into what is
possible to the human mind, into what the human mind can
experience through its own inner activity. You must now consider
how, through all the preparatory exercises which those about to
be initiated had to go through, it was possible that as by magic,
landscapes as they are usually spread out before human senses
were conjured up before these senses. No religious or fanciful
hallucinatory impressions were thus given, for that which man
was accustomed to look upon appeared before the soul as from
behind a veil, concerning which he knew very well something was
behind. And it was the same in regard to the gazing into his own
inner being in the case of the enchanted vision of the dreamlike
summer landscape. The pupil was prepared beforehand to have
Imaginations which were connected with that which he otherwise
saw with his outer senses. But he really knew when he had these

Imaginations that he was about to penetrate further by means of these Imaginations to something quite different.

"I have shown you how the pupil penetrated through to the vision of the time before earthly existence, and to the time after earthly existence; by vision forwards to the time after death as far as the middle point between death and a new birth, and by vision backward s into the time which immediately preceded the descent to Earth,—again to the middle point between death and a new birth. But something still further happened. Because the pupil had been led further to sink himself deeply into that which he had gone through, and because his soul was strengthened through the vision of the pre-earthly and of the post-earthly life, because he had gained insight into Nature dying and continually being re-born, because of all this he could with yet stronger inner power and energy sink himself into what had happened through the numbness, through his being taken up into world-spaces, through floating out into the blue Ether-distances, and again through what had taken place when he felt himself a personality only within his senses, when he so to speak received nothing through the rest of his whole being as man; but only received anything from existence through the eye, or in the auditory tract, or in the sensation of feeling, etc., when he thus became completely a sense-organ.

"The pupil had learned to revive these conditions in himself with strong inner energy, and out of these conditions to allow that to come over him which worked a still further result. When all this was indicated to him, after he had gone through all that which I have described, quite voluntarily and inwardly to bring again before himself the condition of inner numbness, so that he felt, as it were, his own organism as a kind of mineral thing, that is to say, as something quite foreign to him, when he felt his external being, his bodily being, as a thing strange to him, and the soul, as it were, only floating around, ensheathing this mineral thing, then in the condition of consciousness which resulted he received a clear vision of the Moon-existence, which preceded that of the Earth...

"And now when the pupil felt everything flowing together into his heart which he had experienced earlier, just as I described it to you yesterday, all that he had experienced in his soul, manifested itself at the same time as the experience of the planet. Man has a thought. The thought does not remain within the skin of the man. The thought begins to resound. The thought becomes *Word*. That which the man lives, forms itself into Word. In the [Future] Vulcan-planet the Word spreads itself out. Everything in the [Future] Vulcan-planet is speaking, living Being. Word sounds to Word. Word explains itself by Word. Word speaks to Word. Word learns to understand Word. Man feels himself as the World-understanding Word, as the Word-world understanding Word. While this was present before the candidate for Initiation in Hibernia, he knew himself to be in the [Future] Vulcan existence, in the last metamorphosed condition of the Earth-planet."

Spiritual Hierarchies, **Rudolf Steiner, Lecture V, Düsseldorf, April 14, 1909, GA 110**

"Yesterday, we mentioned that, where Old Saturn had transformed itself into the later Old Sun, the Cherubim worked into the Universe from the periphery. Now you must imagine that the Cherubim were already present around Old Saturn; but they had not yet been called upon to play their part. To put it trivially, although they were present at the periphery of Old Saturn, they had not yet reached the stage where they could accomplish a task of importance. Other beings were also present in the environment of Old Saturn, beings of a loftier rank than the Cherubim, the Seraphim. The Thrones come out of the same realm. We have seen how the substance of the Thrones—beings who stand one degree below the Cherubim—streams downward and provides the heat substance of Old Saturn. We can, therefore, picture ancient Saturn as a gigantic globe of heat surrounded by choirs of extraordinarily lofty spiritual beings. In Christian esotericism they are called Thrones, Cherubim and Seraphim. They are the Dhyanic beings of Oriental wisdom.

"But what is the origin of these exalted choirs of beings? Everything in the Universe is in the course of development. In order to gain a picture of where the Cherubim, Seraphim and Thrones come from, it is advisable to consider first our own solar system and ask what will become of it. Let us briefly sketch the development of our solar system. Ancient Saturn was the starting point, and Old Saturn transformed itself into the Old Sun, which further changed into the Old Moon. A special stage of evolution is reached during the transformation of the Old Sun into the Old Moon. The Moon goes out of the Sun for the first time, so that we have in the Moon a cosmic body that exists outside the Sun. The Sun could go through a higher stage of development because it cast off its coarser substances. The whole system developed so as to become our present Earth, which came about because all the coarser substances and beings of the Moon and Earth were cast off from the Sun.

"But evolution proceeds. The beings who have to live their separate existence on Earth, who have been cast off from the Sun, so to speak, continue to develop to even higher stages cut off though they are from the Sun. They still have to go through the [Future] Jupiter stage; but as a result they gradually mature so that they will again be able to unite with the Sun. During the

[Future] Venus evolution, all the beings who dwell on the Earth today will again be incorporated into the Sun. The Sun itself will have reached a higher stage of development because all the beings that had formerly been cast off will have been redeemed. This is followed by the Vulcan condition, the highest stage in the development of our system. The seven stages in the evolution of our system, therefore, are: [Old] Saturn, [Old] Sun, [Old] Moon, [Present] Earth, [Future] Jupiter, [Future] Venus and [Future] Vulcan. During the Vulcan stage all the beings who have evolved out of the small beginnings of Saturn will have been spiritualized in the highest degree. Together they will have grown not only to being a Sun, but more than a Sun. Vulcan is more than a Sun, and it will have reached the stage of maturity when it will be able to sacrifice itself, when it has attained the maturity necessary for self-disintegration.

"The course of evolution for a system that has its starting point in a Sun proceeds in such a way that, at first, the Sun is too weak and thus has to throw off its planets so that it can develop itself to a higher stage. The Sun then grows in strength, reabsorbs its planets, and becomes a Vulcan. Then the whole is dissolved and the Vulcan globe is emptied. Here we have something similar to the round of the Thrones, Cherubim and Seraphim. The Sun will dissolve into the Cosmos, sacrifice itself, send forth its being into the Universe, and thus become a choir of beings like the Seraphim, Cherubim and Thrones who advance to new creative tasks in the Universe."

Foundations of Esotericism, Rudolf Steiner, Lecture XXV, Berlin, October 27, 1905, GA 93a

"When we consider the successive Planetary evolutions we find that each one is a stage of a particular condition of evolution, which has 7 Rounds, 7 x 7 Globes and 7 x 7 x 7 Races. The purpose of every such Planetary evolution is to lead one condition of consciousness through all its stages. In the different esoteric religions these stages are named in various ways. In Christian esotericism:—

A condition of Consciousness is called Power
A Round is called Kingdom, Wisdom
A Globe is called Splendor, Glory

"When in Christian esotericism we speak of Power we mean 'going through a condition of consciousness.' Going through a Round is going through a Kingdom. In the successive rounds man experiences seven Kingdoms:—

1. First Elemental Kingdom
2. Second Elemental Kingdom
3. Third Elemental Kingdom
4. Mineral Kingdom
5. Plant Kingdom
6. Animal Kingdom
7. Human Kingdom

"Going through the seven conditions of Form or Globes is called 'Glory.' Glory signifies what has external appearance, what takes on shape and form. The Lord's Prayer gives us in its final words: 'For Thine is the Kingdom, the Power and the Glory,' a gazing upwards to Cosmic events. When once again this will be present in consciousness, a knowledge of God will be possible.

"Today all religions, exoteric religions in particular, have fallen away from the true knowledge of God. They are the bearers of egoism for they are not conceived in connection with the whole world, with the 'Kingdom, the Power and the Glory.' When these words regain their meaning through living consciousness, then once more religions will be what they ought to be…

"In the Seventh Round [Vulcan], man will create himself. He will then be able to duplicate, to reproduce himself. In the Seventh Round [Vulcan] everyone will have reached the stage at which our Masters stand today. Then our Ego will be the bearer of all earthly experiences. To begin with this will be concentrated in the Lodge of the Masters. The Higher-Ego then will draw itself together, become 'atomic' and form the atoms of [Future] Jupiter.

"The White Lodge will be looked upon as a unity, an Ego comprising everything. All Human-Egos and all separateness will be given up and will flow together into the all-comprehensive Universal-Consciousness; great circles, expanded from within, each having a special color, all assembled together in one single circle. When one thinks of them as laid one upon the other the result is an all-inclusive color. All the Egos are within it, making a whole. This immense globe, contracted, constitutes the atom. This multiplies itself, creating itself out of itself. These then are the atoms which will form [Future] Jupiter. The [Old] Moon Adepts formed the atoms of the present-day Earth. One can study the atom when one studies the plan of the Adepts Lodge on the [Old] Moon."

"On the [Future] Venus a complete consciousness in the etheric body will develop. Then, while man sleeps, he will gain a consciousness concerning the other side of the world. On [Future] Vulcan the spirit is completely detached; he has then taken the etheric body also with him. This condition endows man with an exact knowledge of the entire world."

Theosophy of the Rosicrucians, **Rudolf Steiner, Lecture VIII,**
Human Consciousness in the Seven Planetary Conditions,
Munich, June 01, 1907, GA 99

"That the human being can pass through seven such planetary
conditions is the meaning of evolution. Each planetary stage
is bound up with the development of one of the seven states of
human consciousness, and through what takes place on each
planet the physical organs for such a state-of-consciousness
are perfected. You will have a more highly developed organ, a
psychic organ, on Future Jupiter; on Future Venus there will be an
organ through which man will be able to develop physically the
consciousness possessed by the initiate today on the Devachanic
Plane. 1. And on Future Vulcan, the Spiritual Consciousness will
prevail which the initiate possesses today when he is in Higher
Devachan, the World of Reason." 2.

Notes:

1. Devachan is a phonetic spelling of the Tibetan term 'bde ba can'
    or 'bde ba chen' (frequently written as 'dewachen'). The term can
    be translated as 'blissful realm' or 'pure land,' and corresponds in
    Mahayana Buddhism to 'sukhāvatī' or in Hinduism to 'devaloka'
    ('place of the shining ones') or 'svarga' ('Heaven'). It has two
    fundamental regions; Upper and Lower (Arupa = Formless and
    Rupa = Form).

    Lower Devachan: 'Rupa Devachan,' or also the 'Mental World.'
    In Rosicrucian terminology it is known as the world of the
    'Harmonies of the Spheres' or the World of Inspiration; because
    sound or tone is the medium of the Inspiration when the
    corresponding senses have been opened. In Rosicrucianism,
    this world has been called the 'Heaven World.' "Lower or Rupa-
    Devachanic world, Devachan, the world of Inspiration, the
    Heaven world—these again are one and the same." Rudolf Steiner

Indian theosophical terminology, Lower Devachan, or Rupa-Devachan, is the term used to describe the four lower realms of the spirit land; i.e., the spiritual world, the heavenly world, the kingdom of heaven or the heavenly paradise according to Western Esoteric traditions. According to Rudolf Steiner's Rosicrucian-Christian esotericism, Rupa-Devachan is also called the *World of the Son*. The three lowest regions of the lower devachan correspond to the three outermost planetary spheres, beginning with the Mars sphere; the fourth region, on the other hand, is the realm of primordial thought. This fourth and highest region is also called the 'Akasha.' It is the region of the spiritual Cosmic Memory, the Akasha Chronicle, in which the spiritual archetypes of all earthly events are inscribed. This is where the 'I' of the Plant Kingdom resides. Corresponds to Old Sun.

2. The three uppermost regions of the spirit land, the spiritual world in the narrower sense, are called the Upper Devachan or Higher Devachan. The Higher Devachan is the actual World of Reason, the World of true Intuition. According to Indian theosophical terminology, the Upper Devachan is also called Arupa-Devachan (Sanskrit: अरूप arupa; 'formless'), because this is where the still unformed germinal points of the soul, the living and the physical arise. According to Rudolf Steiner's Rosicrucian-Christian esotericism, it is also called the *World of the Father God* and on occasion the 'superspiritual world.' This is where the 'I' of the Mineral Kingdoms reside. Corresponds to Old Saturn.

The Riddle of Humanity, Rudolf Steiner, Lecture V, Dornach, August 6, 1916, GA 170

"So much, so inconceivably much, has gone into our becoming what we are. And there is so inconceivably much contained in the Earth evolution that is still to come, and in our passage through the spheres of Future Jupiter, Future Venus, and Future

Vulcan! Only little-by-little does one disentangle oneself from the implications of current thought and approach that which, because it is more spiritual, is more difficult to conceive and is rarely touched on by the habitual thinking of people of today. Observing man as he presently is on Earth, we see that the seeds, so to speak, of what will develop during Future Jupiter, Future Venus, and Future Vulcan already are hidden within him. But the human being is also the result of the Old Saturn, Old Sun, and Old Moon spheres. Yesterday I said that wisdom and everything concerned with truth was established on Old Sun and will be completed on Future Jupiter. The seed that was planted on Old Sun will, more-or-less, complete its development on Future Jupiter. Thus, we can say: The period within which truth develops stretches from Old Sun to Future Jupiter. On Future Jupiter, truth will have become thoroughly inward, and so will have become wisdom: Truth becomes Wisdom!"

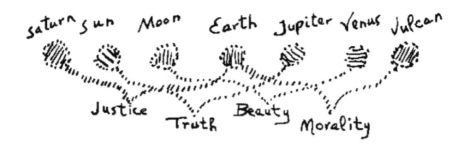

Through these sweeping images of the nature of the Threefold-Ego, we can see outlined a dynamic where the 'Earthly-Ego' comes to birth in the soul realm and merges with the Spirit-Self, manifesting as the reincarnating soul/spirit of the individual. On the other hand, the Higher-Ego, that is a replica of Christ, is intimately connected to the Life-Spirit part of the threefold spiritual constitution of the human being (Spirit-Self, Life-Spirit, Spirit-Human) that may be found in the realm of the Archangels that is the home of the Higher-Ego or Christened-Group-Soul of Humanity. This realm is also called 'Budhi [Buddhi] in theosophical terminology. It is out of this realm that Christ pours forth the Waters of Life to renew the etheric realms of the Earth and the human etheric body. When the soul is purified and the astral body is tamed, the eternal thoughts gleaned from life by the Consciousness-Soul/Spiritual-Soul are offered as the 'Virgin Sophia' to the Spirit-Self as a Bride of Wisdom, ready for the spiritual wedding of the Earthly-Ego to the Higher-Ego, or Spirit-Self to Life-Spirit.

Thus, from Group-Soul to Christened-Group-Soul to union with Christ and the Zodiac, the human three Egos will evolve from the rank of the tenth hierarchy (Human), to the sixth hierarchy and join Christ in the realm of the Elohim at the end of Future Vulcan. Humanity can ascend through the realms of Angels, Archangels, and Archai and become the 'image' of Christ—a trinity of Egos acting as one being.

From many perspectives derived from the works of Rudolf Steiner we have defined, described, and characterized the three Egos as stages, realms, worlds, hierarchical ranks, and mansions in Heaven. These future states (conditions of consciousness or ranks) will take great lengths of time to manifest. Some Spiritual Scientists and initiates can already tap into these realms and communicate with 'supermen' from future worlds, or their own spiritual Egos coming to them from the future. When Moral Imagination, Inspiration, and Intuition move through an initiate or aspirant, the spirit can appear, sound, and speak to the spiritualized Ego of the person. This communication reveals the Divine Plan by using the Language of the Spirit to bring the

'Word' of wisdom and love into the world. We are privileged to
be part of a plan of spiritual evolution that brings the Earthly-Ego
of the human being along a path to becoming a god, a co-creator
with the Divine.

Rudolf Steiner often spoke of the various human principles—
highlighting the importance of understanding their universal
nature in true Rosicrucian-Christian Occultism—and how
through initiation they become purified embodiments of the
Christ-Impulse; what could be called 'Christophorus', or 'bearers
of the Christ' through the 'Three Egos of the Human Being'—by
this is meant the 3-fold nature of the 'I', or the three facets of the
'I'—and how they occupy an important place in developing a
more comprehensive understanding the Fourth Human Principle
the "I Am" or 'I'; sometimes referenced in English translations as
the 'Ego.' In this early lecture from 1905, Rudolf Steiner provides
a clear picture of some of the terms that are helpful to understand
and were used at that time in the Theosophical Society; derived
from the profound esoteric teachings of the Indian literature
from the ancient East. In light of this, once again, the best way is
to let Rudolf Steiner explain this in his own words; and so, it was
thought best to include a complete lecture; therefore it won't be
surrounded by quotation marks; but rather it will be preceded
and followed by a triangle.

Δ

The Foundations of Esotericism, Rudolf Steiner, Lecture V, Berlin, September 30, 1905, GA 93a

It is always stressed that in order to progress in occult matters one
should be as positive as possible and as little as possible negative;

that one should speak less about *what is not*, than about *what is*. When this is practiced in ordinary life it is a preparation for work in the sphere of the occult. The occultist must not ask: *Has the stone life?* But rather: *Where is the life of the stone?* Where is the consciousness of the mineral kingdom to be found? That is the highest form of non-criticism. Particularly in regard to the highest questions this is the attitude-of-mind that must be cultivated.

In ordinary life we differentiate three bodily conditions: the solid, the fluid and the gaseous or airy. The solid must be distinguished from the mineral; for Air and water are also mineral. Theosophical writings add to these, four other finer conditions of matter. The first element which is finer than the air is the one which causes it to expand, which always increases its spatial content. What expands the air in this way is warmth; it is really a fine etheric substance, the first grade of ether, *the Warmth Ether*. Now follows the second kind of ether, *the Light Ether*. Bodies which shine send out a form of matter which is described in Theosophy as Light Ether. The third kind of ether is the bearer of everything which gives form to the finest matter, the Formative Ether, which is also called *the Chemical Ether*. It is this ether which brings about the union of oxygen and hydrogen. And the finest of all the ethers is that which constitutes life: Prana, or *Life Ether*.

Science throws together all four kinds of ether. Nevertheless, it will gradually distinguish them in this way. Our description tallies with that of the Rosicrucians; while Indian literature speaks of four different grades of ether.

To begin with, let us take everything that is solid. What is solid has apparently no life. When one transposes oneself into the life of the solid; which becomes possible through living in waking consciousness in the condition described as the dream world, and when one then seeks to discover the solid; for instance by entering into a rocky mountain landscape, then one feels in oneself that one's own life is altered—*one feels life rippling through one.* One is not there with consciousness, but with one's own life, the etheric body; one is then at a place, in a condition which is called the Mahāparinirvāṇa plane. On this Mahāparinirvāṇa plane the life of the solid is to be found—for this plane is the other pole of the solid. Therefore, through life on the Mahāparinirvāṇa plane one has acquired another means of perception; and when one returns one has experienced the activity of *beings* in the Mahāparinirvāṇa plane. *For it is there that the solid stone has its life.*

Secondly there follows what is fluid, water. When in the dream condition one transposes oneself into the sea, then one becomes imbued with the life of the fluid, on the Paranirvāṇa plane. Through this procedure one learns to know something of the different planes.

Thirdly, when one transposes oneself in dream—into the air-forming element, one finds oneself on the Nirvāṇa plane. Nirvāṇa means literally, 'to be extinguished,' as one extinguishes a fire. When one seeks for life in it, one is with one's own life on the Nirvāṇa plane. Man breathes in the air. When he experiences in himself the life of the air, then that is the way to reach the Nirvāṇa plane. This is the reason for the breathing exercises of the Yogis. No one can attain to the Nirvāṇa plane if he does not actually practice breathing exercises. But they are only Hatha-Yoga exercises when they are carried out on the wrong level. Otherwise they are Raja-Yoga exercises. One actually inhales life: the Nirvāṇa plane.

Fourthly, below the Nirvāṇa plane is the Budhi [spelled 'Buddhi' in Theosophical literature] or Shushupti plane [Sanskrit:

Shushupti = deep sleep consciousness]. There warmth has its life. When Budhi is developed in man, all Kama [desire] is transformed into selflessness, into love. Those animals which develop no warmth are also without passion. At higher levels man must again achieve this passionless condition; because he has his life on the Shushupti plane.

Fifthly comes the Devachan or Mental plane; hence the inner connection between wisdom and light. When in dream consciousness one experiences the light, one experiences wisdom within it. This was always the case when God revealed himself within the light. In the 'burning thorn-bush'; that is to say, in the light, Jehovah appeared to Moses in order to reveal wisdom.[1]

The sixth is the astral plane. On this plane the chemical ether has its life. A somnambulist perceives on the astral plane the qualities of the chemicals, the chemical characteristics; because here the chemical ether actually has its life.

The seventh is the physical plane. There the life ether lives in its own element. With the life ether one perceives life. This ether is also called the atomic ether; because on this plane it has its own life, its own central-point. For what lives on a particular plane has on this same plane its central-point.

As an actual fact everything we have around us contains the seven planes. We must only ask: *Where has each element, the solid, the gaseous, etc., its life?*

We have now heard that warmth has its own life on the Budhi or the Shushupti plane. Thus between all things definite relationships exist. Very striking is the relationship between the ear and speech. In evolution the ear was present much earlier than speech. The ear is the receptive organ; speech is the organ which produces sound. These two, ear and speech, essentially belong together. Sound as it manifests is the result of vibrations in the air, and each single sound arises from a particular vibration. When you study what exists outside, outside yourself, as sound, then you are studying the arithmetic of the air.

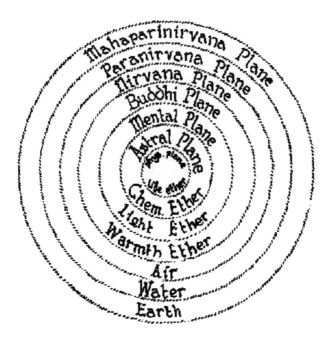

Diagram I.

Undifferentiated space [Akasha] would be soundless. Space which is arithmetically organized produces sound. Here we have an example of how one can look into the Akashic Record. If one can rise to the perception of the inner arithmetic which is preserved from sound in space, then at any time one can hear again a sound which someone has spoken. For instance one can hear what was spoken by Caesar at the crossing of the Rubicon. The inner arithmetic of sound is still present in the Akashic Record. Sound corresponds to something we call Manas [Spirit-Self]. What the ear experiences as sound is the wisdom of the world. In the perception of sound one hears the wisdom of the world. In the act of speaking one brings forth the wisdom of the world. What is arithmetical in our speech remains in the Akashic Record. When he hears or speaks man expresses himself directly in wisdom. At the present time thinking is the form in which man can bring his will to expression in speech. Today it is only in thinking that we can unfold the will. Only later will it be possible for man, rising above the level of thought, to unfold the will in speech.

The next step is connected with warmth. Man's activity is to be sought in what streams out from him as inner-warmth. Out of what proceeds from warmth: passions, impulses, instincts, desires, wishes and so on, Karma arises. Just as the parallel organ to the ear is the organ of speech, so the parallel organ to the warmth of the heart is the pituitary gland, the Hypophysis. The heart takes up the warmth from outside, as the ear does sound. Thereby it perceives world warmth. The corresponding organ which we must have, in order to be able to produce warmth consciously, is the pituitary gland in the head; which at the present time is only at the beginning of its development. Just as one perceives with the ear and produces with the larynx, so one takes up the warmth of the world in the heart and lets it stream forth again through the pituitary gland in the brain. Once this capacity has been achieved, *the heart will have become the organ it was intended to be.* There is a reference to this in words from 'Light on the Path'²: 'Before the soul can stand in the presence of the Masters, its feet must be washed in the blood of the heart.' Then our heart's blood streams out as today our words stream out into the world. In the future, warmth of soul will flood over mankind.

Somewhat deeper in evolution than the warmth organ stands the organ of sight. In the course of evolution the organs of

hearing, warmth and sight, follow in sequence; the organ of sight
is only at the stage of receiving—but the ear already perceives;
for instance in the sound of a bell, its innermost being. Warmth
must flow from the being itself. While the eye has only an image,
the ear has the perception of innermost reality. The perception of
warmth is the receiving of something that rays outwards. There is
an organ which will also become the active organ of vision. This
is today germinally present in the pineal gland, the Epiphysis,
the organ which will give reality to the images which today are
produced by the eye. These two organs, the pineal gland and the
pituitary gland as active organs, must develop into the organ of
vision (eye) and the organ of warmth (heart). Today fantasy is the
preliminary stage leading to a later power of creation. Now man
has at most imagination. Later he will have magical power. This is
the Kriya-shakti power.[3] It develops in proportion to the physical
development of the pineal gland.

In the reciprocal relationship between ear and larynx we have
a prophetic model (example = 'vorbild'). Thinking will later be
interpenetrated with warmth, and still later man himself will
learn to create. First he learns to create a picture; then to create
and send forth radiations; then to create beings. Freemasonry
calls these three forces wisdom, semblance (beauty) and power.
[See: Goethe's Fairy Tale.][4]

Warmth has its life on the Shushupti plane. To make conscious
use of this is possible for one who understands and controls the
life of warmth, as in a certain sense man today controls the life
of the air. In his development man must now approach the forces
of the Shushupti plane (Budhi-Manas) [Budhi = Life-Spirit;
Manas = Spirit-Self]. The Fifth Sub-Race has mainly the task of
developing Kama-Manas. One finds Manas in everything which
is placed in the service of the human spirit. Our age has placed its

highest powers at the service of these needs, whereas the animal is satisfied without such achievements.

Now however Budhi-Manas must also begin its development. Man must learn something beyond speech. Another force must be united with speech, such as we find in the writings of Tolstoi.[5] It is not so much a matter of what he says; but that behind what he says stands an elemental force that has in it something of Budhi-Manas, which must now enter into our civilization. Tolstoi's writings work so powerfully because they are consciously opposed to West[ern] European culture and contain something new and elemental. A certain barbarism which is still contained in them will later be brought into balance. Tolstoi is just a small instrument of a higher spiritual power which also stood behind the Gothic initiate Ulfilas.[6] This spiritual power uses Tolstoi as its instrument.

$$\Delta$$

Notes:

1. Jehovah: Latin translation of the Hebrew יְהֹוָה *Yəhōwā*, the Tetragrammaton יהוה (YHVH), the 'Four-Lettered Name of God,' the God of Israel in the *Old Testament*. The Lunar Exusiai (Spirit of Form) is the leader of Earth evolution that is responsible for separating the Moon from the Earth; which brought about the division of the sexes in the Lemurian Epoch (3rd Epoch), as depicted in the story of Adam and Eve in *Genesis* (2-3)

2. Mabel Collins (September 9, 1851–March 31, 1927) Mrs. Keningale Cook published her many writings under the literary pseudonym of Mabel Collins. She was an English Theosophist and early co-worker of H. P. Blavatsky. Mabel Collins was an author of at least 46 books, including *Light on the Path*, (1885) a

central meditative text amongst Theosophists *Light on the Path*
was the first meditation guidebook Rudolf Steiner used when
he took over the Esoteric Section of the Theosophical Society in
Germany. Regarding its mysterious origins H. P. Blavatsky had
this to say: "[Mabel] saw before her, time after time, the astral
figure of a dark man (a Greek who belongs to the Brotherhood
of our Masters), who urged her to write under his diction. It was
Hillarion [often: Hilarion or Ilarion], whom Olcott knows well.
The results were *Light on the Path* and others." (Source: Michael
Gomes, *Theosophical History*, Vol. 3, No. 7-8 July-October 1991;
pg. 194)

> (See: *Light on the Path and Karma*, written down by M.C. ,
> Theosophical Publishing Society: London, 1904, many editions
> in many languages; Also see: Barnwell, John. *The Arcana of
> Light on the Path: The Star Wisdom of the Tarot and Light of the
> Path*, Verticordia Press: Bloomfield Hills, 1999/ 2nd. Edition
> 2024)

3. Kriya-shakti is the complete 'subject-object unity.' ***Iccha-shakti***
    (Sanskrit: इच्छाशक्ति, romanized: *Icchāśakti*, lit. 'willpower')
    is a Sanskrit term translating to free will, desire, creative urge.
    It functions as the impulse towards manifestation within the
    principle of *shakti,* the concept of divine feminine energy. Along
    with *kriya-shakti* (action power) and *jnana-shakti* (knowledge
    power), *iccha-shakti* is described to constitute the three aspects of
    shakti in Hinduism, regarded to be responsible for the evolution
    of the universe in Tantra. In Shaivism, *iccha-shakti* represents one
    of the five *shakti*s of Shiva, alongside *adi-shakti, parama-shakti,
    kriya-shakti,* and *jnana-shakti.* (Wikipedia)

4. Goethe's Fairy Tale: *The Green Snake and the Beautiful Lily*
    (German title: *Märchen* or *Das Märchen*) is a fairy tale by Johann
    Wolfgang von Goethe published in 1795 in Friedrich Schiller's
    German magazine *Die Horen* (The Horae). It concludes Goethe's

novella rondo *Conversations of German Emigrants* (1795). *Das Märchen* is regarded as the founding example of the genre of Kunstmärchen, or artistic fairy tale. The story revolves around the crossing and bridging of a river, which represents the divide between the outer life of the senses and the ideal aspirations of the human being. (Wikipedia) Rudolf Steiner often made frequent reference to this wonderful tale, characterized by him in: *Old and New Methods of Initiation*, Lecture XII, Dornach, February 25, 1922, GA 210 "In the process, Goethe wrote his fairytale of the *Green Snake and the Beautiful Lily*, which was to depict how the soul forces work in man. Goethe was simply pointing out the path to the world of Imaginations. This fairy-tale of the *Green Snake and the Beautiful Lily* is so very important because it shows that out of his own struggles, and also in his *Faust*, Goethe felt impelled, at a most important moment, to the path towards Imaginations. We see how a personality as great as Goethe strives to find an entry to the Spiritual World. In the fairy-tale of the *Green Snake and the Beautiful Lily* he is seeking for an Imagination which will make the human being comprehensible."

5. Tolstoi: Count Lev Nikolayevich Tolstoy (September 9, 1828–November 20, 1910), usually referred to in English as Leo Tolstoy, was a Russian writer. He is regarded as one of the greatest and most influential authors of all time. He received nominations for the Nobel Prize in Literature every year from 1902 to 1906 and for the Nobel Peace Prize in 1901, 1902, and 1909. Born into an aristocratic family, Tolstoy's notable works include the novels *War and Peace* (1869) and *Anna Karenina* (1878), often cited as pinnacles of realist fiction, and two of the greatest books of all time. He first achieved literary acclaim in his twenties with his semi-autobiographical trilogy, *Childhood, Boyhood, and Youth* (1852–1856), and *Sevastopol Sketches* (1855), based upon his experiences in the Crimean War. His fiction includes dozens of short stories such as *"After the Ball"* (1911), and

several novellas such as *The Death of Ivan Ilyich* (1886), *Family Happiness* (1859) and *Hadji Murad* (1912). He also wrote plays and essays concerning philosophical, moral and religious themes. (Wikipedia)

6. Ulfilas (c. 311-383): Bishop Wulfila was a 4th century preacher of Cappadocian Greek descent. He was the apostle to the Gothic people; who oversaw the translation of the *Bible* into Gothic. Known as the *Gothic Bible* or *Wulfila Bible* is the Christian *Bible* in the Gothic language spoken by the Eastern Germanic (Gothic) tribes in the Early Middle Ages. During the third century, the Goths lived on the northeast border of the Roman Empire, in what is now Ukraine, Bulgaria and Romania. During the fourth century, the Goths were converted to Christianity, largely through the efforts of Bishop Wulfila, who is believed to have invented the Gothic alphabet. The translation of the *Bible* into the Gothic language is thought to have been performed in Nicopolis ad Istrum in today's northern Bulgaria. Traditionally ascribed to Wulfila. The German word for 'I' is 'Ich'; which we know from Rudolf Steiner was first coined by the initiate Ulfilas;† when he first began Gothic as a written language; which subsequently became the German language.

> "Through Christianity much that is of a communal nature has been brought about, which previously was not communal. The active power of this substitution is expressed in the fact that through inner vision, through true mysticism, community with Christ is possible. This has also been embodied in language. The first Christian initiate in Europe, Ulfilas, himself embodied it in the German language, in that man found the 'Ich' within it. Other languages expressed this relationship through a special form of the verb, in Latin for instance the word 'amo,' but the German language adds to it the Ich. 'Ich' is J. Ch. = Jesus Christ. It was with intention that this was introduced into the German

language. It is the initiates who have created language. Just as in Sanskrit the AUM expresses the Trinity, so we have the sign ICH to express the inmost being of man. By this means a central-point was created whereby the tumultuous emotions of the world can be transformed into rhythm. Rhythm must be instilled into them through the Ich. This center-point is literally the Christ."

Rudolf Steiner, *Foundations of Esotericism*, Lecture II, Berlin, September 27, 1905, GA 93a

Understanding the "I Am" and its Relationship to Nerves and Blood

Karma of Untruthfulness, Vol. II, Rudolf Steiner, Lecture XIX, *Secret Societies, the Media, and Preparations for the Great War*, Dornach, January 14, 1917, GA 174

"The nature of man is complicated, and very much of what actually goes on within the human being remains more-or-less beneath the threshold of consciousness, merely sending its effects up into consciousness. True self-knowledge cannot be won without first obtaining insight into the working of the sub-consciousness weaving below the surface in the impulses of soul. These, it could be said, move in the depths of the ocean-of-consciousness and come to the surface only in the wake of the waves they create. Ordinary consciousness can perceive only the waves that rise to the surface, and on the whole one is not capable of understanding their significance—*so true self-knowledge is not possible*. Merely pondering on what is washed up into consciousness does not lead to self-knowledge; for things in the depths of the soul often differ greatly from what they become in ordinary, everyday consciousness. Today we shall look a little into this nature of man in order to gain, from this point-of-view, an idea of how the subconscious soul-impulses in the human being really work.

"In this field we can, of course, to a greater or lesser extent, speak only in pictures. But if you bring together much of what we have hitherto discussed within our Anthroposophical Movement, you will be able to understand the realities that want to speak through the pictures. We can say:— *The invisible nature of man, his Ego, his astral body, his etheric body, work through his visible nature, so what is not manifest works through what is manifest.*

"However, the manner in which what is evident works through what is not evident is very complicated. But if we work our way bit-by-bit through the various parts of this complicated process, and place them all together, we shall, in the end, attain an overall view of the being of man. Even this, though, will always remain incomplete—*for the being of man is infinitely complex.* But at least we can gain a certain basic knowledge of human nature as a valid foundation for self-knowledge.

"Today we shall examine how the separate components of human nature express themselves in a more or less pictorial or formalized manner through physical life. Here is a human being. To illustrate what I want to tell you, I shall start with what we recognize for earthly man as the aspect of which we are conscious: the Ego ['I']. I must emphasize that pictorial explanations can very easily lead to misunderstandings; because things said earlier seem to contradict other things said later. Follow carefully, and you will soon notice that such contradictions are, in fact, non-existent.

"So let us start with the Ego-nature of man, with that component we call our Ego ['I']. This Ego-nature is, of course, entirely super-sensible—*it is the most super-sensible part we have as yet acquired*—but it works through the physical. In the intellectualistic sense the Ego works in our physical being chiefly through the nervous system which is called the system of ganglia, the nervous system radiating from the solar plexus. ... It is active in a way which, at first glance, does not appear to have much to do with what, in a materialistic sense, we could call the life of the nerves. Yet it is the actual point-of-contact for real Ego-activity. This is not a contradiction of the fact that when we begin to see ourselves spiritually, we have to seek the center of the Ego in the head. Since the Ego-component of the human being is super-sensible, the point at which we experience our Ego is not the same as the point at which it chiefly works in us.

"We must be quite clear what we mean when we say: The Ego works through the point-of-contact of the solar plexus. What it means is this: The Ego itself is equipped with only a very dull consciousness. For the Ego-thought is not the same as the Ego. The Ego-thought is what is washed up into consciousness—*but the Ego-thought is not the Real-Ego.* The Real-Ego intervenes as a formative force in the whole human organism through the solar plexus.

"Certainly you can say that the Ego distributes itself over the whole body. But its main point-of-contact, where it particularly intervenes in the formative element of the human organism, is the solar plexus. A better expression would be the system of ganglia, because all the ramifications are part of this process—as the system of ganglia. It is a process that lives in the subconscious and works within this system of ganglia. Since the system of ganglia plays its part in the circulation of blood as well, this does not contradict the fact that the Ego expresses itself in the blood. The exact meaning of everything that is said must be considered. It is one thing to say:—

The Ego intervenes through the system of ganglia in the formative forces and in all the life-processes of the organism.

"But something else is meant when we say:— The blood with its circulation is an expression of the Ego in the human being.

"For the nature of the human being is, as I said, complicated. To understand the significance of what has been said, it will be useful to answer the following question: What is the relationship of the Ego with the system of ganglia and all that is connected with it? How is this Ego anchored, as it were, in the abdominal organs of the human being?

"When the human being is in a normal state of health, the Ego is chained to the solar plexus and all that is connected with it. It is bound by the solar plexus. What does this mean? This Human-Ego, given to man during the course of earthly evolution as a gift from the Spirits of Form [Exusiai; Elohim], has been, as we know, subjected to the temptation of Lucifer. The Ego, as it now exists in mankind, and because it has been infected by luciferic forces, would be a bearer of evil forces. The truth of this fact must definitely be recognized. The Ego is not a bearer of evil forces because of its own nature; but because it has become infected with luciferic forces through the temptation by Lucifer; it is in fact the bearer of truly evil forces—*forces which, because of the luciferic infection, tend to distort the thought life of the Ego towards evil*. Since the moment when the Ego was given to him, man has been able to think. If there had been no luciferic temptation, man would think only good thoughts about everything. But as the luciferic temptation did, in fact, take place, the Ego does not think good thoughts; but thoughts infected by Lucifer. This is a fact of earthly evolution: the Ego is malicious and dastardly. It thinks only of showing itself in a good light and consigning everything else to the shadow. It is infected with all kinds of egoisms. This is how it is—*because it is infected by Lucifer.*

"Now the system of ganglia, the solar plexus, is something in man that has come over from the Old Moon incarnation of the Earth. It is a kind of 'house' for the Ego; the Ego fits into it in a certain way. In fact, it can be held a prisoner there. So we have the following state-of-affairs: Because of its luciferic infection, the Ego tends all the time to behave in a dastardly, lying manner and place itself in the light, while consigning everything else to the shade. But it is held prisoner by the nervous system of the abdomen. For there it has to behave itself. By means of the nervous system of the abdomen the properly progressing forces, which have come to us from Old Saturn, Sun and Moon, compel the Ego not to be a demon in the bad sense of the word. So the manner in which we bear our Ego within us is to have it bound by the organs of the abdomen.

"Assume now that these abdominal organs are unhealthy in some way, or not in a normal state. Not to be in a normal state means not to want to take in fully what fits into them spiritually, what spiritually belongs to them. The Ego can be somewhat freer in its activity if the abdominal organs are not quite healthy. If this freeing is brought about by some physical hyperactivity, this can express itself in the human being in that the Ego is let loose on the external world, instead of remaining bound. When the Ego behaves freely in this way, we have a case of psychological illness: the human being displays the characteristics of the Ego infected by Lucifer. The characteristics of the Ego of which I have spoken then make their appearance. There is certainly no need to be a materialist in order to understand fully the manner in which the spiritual—in this case the Ego—can be bound to the physical organs in the life between birth and death; though in a way that

differs from what is perceived by a materialist. There is no need
to be a materialist to see how, in a manner of speaking, the devil
can throw off his chains and break loose. This is one instance of
psychological illness.

"The freeing of the Ego, however, is not necessarily a question
of psychological illness, because another state of affairs is also
possible. In such an instance it is not a question of illness in
the abdomen but rather a 'switching off' of its normal activity.
This is what happens in the great majority of cases of hypnotic
consciousness. The functioning of the system of ganglia in the
abdomen is put into a state—either by natural causes or by all
kinds of mesmeric effects—in which it is unable properly to
keep the Ego under control. Thus in this way, too, the Ego has
an opportunity to become more involved with its environment.
It is not embedded in the system of ganglia and is therefore free
to make use of channels to the outside world which enable it
to perceive from a distance all kinds of processes in space and
time which, when it is embedded in the system of ganglia, are
processes which it cannot normally perceive.

"So it is important to know that a certain relationship exists
between the hypnotized state, which in a mild way switches
off the normal activity of the processes bound to the system
of ganglia in ordinary consciousness, and certain forms of
madness, where the switching-off is caused by deformation
or illness in certain abdominal organs. If the Ego is freed,
if it feels, you might say, free of its chains and is linked, not
with its body—but with [unwholesome] spiritual forces in its
environment, this is always, in a way, a pathological state, just as
is also the case in madness. That is why some forms of madness
are characterized by the appearance of spite, mendacity,
cunning and craftiness—*everything that comes from luciferic*

infection—the urge to place oneself in the light and consign others to the shadow, and so on.

"Now you will understand why a person's constitution of soul depends on the very way the shell which binds his Ego is fashioned. In order not to focus too closely on the human being and perhaps offend some human souls, let us instead look for a moment at a lion, a savage carnivore, and how it compares with a bull or an ox. You can see the difference. Even though the lion has a Group-Ego while the human being is endowed with an Individual-Ego, we can still use this comparison. What is the difference between the lion's nature and the ox's nature? The lion is definitely a carnivore while the ox is for the most part a vegetarian. The difference is this: What in the lion corresponds to his Group-Ego is less bound; the forceful activity suitable for his abdominal organs makes the Ego freer, lets it loose more on its environment; whereas in the vegetarian ox the group ego is more bound to the abdominal organs. The ox lives more bound up in itself.

"You can see why it can be good sense for human beings to become vegetarian—of course, only if they so wish. For what does a vegetarian diet bring about? It makes the abdominal organs even more capable of binding the Ego, which, if this does not sound like a paradox, leads to the human being becoming more gentle. His evil demon is more internalized and lives less in the environment. Nobody, however, should persuade himself that he does not possess this demon, for he does—*but it is more imprisoned within him…*

"Human nature is indeed exceedingly complicated. One very good way of attaining some knowledge as a basis for true, genuine self-knowledge in life is to pay attention to the connection between the spiritual and bodily parts. I should add,

though, that vegetarians should take care not allow themselves
to become too undernourished. If they are undernourished they
are in danger of damaging themselves, and then their chains—
the 'prison for their devil,' who shows himself in wiliness, lies
and so on—are weakened. They then let their devil out into the
environment, and the environment is troubled by their problems.
Either that, or else they themselves have the trouble. They fail to
cope with themselves; for they either constantly have a mania
for manifesting the various bad qualities of the Ego, or—if they
are well brought-up—they have the urge to keep all this to
themselves, in which case, too, it can happen that they fail to cope
with themselves. All kinds of dissatisfactions arise in their soul. It
is important to see this.

"Just as the Ego has its point-of-contact in the system of
ganglia—*so does the astral body have its point-of-contact in all
those processes which are linked with the nervous system of the
spinal cord*. Naturally, the nerves run through the whole body;
but in the nervous system of the spinal cord we have a second
point-of-contact. Included in this, of course, are once again
all the processes connected with this spinal nervous system.
I am not speaking of the cerebral nervous system. I mean the
nervous system of the spinal cord which has to do, for instance,
with our reflex actions, and is a regulator for much that goes
on in the human body. In the present context we must include
all the processes regulated by this nervous system. Again we
have to see that the astral body is either bound to everything
connected with this spinal system or that it can become free
of it, through illness or through partial somnolence brought
about by mesmerism or something similar. The entity which is
bound here received its luciferic attributes—which are mingled
a little with ahrimanic attributes—as long ago as the time of

Old Moon. Therefore, while these are weaker than the luciferic attributes of the Ego, they are present in the astral body too. If you want to turn your soul to a contemplation of the process by which this luciferic infection crept into the astral body, you will have to study what I said in my book *Occult Science* about the separation of the Moon from evolution as a whole. This infection made its appearance during the time of Old Moon. Here you will discover another reason for certain characteristics in the human being, characteristics of a hypnotic nature— higher hypnotic characteristics which are bound, in the main, to the organs of the chest and which bring in higher experiences than do the organs of the abdomen. At the same time you will see that if something is not in order, so that the astral body cannot be bound as it should be, something can again come about which is a psychological illness, a psychological disorder. Just as the Ego can be released, causing signs of madness, so also can the astral body be released, which again leads to signs of madness.

"When the Ego is released, this leads, as I have said, to characteristics such as spite, cunning, wiliness, fraudulence, giving prominence to oneself and putting everyone else in the shade, and so on. When the astral body is released, this leads to volatility of ideas and lack of cohesive thought, manic states on the one hand or, on the other, to withdrawal, depression, hypochondria. Again, these conditions could be brought about by hypnotic or mesmeric intervention; but in this case the organs are not ill—but have had their normal physical function suppressed by the intervention of a hypnotist or mesmerist.

"There is much in our human nature which must be held in check—*for in a way we do belong to the devil.* We are at least partially decent human beings solely because the devils in us

are held in check by the Divine-Spiritual-Forces which have
developed in the proper way through the periods of Old Saturn,
Sun and Moon. Nonetheless, because of the various temptations,
we do not possess all that great an aptitude for decency. A good
many bad dispositions and moods of soul-life are the result of
meeting with the demon in us. The appearance of the demonic
element comes about because what is bound can become
unbound.

"We shall speak on another occasion about what it is in the
life between death and a new birth that binds those aspects that
are bound by our physical body now, during life between birth
and death. You will agree that we owe a great debt of gratitude to
the Cosmic Order that here, between birth and death, we possess
our physical organism; for without it we would have no 'prison'
for our higher components. For when these higher components
are set free, after we have laid aside our physical body, different
conditions come into operation; which we will discuss at another
time. Suffice it to say that the higher components still retain some
fetters, even then.

"Now, just as the astral body is bound in this way by the
system of the spinal cord and all the processes of organic life
connected with it—*so is the etheric body bound by the cerebral
system and everything that belongs to it.* Therefore, the etheric
body has its point-of-contact by means of the cerebral system.
Similar things could be said here, too; for in our head there is
a 'prison' for our etheric body. Madness or hypnotic conditions
come into operation if the body is not quite well and the etheric
body is let loose. Left to itself, i.e., not enclosed in the prison of
the head, the etheric body has the tendency to reproduce itself,
thus becoming a stranger to itself and spilling over into the
world, carrying its life into other things. This is a description of

the conditions that come about if the 'prison warden' releases the etheric body.

"So we have three possibilities for psychological illness, and also three possibilities of escaping from the physical body. These three possibilities must definitely be taken into consideration—but of course in quite a different way—when a person is to become free of his physical body through Initiation. As what we have been speaking about so far is a freeing brought about by illness, when the organs of the physical body do not remain healthy and are then incapable of containing the higher components. Somnolence of the brain would result if brain activity were damped down. The etheric body would be freed and a somnolent condition would take over. But when the brain is defective, the prison can no longer hold the prisoner—that is, the etheric body—which then embarks on its own adventures, endeavoring to live and create its own disordered, muddled life by opening out into the world. So you see clearly that psychological illnesses are, in the main, caused by a kind of freeing from the physical basis to which the various higher components of man belong during life between birth and death.

"*The etheric body, when it is freed, has mainly ahrimanic characteristics.* Envy, jealousy, avarice and similar states will be pathologically exaggerated, always in connection with a kind of spreading into the environment, a kind of letting oneself go. Try to understand it like this:— The only point of attraction for the Ego is, more-or-less, the system of ganglia and whatever is connected with it; the astral body's point-of-contact is with the spinal system; but together with the system of ganglia; and the etheric body is linked with the cerebral system, but jointly, with both the spinal system and the system of ganglia. So, from this point-of-view, the system of ganglia also has to do with the brain, for instance, insofar as it serves all subconscious organic processes. If the system of ganglia brings about a process of illness which runs its course in the brain, then it could be the etheric body which is freed, even though the root cause lies in the system of ganglia. You see how very complicated things are.

"Psychiatry today has, as yet, no means of distinguishing between these three forms of soul sickness. Psychiatry will only achieve some degree of perfection when distinction is made between psychological abnormalities brought about by the freeing from bondage of the etheric body, or the astral body, or the Ego. Then there will be a really significant way of distinguishing between, and assessing, the various symptoms of psychological abnormality—and it will be important to assess them in this way.

"You see from all this how self-knowledge can only be built up on a penetrating view of the complicated nature of the human being. Knowledge can certainly have disagreeable sides to it. But knowledge is not supposed to be a toy; for it is the most serious matter in the whole of human life. Someone who knows everything there is to know about human nature—if he is even only somewhat inclined to understand it in a way which is not *egoistic*, if he is inclined to think and feel about it in an objective way—can have in this knowledge an important healing factor at his disposal. One might be too weak to use this healing factor; but this knowledge is an important healing factor. It cannot be gained by remaining in one's subjective nature; it cannot be gained by failing to extricate oneself from this.

"This is a great problem for a movement such as ours. On the one hand, it is necessary to strive earnestly for the highest knowledge; but on the other hand, not everybody who decides to join such a movement is inclined to accept such knowledge with total objectivity and with full earnestness. Such knowledge brings health to personal life only if one is not constantly busy reflecting upon one's own personality, if one is not constantly wondering: How do *I* feel, what is going on in *me*, how am *I* getting on in the world, what is living in *my* soul, and so on. *It brings healing only if we free ourselves from all that and concern ourselves instead with the affairs of mankind as a whole, matters which concern every human being.* Difficulty arises only if one wants to concentrate on oneself, if one cannot get away from oneself. The more one is capable of turning away from oneself and towards all that concerns people and the world in general—*the more can knowledge become a healing factor.*

"How glad I would be if only you would believe this! A movement like ours gives plenty of opportunity for observing the very opposite of what I have been saying. It is, of course, natural and justified that people who cannot easily get away from themselves should turn to our Movement for comfort and hope and confidence. But if they do not honestly strive to get away from themselves, if they continue to concern themselves with their own head and their own heart—not to mention whatever else very many people in our Movement are concerned with— then knowledge cannot become for them what, in truth, it is. It is possible to be interested in knowledge in such a way that it becomes not only a personal—*but also a general human affair.* The more personal considerations are involved—*the more one is distracted from what is healing in all the knowledge about the deeper aspects of the world.*

"From the points-of-view we have now reached we must endeavor to gain clarity about how certain impulses in human nature are connected with the freeing of the soul and spiritual element, either in states brought about by hypnosis or mesmerism, or in madness. A process of freeing is always connected with a merging into the spiritual element. But this is in-turn bound up with a certain feeling of voluptuousness, with real voluptuousness, both direct and indirect. For whatever has become free—be it the etheric or astral body, or the Ego—in a way pours itself into the spiritual world. And this pouring forth is definitely connected with inner-feelings of bliss.

"Somebody with a psychological abnormality gains a certain satisfaction from his abnormal soul activity and is therefore loath to depart from it…

"There is truly nothing in the physically-perceptible world as complicated as the nature of the human being. It is more complicated than anything else in the world. To understand man in his totality you have to view him in the way I have been describing. We have seen, for instance, that in the human being as he stands before us with his head, the activity of this head depends in some degree on the etheric body connecting up in the right way to it. Abnormal activity comes about if the etheric body is freed, if it is unbound. Because of the way the human being is normally organized with regard to his sense organs and the nerves of his brain, the etheric body can have a normal relationship with the ordinary environment. What man is as a result of the special connection between his etheric body and his head makes him into a human being like all others in his existence between birth and death in the physical world. If we had nothing else about us except the normal connection of our etheric body with our head, all human beings would be the same—*and there would also be no way of feeling connected with that part of our being that is immortal.* For our head brings to us the experiences we have in life between birth and death through our senses, through the nerves of the brain.

"Consider this in connection with what I have said about the loss of the head during the course of reincarnation: *What is now our head was in our previous incarnation our body, and what is now our body will become our head in our next incarnation.* We know about this connection with our immortal part which runs through all births and deaths—*even though without the wisdom of Spiritual Science this knowledge can only take the form of a belief.* Through our head we can understand this connection; but we can only have this knowledge because we have the system of the spinal cord as an organ of our astral body. For this is where those ideas and feelings are wrought which bring us into a mutual relationship with our immortal, our super-personal, part.

"Everything we possess only for this life between birth and death is given to us through the earthly, solid element in our organism. On other occasions I have pointed out that there is indeed very little of the solid element in our make-up, of which ninety-five percent consists, in fact, of fluid—*of a pillar of fluid.* The human being is a pillar of water containing only five percent of solid ingredients. Yet only this solid element can be the bearer of our ordinary thoughts in physical life; and only insofar as we are permeated by the fluid element with its pulsation can we know about our super-personal part. And this fluid element with its pulsation is linked with the spinal system; which, for the most part, regulates this fluid element and its pulsation.

"How all this is related to certain things I have described on other occasions, to the pulsating rise and fall of fluid between the abdomen and the brain … Now, because the human being bears the fluid element within him he is linked with his super-personal part. But this fluid element also establishes his specific personality. If we had only heads, we would all think the same, feel the same. But because we also have hearts, the fluid element, blood and other juices in us, we are specific in some degree; for through this element the hierarchy of the Angeloi can have a part in our being. The hierarchy of the Angeloi can intervene in us via the fluid element.

"A third possibility for intervening in our being is given because even with the normal working together of the higher components with the system of ganglia, it is possible for the airy element and everything connected with it to have an effect on us. This happens in the process of breathing. It is very complicated, and it varies depending on where we breathe, on how much oxygen, how much humidity, how much Sun-warmth is in the air and so on. It is the hierarchy of the Archangeloi, the Archangels, who work on us via the airy element. And everything that works in us from the hierarchy of the Archangeloi—both those who have progressed normally and those who are retarded—works via the system of ganglia. Also this is the route by which the folk-spirits work; for they belong to the hierarchy of the Archangeloi. The work done by the folk-spirits in the human being takes its effect through the organs which are connected with the system of ganglia. This is why nationality is something so far removed from consciousness—*something that works in such a demonic way*. And for the reasons I have pointed out it is linked so strongly with everything to do with one's locality. For the locality, the local climate, is far more closely connected with the working of the hierarchy of the Archangeloi than one might imagine. Climate is nothing other than what works on the human being via the air.

"So you see that by discussing the system of ganglia one is indicating how the impulses of all that belongs to the folk-soul work in man's unconscious. You will now also understand why, more than one might ordinarily think, belonging to a particular nation is connected with certain characteristics which are linked to the system of ganglia. More than one might think, the problem of nationality has to be seen in relation to the problem of sexuality. Belonging to a nation has the same organic foundation—the system of ganglia—as the sexual element. Quite externally you can understand this when you remember that you belong to a nation by birth, that is, your body develops inside that of a mother who belongs to a particular nation. This of itself creates a link. So you see what subterranean soul foundations connect the problem of nationality with the problem of sexuality. That is why these two impulses in life manifest in such related ways. If your eyes are open to life you will see a tremendous amount of similarity between the way people behave in an erotic sense and the way they show their connection to their nationality. I am not speaking either for or against either of these things; but the facts are as I have described them. Arousal of a nationalistic kind, which works particularly strongly in the unconscious if it is not brought up into Ego-consciousness by making it a question of karma as I described the other day, is very similar to sexual arousal. It is no good glossing over these things by making out that the emotional illusions and longings of national feeling are noble, while sexual feelings are rather less so. For the facts are as I have described them to you.

"From all this you will see that a good amount of agreement can be reached amongst people in matters of the head—*for in the head everyone is the same.* If we consisted of heads only, we would understand one another famously. It is peculiar to say: *If we consisted of heads only.* But when life has brought one together with all kinds of people one grows accustomed to speaking in paradoxes such as this…

"If, as I said, we were heads, it would be easy for us to reach an understanding about all kinds of things. It is less easy to reach

an understanding about matters which have to be comprehended
via the tool of the spinal system. That is why people are embattled
with regard to their view of the world, their religion and
everything else they connect with what is super-personal. And
there is no doubt at all that today they are embattled also with
regard to everything for which the system of ganglia is the organ.
By this I do not mean the external war; I mean the war that
speaks in the language of hate-against-hate; for the external war
need not necessarily have anything to do with all that is unfolding
in such a terrible way in the form of hate-against-hate.

"It is essential for people to become conscious of these things.
Only if people can come to understand the nature of the human
being will it be possible to find a way out of that chaos into which
mankind has entered. Tomorrow we shall speak more about this
chaos. But we must be clear about one thing: The knowledge
and understanding we gain about the complicated nature of the
human being must be filled with a mood that I described just now
as an impersonal mood.

"So far I have only described harmless, personal moods such
as those in people who cannot cope with themselves, who go
on-and-on about their heart, or one thing and another. But in the
world at large we meet with less harmless moods, either personal
or belonging to the egoism of a whole group. Occult knowledge
is not always applied in a selfless manner, as you saw during
our considerations over the past few weeks. We can certainly
look more deeply into the impulses at work in human history if
we have an understanding of the complexity of human nature.
For what we can come to know with regard to the individual is
connected in turn with all that happens between people, both on
a one-to-one basis and also between the different groupings that
come about during human evolution."

Esoteric Lessons, 1904-1909, Vol. I, Rudolf Steiner, Part III, *Esoteric Lesson*, Munich, January 16, 1908, GA 266/1

"Those who are engaged in esoteric training are, in a certain sense, 'waiting,' are seekers. They are waiting for the day a new world will open to them, a world other than the one they usually perceive. They are waiting for the day when they can say:—

> 'I see a new world: between all the things I could perceive in space around me, I see a fullness of spiritual beings that were previously hidden from me.'

"To make this quite clear to you about this, you must, once again, recall the seven conditions of consciousness that human beings go through in the course of evolution. The first state-of-consciousness that the human being had to pass through was a dull, dim state-of-consciousness in which the human beings felt themselves to be at-one with the Cosmos; this state or condition is called Old Saturn-existence. In the Old Sun-existence, the compass of consciousness decreased—*but it became all the brighter for it.* When human beings then lived through Old Moon-existence [astral], their consciousness was similar to what we experience as a last remnant in our dreams; it was a dim picture-consciousness. Here on Earth we have a bright day-consciousness; which will remain when man rises once again to picture-consciousness on Future Jupiter evolution, so that we then have a bright consciousness of pictures [astral].

"Human beings will then raise themselves to two additional, higher states-of-consciousness, the Inspired and Intuitive. Thus our bright day-consciousness stands in the middle between the dim picture-consciousness of Old Moon and the bright picture-consciousness of Future Jupiter. And what the esotericist awaits,

which one day is to be revealed to them, is Jupiter consciousness.[1]
It will one day reach each of you, one person earlier, another
person later—*this depends upon your abilities, and degree of inner
maturity.*

"Now, however, the Future Jupiter-consciousness is already
present in its initial seed-form in every human being. For the
Future-consciousness is already indicated in a very delicate
way; but present-day humans don't know how to interpret it.
The esoteric life consists to a large extent in pupils learning
to interpret the subtle processes in themselves and in their
surroundings. The Old Moon consciousness has not yet entirely
disappeared either; but is still present in its last remainder. In
present-day humans, the two conditions, in which in one case the
Old Moon consciousness is still present, and in the other case the
Future Jupiter consciousness is already present—respectively, as
the *feeling of shame* and the *feeling of fear.* In the feeling of shame,
where the blood is pushed towards the periphery of the body, a
final remnant of the Old Moon consciousness still lives. And in
the feeling of fear, where the blood streams towards the heart in
order to find there a fixed center, the Future Jupiter consciousness
is announced. And so normal daytime consciousness swings in
two directions.

Feeling of Shame------------Normal------------Feeling of Fear

"When we are feeling ashamed about something and our
face turns red, we are experiencing something reminiscent
of the Moon existence. Picture humans of today back on Old
Moon. They could not yet say 'I' to themselves; but rather, they
lived in a dull, dim picture-consciousness, entirely embedded in
astral forces and beings, with which they felt themselves to be in

harmony. Imagine, my sisters and brothers, if one day the feeling were suddenly to dawn on such a Moon- proto-human:— 'I am an I. I am different from the others, I am an independent being, and all the other surrounding beings are looking at me.'

"The entire Moon-proto-human would have been glowing from top to bottom with an incredible feeling of shame. Such a being would have sought to disappear, to be overcome with shame, if he had been able to feel such a premature I-feeling. So we too, my sisters and brothers, when a feeling of shame overtakes us, we would prefer to disappear, to sink under-the-ground, to dissolve our I-ness, as it were. Imagine how the Old Moon proto-humans were embedded in harmony with the forces and beings in their surroundings. If they were approached by a hostile being they did not think about it; but knew instinctively how to avoid it. They acted there with a feeling that, if they had been conscious, could have expressed it as follows:— 'I know that the order of the world is not arranged in such a way that this wild beast will now tear me apart; but rather the harmony of the world is such that there must be means that will protect me from my enemy.'

"Thus the Old Moon-proto-humans felt themselves to be directly in complete, unmediated harmony with the forces of the Universe. And if an I-feeling had awakened in them—*it would have immediately disturbed this harmony*. And as a matter of fact the I-feeling, when it began to permeate human beings on Earth, did increasingly create disharmony with their environment. A clairaudient hears the Universe ringing-out in a mighty harmony, and when they compare it with the sounds that come from individual human beings, then today there is a disharmony—one person more, with another less—*but there is a disharmony nonetheless*. And your task in the course of evolution is to increasingly resolve this discord more and more into harmony. This disharmony arose through I-ness; but it was instituted with wisdom by the spiritual powers who rule and guide the Universe. Had human beings always remained in harmony—*they never would have come to independence.* Disharmony was instituted so that human beings could once again achieve harmony in freedom *out of their own power.* This self-aware feeling for being an 'I' had to develop at first at the expense of inner-harmony. When the time comes for the Future Jupiter-consciousness to light-up, human beings will arrive again at a harmonious relationship with the forces of the Cosmos; *for they will maintain this self-aware I-feeling into the new state-of-consciousness, so that they will be independent, and also in harmony with the Universe.*

"We have now seen that the new consciousness of Jupiter is already being announced in the feeling of fear. However, it is always the case that whenever a future-state begins to appear before its time, then it is premature and not in its rightful place. … So it is with the feeling of fear. It is still out of place today—*but much less so in the future.* What happens with the feeling of fear? The blood is pressed into the center of the human being, into the heart, in order to form a fixed center, in order to make one strong to face the outside world. *It is the innermost power of the 'I' that brings this about.* This power of the 'I' acting on the blood, must become increasingly more-and-more conscious and powerful. For on Future Jupiter, human beings will be able to consciously direct their blood toward the center and be able to make themselves strong. However, what is unnatural and destructive about this today is the feeling of fear associated with this flow of blood. *This must not be allowed to happen in the future; for only the forces of the 'I,' without fear, must be at work there.*

"In the course of human development, the outside world around us is becoming more and more hostile. Increasingly more and more you must learn to confront the encroaching outside world with your inner-power. *But in doing this, fear must disappear.* And especially for those who undergo esoteric training, it is necessary, unavoidably necessary, that they free themselves from all feelings of fear and anxiety. Fear only has a certain justification where it alerts us to stand strong; but all the unnatural feelings of fear that torment people must disappear altogether. What would happen if man still has feelings of fear and anxiety, and Jupiter-consciousness arrived? Then the outside world will be set in opposition to the human being in a much more hostile and terrible way than it is today. A human being who does not cease to fear here will fall into one frightening horror after another.

"Already this condition is being prepared now in the external world; and this will be shown to humans even more clearly in the terrifying age that will arrive under the regency of Oriphiel, concerning whom I spoke to you last time.[2]

"By then humans must have learned to stand solidly! Our present-day culture is itself creating the terrible monsters that will threaten the future of humanity on Jupiter. One need only look at the gigantic machines that human technology constructs today with all of its cunning! *Human beings are creating in those machines the demons that will rage against them in the future.*

"Everything that human beings create today in terms of technological apparatus and machines will in the future come to life and oppose them in a terrible and hostile way. All that is created out of a purely utilitarian principle, out of individual or collective egoism—*is the enemy of humanity in the future.* Today we ask much too much about the utility of what we do. If we really want to foster evolution, then we must not ask about utility—*but rather, we must inquire whether something is beautiful and noble.* Everything that people do today in order to satisfy their artistic needs—*out of pure love of beauty*—this too will come to life in the future; but it will contribute to the higher development of the human being. But today it is terrible to see how many thousands of people are kept from knowing any other activity than those done for the sake of material utility; they are cut off from everything that is beautiful and artistic all their lives. The most wonderful works of art should hang in the poorest elementary schools; that would bring boundless blessings to human evolution. For human beings are themselves building their own future. We can get an idea of what it will be like on Jupiter if we clearly understand that today there is nothing absolutely good and nothing absolutely evil. Today good and evil are mixed in every human being. A good person must always say that he or she possesses only a bit more good than evil within—*but is not at all wholly good.* On Jupiter, however, good and evil will no longer be mixed; but rather, human beings will divide themselves into the entirely good and the entirely evil. And all that we cultivate today in terms of the good and the beautiful serves to strengthen the good on Jupiter, and all that happens only from the point-of-view of egoism and utility strengthens the evil.

"So that human beings in the future are a match for the evil powers, they must gain mastery of the inner-most power of their 'I'; they must be able to regulate the blood consciously in such a way that it makes them strong in the face of evil—*but without fear of any kind.* They must have the power that drives the blood inward within their power. But also that other ability to pour the blood from the heart to the periphery must not be lost to them. Because the state of Jupiter will in a way also mean a return to the Old Moon-consciousness [but with the addition of the wakefulness that was gained through Earth-evolution]. Human beings will again come back into harmony with the great laws of the Universe and feel at one with them. They will once again acquire the ability to flow together with the spiritual powers of the world; *but not unconsciously and dimly as on Old Moon.* But rather, on Future Jupiter they will maintain their clear day-consciousness and self-conscious I-feeling and yet live in harmony with the spiritual powers and laws of the world. Disharmony will then be dissolved in harmony. And to be able to let themselves flow into the harmony of the Universe—*they must learn to consciously let the inner-most-power of their 'I' radiate out from the heart.* They must be able to centralize the inner-power of their blood when an enemy approaches them, and they must also be able to radiate it forth consciously. *Only then will they be equal to future conditions.*

"Those then who strive for inner-development must begin today to gradually get these forces more and more under control. They do this by learning consciously to inhale and exhale. When humans inhale—*the forces of the 'I' enter into activity*—for the forces that bring them into connection with the powers of the Cosmos, are those forces that radiate from the heart. And when human beings exhale, and when they hold their breath—then those forces of the 'I' become active which push toward the middle-point, toward the heart, and create for them a stable center. Thus, esoteric pupils are learning already today when they consciously practice breathing exercises in this manner. They learn gradually to master the powers of the 'I.' However, no one should believe that they are allowed independently to carry out such exercises if they have not yet received instructions on them.[3] Everyone will receive them at the right time. However, even for those who are not yet doing any exercises, it is never too early to familiarize oneself with the meaning of these exercises and to gain an understanding of them. They will then become all the more fruitful for you later on. Thus, my sisters and brothers, you should always strive to gain more and more understanding for the subtle processes within yourselves and in the Cosmos and gradually grow into the future stages of human evolution.

Notes:

1. *Jupiter-Consciousness*: See: Lecture January 3, 1915, "The Future Existence of Jupiter and its Beings," in: *Art as Seen in the Light of Mystery Wisdom*, Rudolf Steiner (GA 275)

2. Rudolf Steiner is referring here to the Archangelic Period of Oriphiel that begins in 2,229 A.D. and will extend for around 350 years after the end of the present Michaelic Age.

3. On breathing exercises: See also: *Soul Exercises* (GA 267)

Michaelic Verse For Our Time

We must eradicate from the soul all fear and terror of

what comes toward us out of the future.

We must acquire serenity in all feelings and sensations about the future.

We must look forward with absolute equanimity to all that may come,

and we must think only that whatever comes is given to us

by a world direction full of wisdom.

This is what we have to learn in our times.

To live out of pure trust in the ever-present help of the Spiritual World.

Surely nothing else will do, if our courage is not to fail us.

Let us properly discipline our will, and let us seek

the inner awakening every morning and every evening.

Diagram 1
Elohim †
Incarnations of the Earth

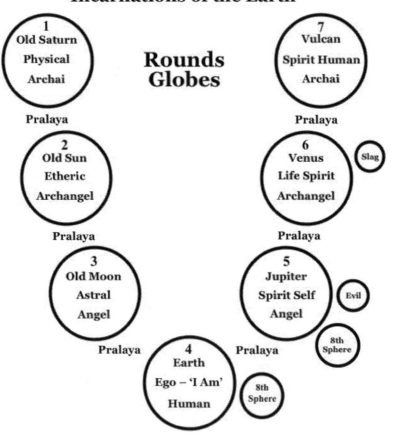

Rounds
Globes

1
Old Saturn
Physical
Archai

Pralaya

2
Old Sun
Etheric
Archangel

Pralaya

3
Old Moon
Astral
Angel

Pralaya

4
Earth
Ego – 'I Am'
Human

8th
Sphere

Pralaya

7
Vulcan
Spirit Human
Archai

Pralaya

6
Venus
Life Spirit
Archangel

Slag

Pralaya

5
Jupiter
Spirit Self
Angel

Evil

8th
Sphere

† Spirits of Form, Greek: Exousíai, ἐξουσίαι; Latin: Potestates; English:
Powers, Authorities; Hebrew: 'Ělōhīm, אֱלֹהִים - plural of אֱלֹוהַּ, 'Ělōah.
"God(s), Heavenly Power(s)."

Diagram 2

7 Conditions of Consciousness

"Neither can they die any more: for they are equal unto the angels; and are the children of God, being the children of the resurrection." Luke (20:36)

Old Saturn
Deep Trance Consciousness
Upper Devachan

Atman Vulcan
Moral Intuition
Universal Consciousness

"Each condition of consciousness can only run its course in seven conditions of life; each condition of life in seven conditions of form. That is 7 x 7 x 7 conditions. In fact, an entire evolution such as that of the Earth passes through 7 x 7 x 7 conditions of form. Our Earth was once Saturn; this went through seven conditions of life and each condition of life through seven conditions of form, Therefore you have forty-nine conditions of form upon Saturn, forty-nine upon the Sun, forty-nine upon the Moon, etc.; 7 x 49 = 343 conditions of form. Man passes through 343 conditions of form in the course of his evolution." †

Old Sun
Dreamless Sleep Consciousness
Lower Devachan

Budhi Venus
Moral Inspiration
Hearing
Music of the Spheres

"Jesus answered them, Is it not written in your law, I said, Ye are gods?"
John (10:34)

Old Moon
Dream Consciousness
Astral World

Manas Jupiter
Moral Imagination
Psychic or Soul Consciousness

Earth
Waking Consciousness

† Rudolf Steiner,
The Apocalypse of St. John,
Lecture X June 28th, 1908 (CW 104)

Diagram 7

Nine-Fold Constitution of the Human Being

1. *Old Saturn*
Thrones – Warmth Ether
Spirits of Will
Primal Physical Body as Warmth

Sphere of Planet Saturn
Mineral Kingdom
4th Stage of the Archai

···

2. *Old Sun*
Kyriotetes – Light Ether
Spirits of Wisdom
Primal Etheric Body as Light

Sphere of Planet Jupiter
Plant Kingdom
4th Stage of the Archangels

···

3. *Old Moon*
Dynamis – Sound Ether
Spirits of Motion
Primal Astral Body as Movement

Sphere of Planet Mars
Animal Kingdom
4th Stage of the Angels

···

4. *Earth*
Exusiai – Life Ether
Donate "I Am" – Ego

Human – Earth & Moon
Sentient-Soul
Intellectual-Soul
Consciousness-Soul

···

5. *Future Jupiter*
Heavenly Sound Ether
Angel Stage

Jupiter + Two Moons
Holy Spirit – Wisdom
Spirit-Self (Manas)

···

6. *Future Venus*
Heavenly Light Ether
Archangel Stage

Venus + One Moon
Son – Love
Life-Spirit (Budhi)

···

7. *Future Vulcan*
Heavenly Warmth Ether
Archai Stage

Vulcan – No Moon
Father – Will
Spirit-Human (Atman)

BIBLIOGRAPHY

- Andreæ, Johann Valentin. *Reipublicæ Christianopolitanæ descriptio.* Argentorati: Sumptibus hæredum Lazari Zetzneri, Strasbourg, 1619.

- Andreæ, Johann Valentin. *Johann Valentin Andreae's Christianopolis; an ideal state of the seventeenth century.* translated from the Latin of Johann Valentin Andreae with an historical introduction. by Felix Emil Held. The Graduate School of the University of Illinois, Urbana- Champaign, 1916.

- Arnold, Edwin Sir. *The Light of Asia, or The Great Renunciation (Mahâbhinishkramana): Being the Life and Teaching Gautama, Prince of India and Founder of Buddhism (As Told in Verse by an Indian Buddhist).* Kegan Paul, Trench, Trübner & Co., London, 1879.

- Avari, Burjor. *India: The Ancient Past: A History of the Indian Sub-Continent.* Routledge, New Edition, 2007.

- Barnwell, John. *The Arcana of the Grail Angel: The Spiritual Science of the Holy Blood and of the Holy Grail.* Verticordia Press, Bloomfield Hills, 1999.

- Barnwell, John. *The Arcana of Light on the Path: The Star Wisdom of the Tarot and Light on the Path.* Verticordia Press, Bloomfield Hills, 1999.

- Blavatsky, H. P. (Helena Petrovna). *Isis Unveiled: A Master-Key to the Mysteries of Ancient and Modern Science and Theology.* J. W. Bouton. New York, 1878.

- Blavatsky, H. P. (Helena Petrovna). *The Key to Theosophy: Being a Clear Exposition, in the Form of Question and Answer, of the Ethics, Science and Philosophy for the Study of Which the Theosophical Society Has Been Founded.* The Theosophical Publishing Company, Ltd. London, 1889.

- Blavatsky, H. P. (Helena Petrovna). *The Secret Doctrine: The Synthesis of Science, Religion and Philosophy.* The Theosophical Publishing Company, Ltd. London, 1888.

- Blavatsky, H. P. (Helena Petrovna). *The Voice of Silence: Being Extracts from the Book of the Golden Precepts.* Theosophical University Press, 1992.

- Bockemuhl, Jochen. *Toward a Phenomenology of the Etheric World: Investigations into the Life of Nature and Man.* Anthroposophic Press, Spring Valley, N. Y., 1977.

- Campanella, Tommaso. *The City of the Sun.* The ProjectGutenberg Ebook, David Widger, 2013.

- Colum, Padriac. *Orpheus: Myths of the World.* Floris Books. Colum, Padriac. The Children's Homer. MacMillan Co., 1946.

- Colum, Padriac. *The Tales of Ancient Egypt.* Henry Walck Incorporated, New York,1968.

- Crawford, John Martin. *The Kalevala: The Epic Poem of Finland.* John B. Alden, New York, 1888.

- Gabriel, Douglas. *The Eternal Curriculum for Wisdom Children: Intuitive Learning and the Etheric Body.* Our Spirit, Northville, 2017.

- Gabriel, Tyla. *The Gospel of Sophia: The Biographies of the Divine Feminine Trinity,* Volume Our Spirit, Northville, 2014.

- Gabriel, Tyla. *The Gospel of Sophia: A Modern Path of Initiation,* Volume 2. Our Spirit, Northville, 2015.

- Gabriel, Tyla and Douglas. *The Gospel of Sophia: Sophia Christos Initiation,* Volume 3. Our Spirit, Northville, 2016.

- Gabriel, Douglas. *The Spirit of Childhood.* Trinosophia Press, Berkley, 1993.

- Gabriel, Douglas. *The Eternal Ethers: A Theory of Everything.* Our Spirit, Northville, 2018.

- Gabriel, Douglas. *Goddess Meditations.* Trinosophia Press, Berkley, 1994.

- Gebser, Jean. *The Ever Present Origin.* Ohio University Press, 1991.

- Green, Roger Lancelyn & Heather Copley. *Tales of Ancient Egypt.* Puffin Books, New York, 1980.

- Harrison, C. G. *The Transcendental Universe; Six Lectures on Occult Science, Theosophy, and the Catholic Faith.* George Redway, London 1893.

- Harrison, C. G. *The Transcendental Universe; Six Lectures on Occult Science, Theosophy, and the Catholic Faith.* Delivered Before the Berean Society, edited with an introduction by Christopher Bamford. Lindesfarne Press, Hudson, 1993.

- Hamilton, Edith. *Mythology.* Little Brown And Co., Boston, 1942.

- Harrer, Dorothy. *Chapters from Ancient History.* Waldorf Publications, Chatham, 2016.

- Hazeltine, Alice Isabel. *Hero Tales from Many Lands.* Abingdon Press, New York, 1961.

- Heidel, Alexander. *The Babylonian Genesis: The Story of Creation.* University of Chicago Press, Chicago, 1942.

- Hiebel, Frederick. *The Gospel of Hellas.* Anthroposophic Press, New York, 1949.

- Jocelyn, Beredene. *Citizens of the Cosmos: Life's Unfolding from Conception through Death to Rebirth.* Continuum, New York, 1981.

- König, Karl. Earth *and Man.* Bio-Dynamic Literature, Wyoming, Rhode Island, 1982.

- Kovacs, Charles. *Ancient Mythologies and History.* Resource Books, Scotland, 1991.

- Kovacs, Charles. *Greek Mythology and History.* Resource Books, Scotland, 1991.

- Landscheidt, Theodor. Sun-*Earth-Man a Mesh of Cosmic Oscillations: How Planets Regulate Solar Eruptions, Geomagnetic Storms, Conditions of Life, and Economic Cycles.* Urania Trust, London, 1989.

- Laszlo, Ervin and Kingsley, Dennis L. *Dawn of the Akashic Age: New Consciousness, Quantum Resonance, and the Future of the World.* Inner Traditions, Rochester Vermont, 2013

- Plato. *The Republic.* Dover Thrift Editions, 2000.

- Sister Nivedita (Margaret E. Noble) & Coomaraswamy, Ananda K.. *Myths of the Hindus and Buddhists.* Henry Holt, New York 1914.

- Steiner, Rudolf. *Ancient Myths: Their Meaning and Connection with Evolution.* Steiner Book Center, 1971.

- Steiner, Rudolf. *Christ and the Spiritual World: The Search for the Holy Grail.* Rudolf Steiner Press, London, 1963.

- Steiner, Rudolf. *Foundations of Esotericism*. Rudolf Steiner Press, London, 1983.

- Steiner, Rudolf. *Isis Mary Sophia: Her Mission and Ours*. Steiner Books, 2003.

- Steiner, Rudolf. *Man as a Being of Sense and Perception*. Steiner Book Center, Vancouver, 1981.

- Steiner, Rudolf. *Man as Symphony of the Creative Word*. Rudolf Steiner Publishing, London, 1978.

- Steiner, Rudolf. *Occult Science*. Anthroposophic Press, NY, 1972.

- Steiner, Rudolf. *Rosicrucian Esotericism*. Anthroposophic Press, NY, 1978.

- Steiner, Rudolf. *Rosicrucian Wisdom: An Introduction*. Rudolf Steiner Press, London, 2000. GA 425

- Steiner, Rudolf. *The Bridge between Universal Spirituality and the Physical Constitution of Man*. Anthroposophic Press, NY, 1958.

- Steiner, Rudolf. *The Evolution of Consciousness*. Rudolf Steiner Press, London, 1926.

- Steiner, Rudolf. *The Goddess from Natura to the Divine Sophia*. Sophia Books, 2001.

- Steiner, Rudolf. *The Holy Grail: from the Works of Rudolf Steiner*. Compiled by Steven Roboz. Steiner Book Center, North Vancouver, 1984.

- Steiner, Rudolf. *The Influence of Spiritual Beings Upon Man*. Anthroposophic Press, NY, 1971.

- Steiner, Rudolf. *The Reappearance of Christ in the Etheric*. Anthroposophic Press, NY, 1983.

- Steiner, Rudolf. *The Risen Christ and the Etheric Christ*. Rudolf Steiner Press, London, 1969.

- Steiner, Rudolf. *The Search for the New Isis the Divine Sophia*. Mercury Press, N.Y., 1983.

- Steiner, Rudolf. *The Spiritual Hierarchies and the Physical World*. Anthroposophic Press, N.Y., 1996.

- Steiner, Rudolf. *The Tree of Life and the Tree of Knowledge*. Mercury Press, NY, 2006.

- Steiner, Rudolf. *The True Nature of the Second Coming*. Rudolf Steiner Press, London, 1971.

- Steiner, Rudolf. *Theosophy*. Anthroposophic Press. New York, 1986.

- Steiner, Rudolf. *Wonders of the World, Ordeals of the Soul, Revelations of the Spirit*. Rudolf Steiner Press, London, 1963.

- Steiner, Rudolf. *World History in Light of Anthroposophy*. Rudolf Steiner Press, London, 1977.

- Tappan, Eva March. *The Story of the Greek People*. Houghton Mifflin Co., Boston 1908.

- van Bemmelen, D. J. *Zarathustra: The First Prophet of Christ*, 2 Vols. Uitgeverij Vrij Geestesleven, The Netherlands, 1968.

- Watson, Jane Werner (Vālmīki). *Rama of the Golden Age: An Epic of India*. Garrard Pub., Champaign.

ABOUT
DR. RUDOLF STEINER

Rudolf Steiner was born on the 27th of February 1861 in Kraljevec in the former Kingdom of Hungary and now Croatia. He studied at the College of Technology in Vienna and obtained his doctorate at the University of Rostock with a dissertation on Theory of Knowledge which concluded with the sentence: "The most important problem of human thinking is this: to understand the human being as a free personality, whose very foundation is himself."

He exchanged views widely with the personalities involved in cultural life and arts of his time. However, unlike them, he experienced the spiritual realm as the other side of reality. He gained access through exploration of consciousness using the same method as the natural scientist uses for the visible world in his external research. This widened perspective enabled him to give significant impulses in many areas such as art, pedagogy, curative education, medicine, agriculture, architecture, economics, and social sciences, aiming towards the spiritual renewal of civilization.

He gave his movement the name of "Anthroposophy" (the wisdom of humanity) after separating from the German section of the Theosophical Society, where he had acted as a general secretary. He then founded the Anthroposophical Society in 1913 which formed its center with the construction of the First Goetheanum in Dornach, Switzerland. Rudolf Steiner died on 30th March 1925 in Dornach. His literary work is made up of numerous books, transcripts and approximately 6000 lectures which have for the most part been edited and published in the Complete Works Edition.

Steiner's basic books, which were previously a prerequisite to gaining access to his lectures, are: *Theosophy, The Philosophy of Freedom, How to Know Higher Worlds, Christianity as a Mystical Fact,* and *Occult Science.*

ABOUT THE AUTHOR, DR. DOUGLAS GABRIEL

Dr. Gabriel is a retired superintendent of schools and professor of education who has worked with schools and organizations throughout the world. He has authored many books ranging from teacher training manuals to philosophical/spiritual works on the nature of the divine feminine.

He was a Waldorf class teacher and administrator at the Detroit Waldorf School and taught courses at Mercy College, the University of Detroit, and Wayne State University for decades. He then became the Headmaster of a Waldorf School in Hawaii and taught at the University of Hawaii, Hilo. He was a leader in the development of charter schools in Michigan and helped found the first Waldorf School in the Detroit Public School system and the first charter Waldorf School in Michigan.

Gabriel received his first degree in religious formation at the same time as an associate degree in computer science in 1972. This odd mixture of technology and religion continued throughout his life. He was drafted into and served in the Army Security Agency (NSA) where he was a cryptologist and systems analyst in signal intelligence, earning him a degree in signal broadcasting. After military service, he entered the Catholic Church again as a Trappist monk and later as a Jesuit priest where he earned PhD's in philosophy and comparative religion, and a Doctor of Divinity. He came to Detroit and earned a BA in anthroposophical studies and history and a MA in school administration. Gabriel left the priesthood and became a Waldorf class teacher and administrator in Detroit and later in Hilo, Hawaii.

Douglas has been a sought-after lecturer and consultant to schools and businesses throughout the world and in 1982 he founded the Waldorf Educational Foundation that provides funding for the publication of educational books. He has raised a great deal of money for Waldorf schools and institutions that continue to develop the teachings of Dr. Rudolf Steiner. Douglas is now retired but continues to write a variety of books including a novel and a science fiction thriller. He has four children, who keep him busy and active and a wife who is always striving towards the spirit through creating an "art of life." She is the author of the Gospel of Sophia trilogy.

The Gabriels' articles, blogs, and videos can currently be found at:

OurSpirit.com
Neoanthroposphy.com
GospelofSophia.com
EternalCurriculum.com

TRANSLATOR'S NOTE

The Rudolf Steiner quotes in this book can be found, in most cases, in their full-length and in context, through the Rudolf Steiner Archives by an Internet search of the references provided. We present the quoted selections of Steiner from a free rendered translation of the original while utilizing comparisons of numerous German to English translations that are available from a variety of publishers and other sources. In some cases, the quoted selections may be condensed and partially summarized using the same, or similar in meaning, words found in the original. Brackets are used to insert [from the author] clarifying details or anthroposophical nomenclature and spiritual scientific terms.

We chose to use GA (Gesamtausgabe — collected edition) numbers to reference Steiner's works instead of CW (Collected Works), which is often used in English editions. Some books in the series, *From the Works of Rudolf Steiner*, have consciously chosen to use a predominance of Steiner quotes to drive the presentation of the themes rather than personal remarks and commentary.

We feel that Steiner's descriptions should not be truncated but need to be translated into an easily read format for the English-speaking reader, especially for those new to Anthroposophy. We recommend that serious aspirants read the entire lecture, or chapter, from which the Steiner quotation was taken, because nothing can replace Steiner's original words or the mood in which they were delivered. The style of speaking and writing has changed dramatically over the last century and needs updating in style and presentation to translate into a useful tool for spiritual study in modern times. The series, *From the Works of Rudolf Steiner* intends to present numerous "study guides" for the beginning aspirant, and the initiate; in a format that helps support the spiritual scientific research of the reader.

Printed in Great Britain
by Amazon